WITHDRAWN
FROM THE VPI & SU
LIBRARY COLLECTION

Communist Armies in Politics

Also of Interest

Soviet Allies: The Warsaw Pact and the Issue of Reliability, edited by Daniel Nelson

From Muskets to Missiles: Politics and Professionalism in the Chinese Army, 1945-1981, Harlan Jencks

Civil-Military Relations in Communist Systems, edited by Dale R. Herspring and Ivan Volgyes

The Military and Security in the Third World: Domestic and International Impacts, edited by Sheldon W. Simon

Military Power and Policy in Asian States: China, India, Japan, edited by Onkar Marwah and Jonathan D. Pollack

*The Armed Forces of the USSR, Second Edition, revised and updated, Harriet Fast Scott and William F. Scott

*The Soviet Art of War: Doctrine, Strategy, and Tactics, edited by Harriet Fast Scott and William F. Scott

*The Chinese Military System: An Organizational Study of the Chinese People's Liberation Army, Second Edition, revised and updated, Harvey W. Nelsen

Arms Control and Defense Postures in the 1980s, edited by Richard Burt

Arms Transfers to the Third World: The Military Buildup in Less Industrialized Countries, edited by Uri Ra'anan, Robert L. Pfaltzgraff, Jr., and Geoffrey Kemp

*Available in hardcover and paperback

A Westview Special Study

Communist Armies in Politics
edited by Jonathan R. Adelman

This book analyzes the historical and contemporary political roles of armies in the majority of the world's Communist countries, stressing the problems faced and overcome by Communist parties in the creation and development of legitimate and effective armies. The authors, all area specialists, explore the sources of the dramatic differences between the highly visible and powerful political roles of the Chinese, Vietnamese, and Cuban armies, the small but increasing political role of the Soviet army, and the minimal political roles of most Eastern European armies. Emphasized are such variables as the nature of revolution, the role of civil war, and the extent of external interference (particularly from the Soviet Union). The authors show how these variables are key factors in determining the path of army political development.

Jonathan R. Adelman is an assistant professor in the Graduate School of International Studies at the University of Denver. After receiving his Ph.D. in Soviet politics from Columbia University in 1976, he served as a Charles Phelps Taft Postdoctoral Fellow at the University of Cincinnati and visiting assistant professor at the University of Alabama. He is the author of The Revolutionary Armies and will edit a forthcoming volume for Westview Press entitled Terror and Communist Politics.

Communist Armies in Politics

edited by Jonathan R. Adelman

Westview Press / Boulder, Colorado

JF
195
C5
C65
1982

A Westview Special Study

All rights reserved. No part of this publication may be reproduced or transmitted in any form or by any means, electronic or mechanical, including photocopy, recording, or any information storage and retrieval system, without permission in writing from the publisher.

Copyright © 1982 by Westview Press, Inc.

Published in 1982 in the United States of America by
     Westview Press, Inc.
     5500 Central Avenue
     Boulder, Colorado 80301
     Frederick A. Praeger, President and Publisher

Library of Congress Catalog Card No.: 82-70561
ISBN: 0-89158-880-9

Printed and bound in the United States of America

For my parents,
Benjamin and Kitty Adelman

Contents

Acknowledgments xi

1 Toward a Typology of Communist Civil-Military
   Relations, Jonathan R. Adelman 1

2 The Soviet Army, Jonathan R. Adelman 15

3 The Chinese Army, William Pang-yu Ting 31

4 The Cuban Army, Jorge I. Domínguez 45

5 The Vietnamese Army, William Turley 63

6 The Yugoslav Army, Robert W. Dean 83

7 The Polish Army, Andrzej Korbonski 103

8 The Czechoslovak Army, Jiri Valenta
   and Condoleezza Rice 129

9 The Romanian Army, Alex Alexiev 149

10 The Mongolian Army, Robert A. Rupen 167

11 The Chinese Militia, June Teufel Dreyer 187

12 Conclusion, Jonathan R. Adelman 207

Contributors 217

Index 219

Acknowledgments

It is always a pleasure to thank those who helped make this book possible. The intellectual origins of this book lay in conversations with Seweryn Bialer on the nature of Communist civil-military relations. The editors at Westview, particularly Miriam Gilbert, were especially encouraging and helpful in putting this work together. Carol Young was always cheerful and efficient in typing this manuscript. Liz Isaacson was an especially careful and accurate proofreader.

J.R.A.

1
Toward A Typology of Communist Civil-Military Relations

Jonathan R. Adelman

A conspicuous void in the literature on civil-military relations has been the minimal attention paid to the sixteen Communist armies, especially outside of the Soviet and Chinese armies. The difficulties inherent in studying such armies (secrecy, lack of data, language) have contributed to this inattention. So too has been a vague awareness that Communist armies cannot be fitted easily into standard theories of civil-military relations. For although a majority of Communist countries (including the Soviet Union from 1917-1940) have been developing countries, not one has witnessed a successful, and possibly even an attempted, military coup. The British revolution, leading to Cromwell's rule in the seventeenth century, and the French revolution ended in military dictatorships; the Russian and Chinese revolutions avoided this fate. Furthermore, while the Chinese, Vietnamese, and Cuban armies have played powerful political roles in developing Communist countries, the Soviet and East European armies have been relatively isolated from the policymaking process. These differences are particularly striking given the fact that most Communist armies were explicitly based on the Soviet model. No completely satisfactory theory has emerged to explain the basic similarities and differences in Communist civil-military relations.

The creation of such a theory is a significant task for the fields of comparative communism and civil-military relations. Communist countries have manifested a number of important differences from non-Communist countries in such areas as ideology, role of the party, politicization of society, implementation of socialist goals, and unique institutional structures. Given these similarities, sharp differences in the nature of army-party relations among Communist countries are of particular interest to the burgeoning field of comparative communism. This is especially true since the state of the army tends to reflect the state of the revolution. At the same time, differences in the nature of Communist civil-military relations from those that prevail in non-Communist countries should be of particular interest to students of civil-military relations.

For many years the dominant model of civil-military relations in Communist countries has been the unitary "Communist" or "totalitarian" model expounded by Samuel Huntington and Morris Janowitz in the 1960s. Their theory drew heavily on the concept of totalitarianism developed by Arendt, Friedrich, Brzezinski, and others in the 1950s. Janowitz and Huntington stressed that the party rigorously subordinated the army to its will and checked its potential power. Terror and purges were key elements in the party's dominance over the army. Using secret police and party cells in the army, commissars, large independent secret-police formations, political socialization of soldiers and officers, and careful selection and advancement of officers, the party has controlled the army. Janowitz concluded: "While he helps fashion defense policy, the organizational independence of the professional officer is weakened and he is eliminated from domestic politics."[1]

The totalitarian model possesses deficiencies in analyzing Soviet civil-military relations. Even for the Stalinist era, the period in which it has the greatest analytic value, it merely describes the nature of such relations. It provides neither clues as to the source of the creation of such a relationship nor orientation toward uncovering the wellsprings of possible change. It offers little guidance to the evolution of the political role of the Soviet army into a significant and legitimate interest group after Stalin's death.

The totalitarian model is of little value in analyzing army-party relations in such Communist countries as China, Vietnam, Yugoslavia, North Korea, and Cuba where the army has emerged as a powerful political actor with a key role in policymaking. In Cuba, Jorge Domínguez has argued that an ongoing army-party fusion has promoted a powerful and diverse role for the army. Career officers constituted 58 percent of all members in the Central Committee in 1965 and 38.9 percent in 1975.[2] In China in 1969, after the end of the Cultural Revolution, army men held twelve of twenty-five Politburo seats, and Defense Minister Lin Biao, a career officer, was Mao's declared heir apparent. Even after Lin's demise in 1971 the People's Liberation Army remained a significant, if diminished, political force with Defense Minister Ye Jianying currently a member of the ruling triumvirate. William Turley has concluded that the Vietnamese army has been the most important institution in the country after the party.[3] The North Korean army, in Choong-sik Lee's estimation, has played a significant political role with one-third to one-fourth of all Central Committee seats.[4] Finally, the Yugoslav army is viewed as a possible arbiter of Yugoslav policies after Tito's death.

THE SEARCH FOR A MODEL

In the last few years several works have begun the process of trying to explain the highly visible differences in the political roles and military effectiveness of Communist armies. Catherine Kelleher's edited work, Political-Military Systems--Comparative Perspectives (Beverly Hills, California: Sage, 1974) contains several stimulating articles on Communist civil-military relations, as does Dale Herspring and Ivan Volgyes's more specialized edited work, Civil-Military Relations in Communist Systems (Boulder, Colorado: Westview Press, 1978). David Albright and Dale Herspring with Ivan Volgyes have written valuable articles in this area. In addition, a number of scholars have contributed journal articles on the development of individual Communist armies.

In the Herspring and Volgyes work the three theoretical chapters by Kolkowicz, Odom, and Colton focus almost exclusively on the Soviet model. These chapters have the limited purpose of reconceptualizing the role of the army in Soviet politics in light of the obvious inadequacies of the totalitarian model.

For the Soviet case the Kolkowicz model of the army as an emerging special interest group, guildlike in character and engaged in "perpetual tension in its relationship with the Party leadership," has considerable validity. Paralleling the work of Griffiths and Skilling, his thesis points to both the potentiality of and the limitations on the power of the Soviet army. The major difficulty of this concept is that it offers little guidance to the minimal and passive role of the Soviet army in the period from 1917-1953.[5]

Odom's institutional congruence approach argues for an army-party symbiosis in which the army leaders are "left to act as executants...[and] are not in a position to frame the issues; they can only respond to the way issues are framed above them." He sees this relationship as rooted in czarist, and even Petrine, civil-military relations. Yet he does not show how these traditions were transferred from a traditional czarist army to the revolutionary Red Army led by Communists and commissars. This approach ignores the strong tensions in army-party relations characteristic of the Stalinist era, which saw the Great Purges decimate the officer corps. It downplays the genuine fear of Bonapartism that played a role in the purges of Trotsky (1925), Tukhachevsky (1937), and Zhukov (1957). This approach, too, considerably underestimates the power achieved in the last two decades by the Soviet military-industrial complex.[6]

Finally, Colton puts forth a participatory model that rejects Kolkowicz's stress of party control of the military.

Instead he emphasizes military participation in politics and the existence of potential but unused military power. He downplays tensions within the political system among the army and other actors. Obviously this mode, too, has little explanatory power for the Stalinist era. Also, he fails to suggest why the Soviet army might not use the power that is available to it.[7]

If we try to apply these models to an analysis of powerful and effective Communist armies, we run into serious difficulties. The Kolkowicz interest group model hardly applies to countries such as China, Vietnam, and Cuba where legitimate and effective armies have emerged as powerful political actors, intimately tied to the party, in constricted policymaking environments. Nor would Odom's institutional congruence approach fare better for the Chinese, Vietnamese, and Cuban armies have been far more than mere "executants" of power. Colton's participatory model is somewhat more relevant but suggests a shyness at the use of power that hardly would be the case in these countries. His approach does not suggest the basis of the power of the army.

Similarly, if we project these models onto the experience of the East European armies, we run into problems. In Eastern Europe a combination of limited legitimacy and external Soviet military interference has prevented the armies from becoming interest groups in the Kolkowicz sense. Odom's institutional congruence approach and Colton's participatory model would not be relevant to most East European armies, except possibly the Romanian, which have not attained that particular relationship with their parties.

Volgyes and Herspring in two recent articles have propounded a political socialization model for Communist civil-military relations. Stressing the antagonism between army and party, the model sees the party Political Administration and party control over the army as the focal points of party-military relations. Their model focuses on the change over time from the transformation phase to the consolidation period to the system-maintenance period. As Herspring has acknowledged, this model has no utility outside of the East European experience. In Eastern Europe it does have significant value, although not explicatory of significant differences among these countries.[8]

Finally, David Albright recently has written a significant article in World Politics in which he argues for a contingency approach to Communist civil-military relations. He eschews the notion of army-party conflict, opting instead for a continuum approach ranging from total cooperation to total conflict between army and party. Albright sees seven variables as significant in explaining differences in Communist civil-military relations:
(1) path to power, (2) foreign relations, (3) extent of

functional specialization in upper echelon of ruling elite, (4) extent of factional strife within the governing elite, (5) amount of bureaucratization of politics, (6) military doctrine, and (7) extent of domestic order. This contingency model represents a serious advance in the state of theorizing about Communist armies. Its only deficiency is that it fails to specify the relative importance of each variable and the interrelationship between variables. All seven variables obviously cannot be of equal importance. In our model discussed below we will emphasize that the first two variables are by far the most important variables and will demonstrate their value in explaining the role of Communist armies in politics.[9]

OUR ATTEMPT

The creation of a theory of Communist civil-military relations is hampered by a number of problems. There exists a significant literature only on the Russian and Chinese armies. For many of the other fourteen Communist armies not a single book and only a few scattered articles and chapters in books have ever been written. This is even true of such important armies as the Cuban, North Korean, and Vietnamese. The number of academic specialists in these areas is tiny. The large number of languages involved in the study of Communist armies and the minimal amount of available data have retarded the development of the discipline. The extensive Soviet influence, especially in Eastern Europe, has obscured the study of the development of Communist armies. Also, any theory of Communist civil-military relations must account for states at different levels of economic development and revolutionary transformation.

Against this background, we wish to propose a historical developmental model that will help rectify the ahistorical tendencies of most Soviet-based theories. We take our lead from Philip Selznick who has stressed the genetic nature of institutional development.[10] We argue that the nature of revolutionary development and degree of external Soviet interference have been decisive factors in determining the nature of Communist civil-military relations. Taking as our point of departure the literature on revolution developed by Huntington, Johnson, Wolf, Tucker, and others, we argue that the path to power has significantly determined the nature of civil-military relations in the first two decades after the seizure of power.

We hypothesize the existence of three main patterns of Communist civil-military relations derived from different paths of revolutionary development. The first pattern, that of a powerful political role for the military, is intimately connected with the nature of the revolutionary path to power and the resultant civil war. In countries such as China, Vietnam, and Yugoslavia the road to power lay through a protracted agrarian insurrection, directed against both internal and external enemies. Power was neither simply handed to the party through external Soviet army intervention nor won in a simple stroke by a workers' insurrection. Rather power could only be seized in a lengthy and difficult struggle against powerful enemies. The foreign enemies were exceedingly strong--the Germans in Yugoslavia, the Japanese in China and Korea, the French in Vietnam. The internal enemies, too, were often cohesive and far from weak--the Guomindang in China and Batista in Cuba. Indeed, Stalin in the 1940s would counsel the Chinese and Yugoslav Communists not to seize power.

Defeat was the norm in the early years (for example, the Long March and Moncado Barracks), and losses to the technologically and numerically superior enemy were often staggering. The nascent army had to learn to compensate for primitive military equipment. Treason and desertion were recurrent problems in the beginning. The creation of a legitimate and effective army under those conditions in remote rural areas was a sine qua non for survival itself. Without such an army, physical extermination was inevitable. The party devoted great efforts to creating an effective army. Over time the new Communist-dominated officer corps, virtually fused with the party elite, began to function effectively. The reliable Communist officers acquired the necessary military experience; incompetents were weeded out. Desertion in the ranks was sharply reduced by the recruiting of a large and reliable Communist stratum to lead primary units in battle. The party, institutionalizing an elaborate system of indoctrination and control, skillfully utilized the potent appeals of nationalism and agrarian reform that were highly popular among the peasant soldiers.

The path to victory was long and arduous for all such armies. The Chinese Communists fought twenty-two years before achieving final victory, the Vietnamese Communists eight years before the convening of the Geneva Conference. In the process the party created its first legitimate and effective institution--the army. Too, the party created a core of experienced Communist government bureaucrats who would help run the government after victory was obtained. The popularity of the revolution and the effectiveness of the army precluded a large role for the secret-police forces, which often came under the direct control of the army.

Thus, after victory, the Communist armies emerged as fully effective and legitimate institutions, closely tied to the parties. This effectiveness has often been demonstrated in military campaigns against powerful enemies. The Chinese army pushed the American army out of North Korea and ultimately stalemated it near the original border lines in the Korean War. The North Vietnamese army triumphantly entered Saigon in April 1975. These armies were among a handful of legitimate and effective institutions in underdeveloped countries where such institutions have been traditionally uncommon. Their role exceeded that of interest groups, for they were usually powerful actors in constricted decision-making environments. As a consequence, armies in countries such as China, Vietnam, and Yugoslavia have become politically significant and highly valued by the ruling parties.

A second pattern is that of minimal political influence exerted by the army. This pattern, predominant in Eastern Europe, is deeply rooted in the path to power and external Soviet role. Unlike the parties previously mentioned, the East European parties suffered from a widespread lack of support and legitimacy. In Eastern Europe there was no revolution and civil war in which the parties would have garnered support and created legitimate and effective institutions. Communist resistance forces were relatively weak, compared to nationalist forces, even at the end of the war. Rather, power was handed to the local Communists in the wake of the Red Army occupation of Eastern Europe in the closing phases of World War II. Apart from Czechoslovakia, where the Communists captured nearly 40 percent of the vote in popular elections, it is generally agreed that the local Communists would never have come to power on their own efforts. Indeed, anti-Russian and anti-revolutionary sentiments were especially strong in countries such as East Germany and Poland. In Romania there were less than 1,000 Communists in the country at the time of the Red Army invasion.

But the weak parties could not look to the weak and illegitimate armies for significant support. The lack of a revolution and civil war had dire consequences for the development of the army. Forces that fought for the Allies were unacceptable (such as the Polish Home Army), and those that fought for the Soviets were small in number. The East European armies either had fought openly for the fascists (as had the German and Romanian armies) or had displayed profascist sentiments. Their officer corps had been dominated by aristocratic and upper-class elements, thoroughly reactionary in political attitudes. Their competence had been limited, as seen in the rout of the Polish army by the Germans in 1939 and the destruction of the Romanian army by the Russians at Stalingrad in the winter of 1942. The army had faithfully reflected the anti-Communist, profascist politics of most East European countries during the 1930s and World War II.

Under these conditions the creation of a legitimate and effective army in any East European country was an extremely lengthy and protracted process. Initially, the old armies were demobilized and the primary responsibility for external defense was taken over by the Soviet army. Given the demobilization of the Red Army from over 11 million men in 1945 to 2.8 million men in 1948, this was not an insignificant task. The nascent East European armies were heavily penetrated by networks of secret police and cross-checked by large, independent secret-police units. The loyalty of the new units, reflecting the mood of the populace, was dubious. In 1956 the Hungarian army would splinter in several directions with some units going over to the rebels while others remained passively in their barracks. That same year the fear that the Polish army would resist a Soviet invasion, despite the presence of Marshal Rokossovsky and 10,000 Soviet advisors in the Polish army, played a definite role in the peaceful resolution of the crisis. Under these circumstances the average, relatively ineffectual East European army, feared for possible Bonapartism and political disloyalty, would play a minimal political role.

Although the creation of the Warsaw Pact in 1956 highlighted the need for competent and effective East European armies, serious constraints have remained on their development. The Soviet Union, wary of the creation of overly powerful local armies, has strived to maintain its control over these armies. Internal economic difficulties and continued presence of Soviet troops on their soil have prompted East European countries to continue to rely heavily on the Soviet Union for their external defense. Under these conditions the armies of Eastern Europe have tended to remain peripheral and limited actors in policymaking.

The final pattern is that of the Soviet army, with a historical trend of a minimal but significantly increasing political role. From being a passive object of policymaking under Stalinism, the army has become a legitimate interest group in Soviet policymaking under Khrushchev and especially under Brezhnev. Far from being universal, the Soviet model, like the October Revolution, has proved unique among Communist countries. Unlike East European armies, the Red Army was formed by a revolution and civil war. But also unlike the Chinese, Vietnamese, and Yugoslav armies, the Red Army lacked a prior gestation period and broad popular peasant support.

The nature of the October Revolution and Russian civil war profoundly influenced the development of the political role of the Red Army. The October Revolution, a workers' insurrection paralleled by spontaneous and uncontrolled peasant uprisings, required no army to achieve victory. At the outset of the civil war in May 1918 the Bolsheviks had no army of their own, as the old czarist army had disintegrated and the call for volunteers had met a meager response. Under these circumstances the Red Army, lacking a gestation period, would be formed literally on the field of battle under dire conditions.

With White Russian and foreign troops occupying three-fourths of the country by the summer of 1918, the Bolsheviks had to rely heavily on the czarist officers (<u>voenspets</u>) from sheer desperation. The two commanders in chief of the Red Army during the civil war (Kamenev and Vatsetis) were senior <u>voenspets</u>. Their very use sharply split the officer corps by virtue of their prior intimate association with czarism.

The situation was even worse in the ranks. Unlike the Chinese and Vietnamese Communists, the Russian Communists lacked broad appeal in the countryside. The lack of a gestation period here also meant the lack of institutionalization of proper procedures of control and organization. Desertion from the ranks was enormous during the civil war. Bubnov has even estimated that only 700,000 to 800,000 of the over 5-million-man army could be considered battle effective.[11]

The battlefield performance of the Red Army was very weak. Against every major enemy, from Denikin to Kolchak, the Red Army had to initially retreat, sometimes more than once. Only through the large-scale mobilization of Communists, workers, and <u>kursanti</u> (military cadets); the constant transfer of reliable commanders (such as Tukhachevsky) and units (such as the First Cavalry Army) to the threatened fronts; the extension of political concessions; and the application of secret-police force did the Red Army finally achieve victory. Even then the Red Army was smashed by a weak Polish army in front of Warsaw in August 1920 and was unable to prevent the loss of such key border areas as Latvia, Lithuania, Estonia, Bessarabia, western Belorussia, and western Ukraine.

At the end of the civil war the Red Army emerged as a weak and vaguely legitimate force, often as much a threat to the regime (as in the Kronstadt revolt) as an asset. Its political role was thereby minimal. With 90 percent of the officers not belonging to the party, its ties with the ruling elite were tenuous at best.[12] The lone army man on the Politburo, Trotsky, and three of four army men on the Central Committee (where they made up only 10 percent of the membership) were party figures in the army--they lacked military experience and owed their primary loyalty to the party. The massive demobilization of 90 percent of all soldiers in the early 1920s and the impoverished state of the Soviet economy guaranteed that the transition to a legitimate and effective army would be a lengthy one. In the interim the Red Army would continue to play a minimal political role.

Only in the crucible of World War II did the Red Army finally emerge, in large part as a result of the massive societal transformations of the 1930s, as a truly legitimate and effective force. The reimposition of Stalinist norms of control after the war prevented the army from exerting the influence that normally would have accrued to it. Instead, the army found its leaders again demoted and the secret police in a powerful counterbalancing role.

After Stalin's death this powerful and legitimate force would naturally emerge as a significant interest group with considerable authority in defense and related matters. This new role coincided with the creation of a new policy-making environment, especially under Brezhnev.

Several armies, notably the Romanian, Cuban, and North Korean, present certain problems in terms of this analysis. The Romanian army, although initially following the East European mold, has recently moved toward a symbiotic relationship with the party. This may be caused by the party's felt need of protection from the Soviet threat to its independence. The Cuban army, although possessing far less of a prerevolutionary past than other similar armies, has emulated their extensive political roles. In January 1959 the guerillas under Castro numbered less than 1,000. It was, however, the myth of guerilla power, not the reality, that was important. Finally, the North Korean army has also evolved toward a significant political role although Soviet troops brought the regime to power. This may be due to the important role of the army in the projected forcible reunification of Korea.

CONCLUSIONS

We have seen the powerful role played by revolution and civil war in shaping the political role of the army in the first several decades after the seizure of power. The Soviet case alerts us to the fact that this impact naturally wanes as the first revolutionary generation fades from power and is replaced by a new generation of leaders. This historical developmental approach may also be used profitably to look at several other related problems in the areas of military development and comparative communism.

The basic analysis could be applied to the study of non-Communist revolutionary armies. The ultimate success of revolutions in countries such as the United States, Great Britain, and France depended to a significant extent on the creation of a legitimate and effective army. The existence of a gestation period, the popularity and social bases of revolutionary appeals, and the attitude of prerevolutionary officers to the revolution were key factors in shaping the nature of the army and its political role.

The American revolution is an example. Traditionally, historians have sought the roots of the minimal political role of the American army in the democratic nature of American institutions, American political culture, and the lack of external threat after victory. An analysis of the nature of the American army in the revolution might suggest that a significant reason should also be sought in the lack of legitimacy and relatively minimal effectiveness of the army. The American army was repeatedly plagued by mass desertion in the ranks (the "melting away" at Valley Forge) and treason in the officer corps (Benedict Arnold). Military historians have credited the British army, despite its mercenary complement, with winning at least half of the battles in the war. Too, at Yorktown in 1781 the Americans present to receive British surrender were significantly outnumbered by French sailors. The enormous lines of supply and communication of the British army, active French support, and American guerrilla warfare may well have contributed more to ultimate American victory than did the American army.[13]

Second, this analysis may be applied to other paramilitary forces, particularly the reserve forces and the militia. Their role has often correlated inversely with that of the army. Thus, in 1958 the accent on the militia in the "everyone a soldier" campaign in China reflected the lessened role of the army in the Great Leap Forward. In Russia in the 1930s the abolition of the territorial reserve system signified the transition to a thoroughly professional mass army.

Third, we could examine the role of the secret police. This analysis could help to explain the different roles of the secret police in Communist countries. In countries where the regime suffered a lack of legitimacy and support, such as in Eastern Europe, the secret police played a powerful role. Here the lack of revolution and civil war created a powerful role for the forces of repression, especially given the lack of a capable army. In the Soviet Union the weakness of the Red Army similarly created a strong role for the secret police in penetrating the army, crushing internal revolts, and watching the population. In countries such as China and Vietnam, however, the party and government gained considerable support through an arduous road to power. The army was capable of discharging its proper duties. Thus, the role of the secret police was sharply curtailed by the capabilities of rival institutions and the existence of mass support.

Finally, this analysis could be extended to other key Communist institutions with no control over the instruments of violence. It could help answer the basic question of why the government bureaucracy has traditionally played a powerful role in China under Liu Shao-yi and Zhou En-lai but played a relatively minimal role in Russia until the 1950s. Again, the Chinese revolution created a nascent core of government party bureaucrats who ruled 100 million people by 1945. By the time the Chinese Communists had seized power, they had created the basic government infrastructure and core of cadres necessary to man it. In this context, the central government bureaucracy emerged as an effective and legitimate force with significant political power. Liu Shao-yi would be Mao's first heir apparent until his demise in 1966. In Russia the path to power precluded such development. The party was forced to rely (as had the army) on bourgeois specialists and czarist <u>chinovniki</u> (civil servants) for the first two decades. In this context the central government bureaucracy, not even to speak of provincial government apparats, largely represented a continuation of the old czarist apparat. The political role of such alien institutions was inevitably minimal.

The study of variables such as the nature of revolution and civil war can aid us in understanding the critical first several decades of Communist rule and divergence of policies and institutions. It is to such variables that we should turn for a better analysis of key differences among Communist states.

NOTES

1. See Hannah Arendt, <u>The Origins of Totalitarianism</u> (London: Allen and Unwin, 1951); Carl Friedrich and Zbigniew Brzezinski, <u>Totalitarian Dictatorship and Autocracy</u> (Cambridge: Harvard University Press, 1956); Morris Janowitz, <u>The Military in the Political Development of New Nations</u> (Chicago: University of Chicago Press, 1964), p. 4; and Samuel Huntington, <u>Political Order in Changing Societies</u> (New Haven: Yale University Press, 1968).

2. Jorge Domínguez, "The Civic Soldier in Cuba," in Catherine Kelleher, ed., <u>Political-Military Systems--Comparative Perspectives</u> (Beverly Hills, Calif.: Sage, 1974).

3. William Turley, "The Political Role and Development of the People's Army of Vietnam," in Joseph J. Zasloff and MacAlister Brown, eds., <u>Communism in Indochina: New Perspectives</u> (Lexington, Ky.: Lexington Books, 1975), p. 135.

4. Robert Scalapino and Choong-sik Lee, <u>Communism in Korea</u> (Berkeley: University of California Press, 1972), 2:1007.

5. Roman Kolkowicz, "Interest Groups in Soviet Politics: The Case of the Military," in Dale Herspring and Ivan Volgyes, eds., <u>Civil-Military Relations in Communist Systems</u> (Boulder, Colo.: Westview Press, 1978), pp. 9-26.

6. William E. Odom, "The Party-Military Connection: A Critique," in Herspring and Volgyes, eds., <u>Civil-Military Relations in Communist Systems</u>, pp. 27-52.

7. Timothy J. Colton, "The Party-Military Connection: A Participatory Model," in Herspring and Volgyes, eds., <u>Civil-Military Relations in Communist Systems</u>, pp. 54-78.

8. Dale Herspring and Ivan Volgyes, "The Military as an Agent of Political Socialization in Eastern Europe," <u>Armed Forces and Society</u> 3, no. 2 (Winter 1977):249-269; and Dale Herspring, "Introduction" and "Concluding

Thoughts," *Studies in Comparative Communism* 11, no. 3 (Autumn 1978):207-212, 325-331.

9. David Albright, "A Comparative Conceptualization of Civil-Military Relations," *World Politics* 32, no. 4 (July 1980):553-576.

10. Philip Selznick, *Leadership in Administration* (Evanston, Ill.: Row, Peterson and Company, 1957), p. 141.

11. A. S. Bubnov, S. S. Damenev, M. N. Tukhachevsky, and R. P. Eidemann, eds., *Grazhdanskaya voina 1918-1921* (Moscow: Gosizdat, 1930), 2: p. 81.

12. Yuri Petrov, *Partiinoe stroitel'stvo v sovetskoi armii i flote* (Moscow: Voenizdat, 1964), p. 179.

13. For recent work on this period see William Skeleton, "Officers and Politicians: The Origins of Army Politics in the United States Before the Civil War," *Armed Forces and Society* 6, no. 1 (Fall 1979):22-48; and Richard Kohn, *Eagle and Sword: The Beginnings of the Military Establishment in America* (New York: Free Press, 1978).

2
The Soviet Army

Jonathan R. Adelman

The role of the Soviet army in decision making in over six decades since the October Revolution forms a fascinating strand in the history of Soviet politics. As the Soviet Union has evolved from a weak and underdeveloped country in the 1920s into one of the world's two superpowers after World War II, so too has the role of the Soviet army changed from that of an ineffective and passive participant in politics in the 1920s to a powerful and self-confident interest group in the 1970s. In this chapter we will trace this development by sketching the major periods of army-party relations and the reasons for the role of the army in a given period.

CIVIL WAR

The nature of the October Revolution and civil war profoundly influenced the development of the political role of the Red Army. The October Revolution with its mass urban working-class support and large independent peasant revolts obviated the need for an army in October 1917. A small force of ill-trained and poorly disciplined Red Guards was sufficient to topple the Provisional Government. By March 1918 the revolution had swept the Bolsheviks into power, often with little opposition, throughout Russia and even in many nationality areas. But in May 1918 the Czech Legion uprising in Siberia triggered a bloody civil war that lasted two and a half years. At the outset the Bolsheviks had no army of their own, as the old czarist army had disintegrated and the call for volunteers had met with a meager response. Under these circumstances the Red Army, lacking the gestation period and popular agrarian and nationalist appeals so important to the success of the Chinese and Vietnamese armies, was formed literally on the battlefield.

The creation of an effective and legitimate officer corps is inevitably a lengthy process. A homogeneous officer corps is formed over many years through prolonged socialization of men with common background characteristics (class, education, and urban or rural origins) who are isolated from society. In 1918 the Bolsheviks had almost no officers of their own. Nearly all party leaders had spent the years before the revolution in jail, exile, or the underground. Worse, the bulk of the czarist officer corps was upper class in origin and monarchist in sentiment. Nevertheless, with the majority of the country in enemy hands by July 1918, the Bolsheviks from necessity turned to mass recruitment of czarist officers (<u>voenspets</u>).

The <u>voenspets</u> (literally "military specialists"), who were 75 percent of all officers in 1918 and 35 percent in 1920, occupied nearly all staff positions and many top command posts during the civil war. The two commanders in chief during the civil war, (Kamenev and Vatsetis), as well as the chief of staff in 1920, Lebedev, were <u>voenspets</u>. The theoretical knowledge and military experience of the <u>voenspets</u> made them invaluable to the Red Army. Hemmed in by commissars, secret-police agents, and the policy of holding as hostages the families of errant officers, the majority of the 48,400 <u>voenspets</u> faithfully served the revolution. However, a significant minority committed treason or deserted to the enemy. Given their prior intimate association with czarism, the use of the <u>voenspets</u> sharply divided the officer corps.

The party relied on many diverse and heterogeneous elements to fill the ultimately 130,000-man officer corps that directed a 5.5-million-man Red Army by the end of the civil war. Besides the alien <u>voenspets</u>, inexperienced but enthusiastic Communists formed a thin 10 percent of the officer corps. The bulk were new Communists with a leavening of several thousand Old Bolsheviks (such as Frunze, Voroshilov, and Trotsky) who filled key positions. Former czarist NCOs (such as Budenny), with their practical military experience and peasant origins, played a significant role. So, too, did temporary junior officers (those who became officers only in the course of World War I), often of bourgeois origins. Partisans, who played a key role in Siberia and the Ukraine, often refused to follow central directives. Not only was the officer corps divided sharply along class and political lines, but its competence was minimal. In 1920 an astrounding 43 percent of all officers had no military training at all. The officer corps was neither red nor expert.

The situation was even worse in the ranks. After four years of World War I and the peasant revolution in the countryside, the majority of peasant soldiers were eager to return home and farm their newly seized lands. The Bolsheviks, however, needed to recruit millions of soldiers to fill the ranks of the fledgling Red Army. Inevitably in underdeveloped Russia this meant that 70 to 80 percent of all soldiers would be peasants. But the urban-oriented Bolsheviks, with their radical social experimentation, antireligious propaganda, forced food requisitioning, and significant Jewish leadership (Trotsky, Zinoviev, Kamenev, Sverdlov, Radek, etc.), lacked broad appeal in the countryside. Furthermore, the lack of a gestation period meant the lack of institutionalization of proper procedures of control and organization. Thus, only 4 to 5 percent of all Red Army men belonged to the party in the civil war.

The result was inevitable. In 1918 desertion from the ranks was enormous. In 1919 and 1920, according to the Soviet historian Olikov, the army apprehended in raids or saw return voluntarily under an amnesty the staggering total of 2.85 million men. This almost equalled the number of men mobilized into the army. Bubnov has even estimated that in 1920 only 700,000 to 800,000 men, from an army of over 5,000,000, could be considered battle-effective.

The army, reflecting the low level of development of the country's productive forces (which were further reduced by World War I and the civil war), functioned with primitive military technology. This level of technology was far below that of the Western European armies in World War I. Tanks and airplanes, widely used by the end of the war, were few in number and poor in quality. In 1920 the navy barely existed and was totally dominated by White forces. The Red Army suffered critical shortages of modern infantry weapons and heavy artillery. Transportation was so primitive that only by the end of 1919 were many troops moved eastward on trains. The supply system was outdated, often hopelessly inadequate to cope with the demands of warfare.

As a consequence, the battlefield performance of the Red Army was very weak. As Lenin declared in October 1921, "On each occasion--on the Kolchak front, on the Deniken front, on the Yudenich front, on the Polish front, on the Wrangel front--...we had been badly battered (and sometimes more than once)." Treason by <u>voenspets</u> (from Muraviev to Lundquist), radical allies (such as Makhno), and atamans (such as Grigoriev) repeatedly hampered operations. Army mobilization capacity was so weak that even in the Polish campaign of 1920, a critical campaign on which might ride the fate of international socialist revolution, the Red Army could raise little more than 1 percent of its total manpower. Red Army incompetence enabled Yudenich's tiny army, the Northwest army of 15,000 to 25,000 men, to seriously threaten the capture of Petrograd and Denikin's forces to reach Orel in the fall of 1919.

Victory required frequent mobilizations of Communists and workers, shifting of key units and their commanders, extension of political concessions, and liberal use of secret-police terror. Even in victory, the weakness of the Red Army led to the separation of Poland, Finland, the Baltics, and parts of the Ukraine and Belorussia from the Soviet Union.

Thus, at the end of the civil war the Red Army emerged as a weak and vaguely legitimate force. Often it was as much a threat to the regime, as in the Kronstadt revolt, as an asset. Its political role was thereby minimal. With 90 percent of the officers and 96 to 98 percent of the soldiers not belonging to the party, the army's ties with the ruling party elite were tenuous at best. The lone army man on the Politburo (War Commissar Trotsky) and three or four army men on the Central Committee (where they made up only 10 percent of the membership) were party figures in the army but not of it. The massive demobilization of 90 percent of all soldiers in the early 1920s and the impoverished state of the Soviet economy guaranteed that the transition to a legitimate and effective army would be a lengthy one. In the interim the Red Army would continue to play a minimal political role.

INTERWAR PERIOD

Although armies in developing countries have traditionally played major political roles, the Red Army remained a passive and defensive political actor in the interwar period. The army did not manage to place a single career soldier on the Politburo in the period from 1921 to 1941. Only the war commissars (Trotsky, Frunze, and Voroshilov), party figures in the army, served on the Politburo. Indeed, not a single member of the Politburo in this period had even served as an officer in the civil war! The representation of the Red Army in the Central Committee rose from a minimal 3 percent in 1927 to a still modest, but more respectable, 13 percent in 1939, after the Great Purges. At party congresses Soviet army representatives were barely noticeable. At the 13th Party Congress in 1924 there was not one army man among 51 speakers, and at the 18th Party Congress in 1939 there were only 6 army men among 132 speakers. At four congresses in the 1920s the names of future marshals Blyukher and Yegorov were never even mentioned once. When military leaders, usually Budenny and Voroshilov, spoke, it was invariably only on issues of military relevance.

Although military influence inevitably increased with the rising role of the military factor in policymaking and the growing strength of the Red Army in the 1930s, the army failed to become a significant political actor. In the two significant confrontations between the party and elements in the army, the party decisively crushed opposition by army leaders. In neither case did army leaders initiate the action--and the consequences were sharp purges that rigidly institutionalized army-party relations.

In the early 1920s the Trotskyites retained a thin and tenuous base in the army while the Stalinists increasingly dominated the party. The bulk of all officers remained neutral and outside of the party. Many Communist officers, angered by Trotsky's arrogant behavior, ardent support of the use of voenspets, and rejection of proletarian military doctrine, were hostile toward him. Nevertheless, leading Trotskyites in the army included War Commissar Trotsky himself, head of the Political Administration (PUR) Antonov-Ovseenko, and Moscow garrison commander Muralov. In December 1923 Antonov-Ovseenko, on his own initiative, took the political campaign into the army. Outside of student cells and the Moscow Military District, the Trotskyites were decisively routed everywhere. In retaliation, the Stalinists ousted all Trotskyites from the army (with Trotsky himself being forced out in January 1925), installed loyal Stalinists in their place, and purged and restructured the Political Administration. Party authority in the army was now beyond question.

Similarly, in 1936 the top army leaders were forced to take a stand on the vital question of terror and purges, a question that affected their personal well-being and institutional integrity. At the Central Committee Plenum in August 1936 perhaps two-thirds of the members voted against the extension of the purges. So, too, did all army leaders except for Voroshilov and Budenny, who were personally tied to Stalin. The army leadership voted in roughly the same proportion as the party leadership and in no way led the opposition to Stalin. Nevertheless this opposition was liquidated totally in the Great Purges that lasted from 1937 until 1941 in the army. These purges swept away 3 of 5 marshals, all 11 vice-commissars of defense, all 8 admirals, 60 of 67 corps commanders, 221 of 397 brigade commanders, and 15,000 to 35,000 officers. The Great Purges terrorized the remaining officers (such as future Marshal Rokossovksy, who was twice beaten unconscious by the secret police) and rigidly reimposed absolute Stalinist control over the military. They opened up enormous opportunities for younger officers, who gratefully accepted tremendous promotions that would have previously been unthinkable. They also brought such Stalinist stalwarts as Budenny, Voroshilov, and Timoshenko into unchallenged control of the army.

Only in military-related matters did the army leaders have any notable success. In 1930 Yakir and Dubovoy obtained the release and rehabilitation of a number of voenspets accused by the secret police of trying to murder them. In 1933 these same leaders, together with some party leaders, obtained a cessation of grain shipments from the starving Ukraine on the grounds of demoralization of the Ukrainian peasant soldiers. That same year future Marshal Blyukher successfully obtained a partial restoration of the New Economic Program (NEP) in the Far East on the grounds of military necessity. But given the tremendous stress on the military factor in the 1930s caused by the rising German and Japanese threat, these areas encompassed significant areas of Soviet politics.

The separation and even isolation of the army from the party was evident in a number of ways. With the brief exception of 1934, party membership in the army fluctuated from a low of 7 percent in 1921 to highs of 15 percent in 1930 and 14 percent in 1940. Most Communists were political commissars, army administrators, officers, and non-commissioned officers, rather than soldiers. The bulk of the officer corps was apolitical. Only 20 percent of all officers belonged to the party in 1921, and even by 1929 fully half of the officers were not Communists. During the 1930s this proportion dropped to one-third of all officers. Most officers who belonged to the party emulated future Marshal Shaposhnilov's apolitical professional ethos. The small Stalinist faction, consisting of men such as Budenny, Voroshilov, Timoshenko, and Kulik (who had been associated with Stalin in the First Cavalry Army at Tsaritsyn in 1919), played a key role in the army. This faction was hostile toward modern mechanized warfare. Members of a third loose faction around Marshal Tukhachevsky, including officers such as Yakir, Uborevich, and Fishman, were fervent advocates of modern mechanized warfare and did not rule out possible opposition to Stalin.

The separation of the army from politics was also seen in the nature of societal tasks performed by the army. Like nearly all armies in developing countries, the Red Army performed in its barracks the modernizing functions of producing politically aware, educated, and trained manpower valuable to society. In this task it was notably successful, even producing a corps of future rural <u>aktivs</u> (party activists). But, unlike the Chinese, Cuban, and other armies in developing countries, it performed virtually no role outside of the barracks. Apart from the Kolkhoz Corps in the Far East in the 1930s, the Red Army participated in almost no economic production activities. Unlike the Chinese People's Liberation Army before and during the Cultural Revolution, the Red Army was never extolled as a model for society. It performed virtually no active political leadership role in society. In short, it was confined to its barracks where the emphasis lay on party control of the military and the creation of an effective military machine.

Finally, the lack of party faith in the army's reliability was seen in the recurrent oscillations in the role of political commissar. The one-man rule of commanders was introduced in 1925, but it was abolished in 1937 with commissars again given authority over commanders. This lasted until August 1940 when commissars were again downgraded to deputy commanders for political affairs. Then the power of commissars was again upgraded at the beginning of the war, only to be finally reduced to deputy status in October 1941.

The party used multiple methods to control the army. Coercion, in the form of massive purges and the creation of a secret-police network within the army, played an important role. So successful were these methods that apart from the two hard purges in the 1924-1925 and 1937-1941 periods, the army was virtually exempt from the recurrent purges that swept the civilian party organization. Large independent secret-police formations, replete with tanks, airplanes, and artillery, formed a powerful deterrent to independent army action. Commissars checked the possibility of independent roles for officers, and the party carefully controlled the promotion and selection of officers.

Coercion, no matter how effective, was far from the only reliable means of party control. Utilitarian measures became significant in the 1930s when the officer corps became one of the most elite, lionized, and privileged sectors of Soviet society. As the army expanded from .5 million men in 1930 to over 4 million in 1941, promotions were very rapid, even before the purges. Normative appeals, especially political indoctrination of officers and soldiers, were of some value. Finally, the massive rise in military spending (from 1.6 billion rubles in 1929 to 56.7 billion rubles in 1940) and the tremendous scope of the military-oriented industrialization and modernization campaigns of the 1930s provided the officers with all the equipment of which they had ever dreamed. An army that had 200 old foreign tanks in 1929 now received over 2,000 modern tanks a year by 1940.

By 1941 the Red Army was well on its way toward becoming a modern, effective fighting force. It bore little relation to the ineffectual Red Army of 1929 that would have had difficulty warding off a Polish attack. Yet, the process of army transformation was not completed and had been hampered by the Great Purges. Those same purges had also smashed the possibility that the army might become in the near future a significant political actor in Soviet politics.[1]

WORLD WAR II AND ITS AFTERMATH

The Second World War markedly changed the very nature of the Red Army. Despite a massive technological transformation and tremendous increase in size, the state of the Red Army remained parlous and ill-defined by the end of the 1930s. Both its effectiveness and legitimacy remained in serious doubt. Its considerable accomplishments in the battles of Lake Hassan and Khalkin-Gol against the Japanese in 1938 and 1939 were overshadowed by its very poor showing in the Finnish campaign of the winter of 1939-1940. The Great Purges, which decimated and demoralized the officer corps through accusations of treason leveled against top army commanders, placed in question the very legitimacy of the army.

Nor did the opening phase of the German invasion of Russia in Operation Barbarossa in June 1941 inspire confidence in the Red Army. In the first four months of the war the Germans took the incredible number of 2.5 million Russian soldiers prisoner and occupied vast areas of the Soviet Union. Stymied in front of Moscow and Leningrad in the winter of 1941, the Germans renewed their advance in 1942 and reached Stalingrad by the fall. Stalin responded by shooting some top army commanders (including Pavlov and Klimovskikh, Western Front commander and chief of state, respectively), replacing others (including his cronies Voroshilov, Timoshenko, and Budenny), and revamping the entire system of command and supply.

The Red Army had, however, held fast in front of Moscow and Leningrad in the winter of 1941 and, despite further losses, in front of Stalingrad in the winter of 1942. The inspired heroism of the soldiers and the increasing capabilities of the commanders and war industry began to tell in battle. After smashing the last major Nazi offensive of the war in huge tank battles in front of Kursk in 1943, the Red Army proceeded to go over to a massive offensive. By the time the Allies finally landed on the continent in June 1944, the Red Army had liberated nearly all Soviet territory except in the northern sector. In the last year of the war the newly effective Red Army stormed Berlin, destroyed the Third Reich, and liberated a number of East European countries.

Why the tremendous change between 1941 and 1945, and what did it presage for civil-military relations? The changes had several basic causes. First, there was a considerable shakeup in the officer corps. Battle-hardened and skilled officers were promoted while incompetent officers were pushed aside in the course of the war. Officers with the requisite talent and lower-class background, hastily promoted during the Great Purges and educated in academies in the 1930s, were often given command posts beyond their capacity in 1941. By 1945 the surviving officers had gained the necessary skills and confidence and formed a cohesive and talented officer corps. Thus, the officer corps had finally attained a level of competence concomitant with the massive improvement in the army's level of military technology. And they had mastered modern military technique, especially in defense against the blitzkrieg and deployment of armor. Second, the army had greatly improved the quantity and quality of weaponry during the war. Third, the fighting zeal of the soldiers in the ranks had changed dramatically during the war. In 1941 the horrors of collectivization and dekulakization drained the fighting spirit of peasant soldiers, and the Great Purges demoralized soldiers from urban areas. Lulled by comforting Soviet propaganda, the soldiers neither expected war nor understood the real nature of Nazi Germany. By 1945 the problems of the 1930s had faded in importance, a process aided by Soviet assurances of changes after the war. By now the truly bestial nature of the Nazi "New Order" awoke a burning and fervent Soviet patriotism and nationalism. Finally, the Soviet Union received significant moral and material aid from the Allies, who belatedly opened a second front against the Germans in 1944.

Despite the dominance of the military factor during the war years, Stalin retained his central role in decision making. By August 1941 he was supreme commander in chief, people's commissar of defense, chairman of the State Defense Committee, and chairman of the Stavka (Supreme Military Headquarters). The State Defense Committee, which directed the overall war effort, contained not a single professional military man among its eight members. The entire system was so centralized that even small decisions were made at the top, and information was regularly received from the regimental level. Extensive conflicts within the system, especially between field commands and between the center and field commands, were resolved by Stalin. For military advice Stalin relied heavily on a small group of professional military officers headed by Zhukov and Shaposhnikov. A mixture of fear and admiration marked this relationship. But Stalin, playing on rivalries within the army, alone made the decisions against which the professionals were powerless to protest. This was true even if they thought these decisions disastrous--the failure to make adequate preparations in June 1941 or the failure to evacuate the Kiev salient several months later, for example. The military elite, in the wake of the Great Purges, feared Stalin more than they did the Germans.

The 1945-1953 period saw the reimposition of the prewar political system. Although the army had now demonstrated great effectiveness and achieved genuine popularity, it was not given a concomitant role in the political system. Rather, its popular leader, Marshal Zhukov, was ousted from the Central Committee and demoted to a provincial command in 1946. Stalin took the bulk of the credit for the victory, and police controls were again tightened in the armed forces. Military doctrine remained frozen in the prewar Stalinist mold. A thoroughgoing demobilization brought the size of the army down from over 11 million in 1945 to only 2.8 million in 1948. No professional soldier was promoted to the Politburo (by contrast, in America Eisenhower would become president in 1953), and Central Committee representation would remain low. After 1947 the onset of the Cold War would lead to a significant buildup of the military to over 5 million men by 1953. But the army remained frozen and constrained in the old Stalinist mold.[2]

THE KHRUSHCHEV ERA

The sudden death of Stalin in March 1953 set off a protracted succession crisis that was to last until Khrushchev defeated the Anti-Party Group majority on the Presidium in June 1957. During this period of uncertainty and division in the party leadership, party and police controls over the armed forces were eased. Various party leaders jockeyed for the support of the military, which now was regarded as a powerful and legitimate political actor. The military leaders yearned to be rid of the straightjacket imposed on it by Stalin and the shame of the Great Purges. In the 1953-1957 period the army was to be a significant political actor on no less than three occasions. The year 1957 was to demonstrate the limits of its newfound power.

Immediately after Stalin's death three professional soldiers (Zhukov, Vasilevsky, and Kuznetsov) were named first deputy ministers of defense under Bulganin. Given the military's natural and implacable hatred of its secret-police rival, it was not surprising that in June 1953 Zhukov and Konev evidently helped arrest Beria, the head of the secret police, and denounced him at his trial in December. As a reward, Zhukov was promoted to full membership on the Central Committee and given Beria's seat.

Events did not move to the satisfaction of the military. Malenkov's New Course policies in 1953 and 1954 directly challenged basic military interests. Seeking détente with the West and rejecting the thesis of the inevitability of war, he sought to respond to popular pressure by increasing production of consumer goods. In 1953 Malenkov reduced military expenditures by 9 percent and used state funds earmarked for war reserves for consumer goods instead. In 1954 Khrushchev, stressing external danger from the West and the need for more military weaponry and heavy industrial investment, challenged Malenkov. The military threw its weight behind Khrushchev, especially when Malenkov again cut military spending. The removal of Malenkov as prime minister at the Central Committee Plenum in February 1955 naturally pleased the military. In return, the military garnered numerous rewards from Khrushchev. Military appropriation was increased by 12 percent in 1955 as were funds for heavy industry. Zhukov became defense minister, eleven generals (most of whom had been associated with Khrushchev at Stalingrad during the war) became marshals, and political controls were de-emphasized in the military. Khrushchev became commander in chief of the armed forces.

The Zhukov-Khrushchev alliance lasted over two and a half years. In February 1956 the 20th Party Congress promoted Zhukov to alternate membership on the Presidium, the first time ever for a professional soldier. In his secret speech Khrushchev curried favor with the military by attacking Stalin for liquidating Tukhachevsky and top officers on false charges in 1937, for failing to take defensive measures against Nazi Germany in 1941, and for ineptly interfering with the Red Army high command during the war. In December 1956 the party press praised Zhukov on his birthday. In June 1957 Zhukov helped rescue Khruschev when a majority of the Presidium voted to oust Khrushchev. Zhukov arranged the prompt transport of Central Committee members to Moscow on military planes, and at a Central Committee Plenum directly challenged Molotov, leader of the opposition. He even addressed Moscow military units. After Khrushchev's victory at the plenum, Zhukov was promoted to full membership on the Presidium, political controls were further eased in the army, and officers purged in the late 1930s were rehabilitated.

Khrushchev, now finally rid of his rivals, became increasingly apprehensive of Zhukov's prominence and popularity, especially after a flamboyant speech in July in which Zhukov touted himself and ignored the role of Khrushchev and the party. Fearing incipient Bonapartism, Khrushchev struck first by purging Zhukov in October 1957. At a Central Committee Plenum, Marshals Malinovsky and Konev led a denunciation of Zhukov for his personality cult, elimination of the role of the party in the military, and adventurism in foreign policy. Once again officers associated with Khrushchev in the war (the "Southern Clique"), including Grechko and Moskalenko, were promoted and Malinovsky became defense minister.

The 1957-1964 period was marked by varying degrees of tension between Khrushchev and the military. As he had in the Zhukov case, Khrushchev sought to capitalize on divisions within the armed forces, this time primarily between the more conservative elements in the ground forces and tactical air force and the radical elements in the strategic rocket forces and subsurface navy. In 1958 and 1959 he sought to limit the authority of commanders and increase that of party elements and the Main Political Administration in the armed forces. In January 1960, inspired by moves toward détente with the West and a desire to increase the production of consumer goods at home, he sought to save 17 billion rubles through reduction of the armed forces by one-third. Furthermore, the ground forces and surface navy would be downgraded in favor of the new strategic rocket forces and subsurface navy. The army, which had already borne the brunt of the previous mass reduction from 5.8 million men in 1955 to 3.6 million in 1958, strongly resisted this new slash in its manpower. Such a reduction meant retiring 250,000 officers, many of whom would suffer reduction in status and pay. So stiff was military resistance that Deputy Defense Ministers Sokolovky and Konev were retired in April, replaced by the more pliable Grechko and Zakharov. Nevertheless, by

December half of the cuts had been made. The Berlin crisis and rising tensions in 1961 added to military opposition and led to a suspension of the remaining cuts and the resumption of nuclear testing.

The last three years of the Khrushchev era did little to improve relations between the party and the army. The 1962 Cuban missile crisis debacle severely strained army-party relations and lowered Khrushchev's prestige. This was especially the case as Moskalenko (chief of strategic rockets) and other military leaders had been opposed to the original decision to put the missiles into Cuba. In December 1963 Khrushchev called for a further reduction in the size of the armed forces and sliced the military budget by 5 percent. In February 1964 he attacked the idea of priority for heavy industry over light industry, and in September he reiterated his call for a drastic shift of resources away from heavy industry and military industry. When Brezhnev, Kosygin, and Podgorny overthrew Khrushchev in October 1964, they could rest assured that, unlike the situation in 1957, the military leadership would do nothing to save Khrushchev.[3]

THE BREZHNEV ERA

Although the military played only a minor, supporting role in Khrushchev's ouster, it became one of the chief beneficiaries of his fall. Brezhnev and his colleagues clearly wished to avoid the fatal error of Khrushchev in alienating the key central institutions in Soviet politics. Khrushchev had defamed the secret police, split the party apparatus in two, decentralized the economic ministries, slashed Soviet ground troops, and sent Zhukov into exile. Instead of "harebrained" scheming that had proceeded at a frenetic pace, Brezhnev sought to give each key institution a secure and legitimate place in the decision-making process. The secret police would be restored to an honorable place in the system, the party would be reunited, government ministries would be securely centralized, and the armed forces would no longer find its basic interests under constant attack. Furthermore, all key groups were assured of real increases in their appropriations. Thus, Brezhnev sought to secure his own position by avoiding threats to the key interests of powerful central institutions and without purging their personnel. By 1973 the defense minister (Grechko), the head of the secret police (Andropov), and the foreign minister (Mikoyan) would all be added to the Politburo as a reflection of this process. Given the aging of top leaders over time (inevitable, assuming the avoidance of purges), the process initiated by Brezhnev involved a marked congealing of decision making around conservative central bureaucratic institutions.

As the military shares common views and interests with other key institutions, this decision-making process has been particularly advantageous to it. In four decades of continual stress on heavy industry and defense industry, many of the most talented people who were drawn to its managerial work were later promoted to top governmental and party posts. Unlike the Khrushchev era, top party leaders now hold many of the relatively conservative values and attitudes of the military leadership. The Cuban missile crisis in 1962 had demonstrated to them the importance of building up the power of the Soviet military. Finally, the power of the military-industry complex was reinforced by the fact that, because of tight censorship, the military retains control over crucial information vital to decision making.

Thus, under Brezhnev the Soviet military has again become a privileged sector of Soviet society. Over the past sixteen years it has enjoyed a steady rise in military appropriations of 3 to 5 percent a year. The armed forces have been expanded to over 4 million men and modernized with an array of sophisticated weapons. The navy under Gorshkov has undergone such considerable expansion that, for the first time, it has become a truly bluewater force capable of challenging American naval supremacy. Transport capabilities, as seen in the air and sea lift of the 1973 Yom Kippur War, were greatly expanded. Nor was this expansion limited primarily to those conservative elements of the military that had suffered under Khrushchev. During the 1970s the Soviet Union not only achieved strategic nuclear parity with the United States but threatened to take the lead over the United States in the early 1980s. Receiving 13 percent of the GNP by 1980, the Soviet military had not seen such a golden era of military appropriations since the 1930s. At the same time, the party was solicitous of the material status and professional interests of the armed forces and especially its officer corps.

Nevertheless, as in the 1930s, this military bounty did not mean that the armed forces were dominant in the policymaking process. Formal military representation in the Central Committee remained around 10 percent. After Marshal Grechko died, his seat in the Politburo went not to another professional soldier but to a civilian, Dimitri Ustinov, who had been in charge of military industry. When the top party leadership differed in its views from the military leadership, it retained the power to enforce its own views. Despite military resistance, the Soviet Union signed SALT I (Strategic Arms Limitation Treaty) and initialled SALT II. In another instance, highly sophisticated military weaponry, which had not been made available to Warsaw Pact troops, was shipped to Middle Eastern countries despite fear by the military that this weaponry might ultimately find its way into American hands. Thus, the policymaking role of the armed forces, though significant, has important limitations.[4]

CONCLUSIONS

We have seen that the historical development model is useful in understanding civil-military relations under Lenin and Stalin. Emerging from the civil war as a force lacking in legitimacy and effectiveness, the army played a minimal political role in the 1920s. Excluded from Stalinist decision making in the 1930s, the army was the passive beneficiary of industrialization and modernization and the passive object of the Great Purges. Although World War II saw a natural increase in military influence, Stalin remained firmly in control. After the war he reinstituted the old controls. The death of Stalin in 1953 allowed the armed forces, and other institutions, to throw off many of the Stalinist restraints on their political role. The army, which had emerged as a highly legitimate and effective force by the end of World War II, under Zhukov helped Khrushchev oust Malenkov and defeat the Anti-Party Group. After Khrushchev purged Zhukov as a potential rival in 1957, the role of the armed forces declined amidst recurrent Khrushchevian attempts to reduce and reform it. Under Brezhnev the military had emerged as a legitimate interest group with significant ties to other elite groups.

NOTES

1. For the civil war and interwar period see Jonathan Adelman, The Revolutionary Armies (Westport, Conn.: Greenwood Press, 1980); John Erickson, The Soviet High Command (London: Macmillan and Company, 1962); and D. Fedotoff White, The Growth of the Red Army (Princeton: Princeton University Press, 1944).
2. For World War II see Seweryn Bialer, ed., Stalin and His General (New York: Pegasus, 1966); and Timothy Colton, Commissars, Commanders, and Civilian Authority (Cambridge: Harvard University Press, 1979).
3. For the Khrushchev era see H. Gordon Skilling's chapter on the military in H. Gordon Skilling and Franklyn Griffiths, eds., Interest Groups in Soviet Politics (Princeton: Princeton University Press, 1971); Raymond Garthoff's chapter on the military under Khrushchev in Alexander Dallin and Alan Westin, eds., Politics in the Soviet Union (New York: Harcourt, Brace and World, 1966); Roman Kolkowicz's chapter on the military in Allen Kassof, ed., Prospects for Soviet Society (New York: Praeger, 1968); Michel Tatu, Power in the Kremlin: From Khrushchev to Kosygin (New York: Viking, 1968); and Jerry Hough and Merle Fainsod, How the Soviet Union is Governed (Cambridge: Harvard University Press, 1979).

4. For the Brezhnev era see Seweryn Bialer, *Stalin's Successors* (New York: Cambridge University Press, 1980); Raymond Garthoff, "SALT and the Soviet Military," *Problems of Communism* 24 (January-February 1975); Thomas Wolfe, "Are the Generals Taking Over?," *Problems of Communism* 18 (July-October 1969); and Dale Herspring, "The CPSU and the Military," *Problems of Communism* 25 (March-April 1976).

3
The Chinese Army

William Pang-yu Ting

Two traits characterize Chinese civil-military relationships. First, it is difficult to differentiate the Chinese civilian elite from the Chinese military elite. Since the formation of the Chinese Red Army in 1927, many Chinese elite members have worn civilian and military hats simultaneously. Historically, the Chinese military often played "nonmilitary roles." From 1927 to 1949, when the Chinese Communist party gained national power, the Red Army often performed educational, administrative, propaganda dissemination, and other nonmilitary functions. From 1949 to 1954 (the Reconstruction Period), the Red Army, renamed the People's Liberation Army (PLA), was the only nationwide administrative apparatus available to the Chinese Communist party. During this period, the five field armies of the PLA were each responsible for the administration of one geographic region.

Second, the Chinese political system has oscillated back and forth between favoring moderate policies and pushing for radical reforms. This oscillation often has strained civil-military relations and has created confusion in defining the role of the military in Chinese society. This tension between the Chinese civil and military leaders during periods of intense moderate-radical conflicts occurred primarily after 1952, although such conflicts can be traced back as far as 1932.[1] Given these two traits, Chinese civilian and military relations can best be described as a system that (a) shares the same personnel pool, (b) had a symbiotic existence before the Chinese Communists gained power, and (c) oscillated between tension and cooperation after the Chinese Communists gained power.

THE PATH TO POWER

A common pattern shared by all politically powerful Communist armies is that they played a crucial role in determining the outcomes of civil wars and/or foreign invasions prior to their gaining power. From a comparative perspective, the PLA ranks among the most politically powerful Communist armies, even though its quotient of political power, as stated above, has varied through times. Thus we need first to examine the PLA's path to power in order to explain China's particular civil-military relations.[2]

The birth of the Chinese Red Army in 1927 signified a major policy shift in the Chinese Communist party. Prior to that time, the Chinese Communist party was a purely political movement with no military backing. At the urging of the Soviet Union, the Chinese Communist party had entered a "united front" strategy with the Chinese Nationalist party (its competitor for national power), believing that China needed to complete a nationalist period before it could begin to attempt socialist reforms. Thus, the Chinese Communist party prior to 1927 concentrated on building labor organizations and organizing strikes in urban centers; a politically conscious Chinese urban working class was thought to be the best guarantee to insure an eventual Communist victory in China. This united front strategy backfired in 1927 when the Chinese Nationalists ordered their troops to attack Communist labor organizers in the major Chinese urban centers. This event, called the 1927 Shanghai Massacre, taught the Chinese Communists two lessons. First, they needed to build an army to counter the Nationalists' monopoly of fire power in order to prevent a recurrence of the Shanghai Massacre. Second, they needed to shift their power base from urban centers to rural areas so that their leaders were no longer easy targets for the urban-based Nationalist troops.

The Shanghai Massacre, more than any other historical event, hastened the birth of a regular Chinese Communist army, the Chinese Red Army. The new Red Army, under the command of Mao Zedong and Zhu Teh, established a strong hold for the rural wing of the Chinese Communist party in rural Jiangxi in 1927. The urban wing of the Chinese Communist movement survived until 1931, but it was the Mao-Zhu wing that is more relevant for our discussion on civil-military relations here. The birth of the rural-military strategy, which eventually led to the victory of the Chinese Communists over the Chinese Nationalists, signified the important role that the Red Army played in the path to power of the Chinese Communist party.

The period from 1927 to 1935 was a formative period for the Red Army. During this period, the Maoist wing of the party started as a dissident group and ended as the dominant force of the Chinese Communist revolution. It was during this period that Mao began to develop and to implement his military philosophy. Mao emphasized the political role of the Red Army and regarded the Red Army primarily as an ideological dissemination organization. He also stressed organizational penetration of the army by the party. A dual command system was implemented in the military whereby unit commanders shared decision-making power with political commissars assigned to the same unit. The commanders were responsible for the technical aspects of warfare, and the commissars were delegated the responsibility of keeping the military politically conscious. Commanders' military orders were to be countersigned by corresponding political commissars. Also, strategically, Mao favored a nonpositional, guerrilla warfare, which is more political than military in nature.

This Maoist view of the military primarily as a political tool for the revolution created both philosophical and strategical problems for many commanders during this period. As early as 1929, military commanders showed resentment of party control and disliked the amount of time devoted to political work by regular Red Army units.[3] Moreover, during this period, the Nationalists organized five massive positional military campaigns against the Communists, which forced many PLA commanders to view warfare from a more professional, nonideological viewpoint. On the other hand, it was also clear to the Chinese Communists that they could not win militarily against an enemy with more powerful fire power unless they could organize the masses politically in order to isolate the enemy. Thus, the civil-military cooperation-tension cycle, which has plagued China ever since, has a history as long as the existence of the PLA.

The period from 1927 to 1935, according to Whitson, also helped to fashion the composition and the military philosophy of the officer corps of the Chinese military.[4] During this period, recruitment to the PLA officer corps came primarily from the southern provinces. These young recruits were promoted rapidly during the campaigns against the Nationalists; therefore, these young southern officers soon began to dominate the elite structures of the PLA. These campaigns also helped to speed up the professionalization process of the Chinese officer corps, and this increasingly came into conflict with the Maoist view of a more political military.

Under constant threat of military annihilation by the better-equipped Nationalist army, the Communists decided to move their base to the remote northwestern part of China by 1935. This difficult journey was the famous Long March. Only 50,000 Communist troops reached the final destination. The rest fell victim to the harsh conditions and pursuing Nationalist troops.

Recruits to the Chinese army officer corps after the Long March, given the geographic constraint, were primarily northerners. This pattern continued until after 1949 when the Communists gained national power and nationwide recruitment was possible. Thus, the officer corps of the Chinese military by 1949 consisted mainly of two types: southern veterans of the Long March who dominated the high command of the Chinese military system, and northern, lower ranked, younger recruits who did not participate in the Long March. North-South tensions among the officers later were to become a major source of intramilitary elite conflict when the northerners' upward mobility was blocked by the southern elite members who refused to make room at the top.[5]

The threat of Japanese invasion forced an uneasy truce in 1936 between the Nationalists and the Communists as they joined once again to form a second united front. From 1937 to 1945, Japanese troops invaded China. This invasion influenced the subsequent development of civil-military relations in China in several ways. First, the Chinese Communists moderated their social-economic reform policies in order to rally a wide spectrum of support. Second, the party initiated a tripartite system of local administration that included one-third Communists, one-third non-Communists, and one-third independents. This deemphasis of radical reforms, coupled with a foreign invasion, created two trends in the Chinese military system. First, the commanders gradually gained the upper hand in decision-making power over the commissars. Second, a decentralized civil-military system was implemented in Communist-controlled areas where, gradually, five independently commanded Red Army branches emerged. These five branches were to become the five field armies that jointly defeated the Nationalist forces in their final struggle for power.

The growth of the Red Army during this period was unparalleled. In 1937, the Red Army only had a total strength of 92,000. By the end of the Japanese invasion in 1945, the Chinese army had a total of 880,000 soldiers, of which roughly 400,000 were recruited in 1944-1945 alone.[6]

After the Japanese had surrendered in 1945, a civil war broke out between the Communists and Nationalists. Communist troops suffered initial defeats, but superior discipline, higher morale, and a more efficient mass support system soon turned the tide for the Red Army. On October 1, 1949, the Chinese Communists reached the long-sought-after goal of establishing a People's Republic of China.

THE PLA IN POST-1949 POLITICS

We can best analyze post-1949 civil-military relations in China by studying the role played by the PLA in various post-1949 political crises. This role followed a common pattern. A crisis was usually initiated by a radical elite coalition that perceived that the Chinese revolution was being betrayed by moderate leaders who valued productivity above equality of distribution of goods and values. This was followed by the subsequent involvement of the PLA into the radical-moderate conflict, usually at the request of one side or the other. However, the PLA always finished up a crisis by supporting the moderate coalition over the radical coalition.

The initial decade of the People's Republic of China (1949-1959) saw no major conflict between the radicals and the moderate leaders. Many of the moderate leaders were from the military. China was busy reconstructing after a bitter civil war and a foreign invasion. The PLA enjoyed tremendous political power during the initial two years of this decade, as China was divided into six administrative regions, four of which were actually headed by purely military men. In addition, every senior commander of the five field armies was rewarded with membership in the Military Affairs Council, the highest party committee for military affairs.

In the early 1950s the PLA was engaged in the Korean War. The net result of the Korean War was the increasing professionalization of the PLA officer corps and the further dominance of the professional commanders over the political commissars. For the first time, the Chinese armed forces had met the awesome fire power of a modern fighting force from the United States. Thus, under Marshal Peng Dehuai, the former commander of the First Field Army and the first defense minister of the People's Republic of China, the PLA began to push for the development of a more modern weapons program and to argue for a more professionally oriented armed force during the 1950s.

The first political crisis in post-1949 China came during Peng's push for military modernization. It was during this time, the mid-1950s, that China launched the Great Leap Forward to speed up the socialist transformation process. Agricultural collectivization was intensified, and backyard local industries were encouraged and organized. However, lack of quality controls, exaggerations of production figures at local levels, and widespread mass resistance resulted, which began to drag China into a state of near anarchy.

There is some debate as to whether the PLA under Peng and other more moderate party elite members supported the ill-conceived Great Leap Forward during its initial stage. However, there is no doubt that by 1959, two years into the Great Leap, Chinese party moderates under Liu Shao-yi and the PLA under Peng began to view the Great Leap Forward with great concern. Also, many generals were very resentful of being sent down to local units to practice "productive labor" with common soldiers, a program initiated by Mao during the Great Leap Forward period.

Consequently, during a plenary meeting of the Chinese Communist party's Central Committee held in Lushan in 1959, Peng criticized bitterly the economically disastrous programs of the Great Leap Forward and blamed Mao for this fiasco. The conflict between Mao and Peng created an intense debate among the Chinese elite. Mao was very disturbed by the Lushan Conference. Reportedly, he even threatened to quit the party in order to lead an insurgent force against the dissidents. After heated debates, the conference finally recommended the dismissal of Marshal Peng as defense minister. During this time, Mao also became increasingly worried about revisionism in the Soviet Union, and he must have viewed Peng's call for more moderate policies as the beginning of revisionism in China.

To replace Peng as defense minister, the party selected Lin Biao, the former commander of the Fourth Field Army. A series of political policies, aimed at strengthening the party's control over the PLA, were initiated by Lin. These policies met strong resistance among the PLA elite members, and military morale during this period was at a very low point. Subsequent events, such as the conservative behavior of the PLA during the Cultural Revolution, indicated that the attempt by Lin to politicize the PLA was a failure particularly among regional and local PLA units. This is not to suggest, however, that the PLA by this time had become a totally political organization. Rather, it is to argue that the PLA, after the Korean War and the Great Leap Forward, now favored an orderly progression over radical reforms that could bring about near anarchy once again. Thus, the political division in China at this time was between a coalition of some radical central military and civilian elite members against a competing coalition of the more moderate party and military elite members primarily at the regional level. Since there were more regional military elite members than central ones (the ratio was about four to one), the majority of the PLA elite actually belonged to the moderate coalition.

By 1965, Mao felt very isolated from his moderate party and military subordinates. Mao had lost his presidency to his chief rival, Liu Shao-yi, in 1959. Liu and Deng Xiaoping, the party secretary, had placed their own people, those who favored moderate policies, in important party positions. This moderate coalition consistently had frustrated Mao's attempts to revitalize the revolutionary spirit of the Chinese Communist party.

It was under such adverse conditions that Mao decided to take drastic measures. Believing that the party apparatus was controlled by "capitalist roaders," a term he used to describe Chinese revisionists, Mao called on the PLA, the sole politically reliable organization, to reform the party. Army commissars were assigned to party units to engage in political work. This eventually led to a period of intense conflict between the moderates and the radicals during the Chinese Cultural Revolution of 1966 to 1969.

Since we are concerned with civil-military relations, only a very limited and relevant part of the Cultural Revolution will be analyzed here. Following a common pattern of crisis development in post-1949 China, the Cultural Revolution was initiated by a coalition of the radical civilian elite who feared that the moderate capitalist roaders were betraying the original goals of the revolution.

The radical elite coalition, headed by Mao, developed two strategies during the Cultural Revolution. First, the PLA, considered to be politically reliable, was called upon to reform the bureaucratic party. Second, youths were encouraged to join a Red Guard movement to attack local moderate party cadres.

It was possible that Mao had never anticipated the degree of violence that resulted from Red Guard actions and the military's ensuing reactions. Moderate party elite coalition members at the central level were dismissed one by one during the first two years of the Cultural Revolution, including the "head capitalists" Liu and Deng. However, the regional and provincial moderate civil and military leaders proved far more transigent and resisted central interferences by disregarding many radical directives. Red Guards, meanwhile, had grown to 10 million in number. These large masses of mobilized young people soon began to engage in intrafactional feuds that drove the nation to the brink of a war. By early 1967, civil disorder and violence had spread nationwide, as competing Red Guard groups and mass organizations battled openly in the streets.

The most serious case of civil-military conflict in Chinese Communist history, as well as intramilitary conflict, occurred in 1967. The central-radical coalition had issued a directive ordering the PLA to get involved directly in the Cultural Revolution by supporting the local radical Red Guard and mass organizations in their attempts to "take power from the capitalist roaders."[7] Unfortunately, many provincial capitalist roaders were military men. Thus, the central directives met with general noncompliance from the regional PLA. In fact, many regional and provincial commanders did exactly the opposite by suppressing the radical mass organizations. To counterattack, the central radical coalition then ordered sixteen of the thirty-six army corps, under the direct command of the Central Military Affairs Commission, to move into dissident provinces to provide military support for radical organizations against the regional and local capitalist roaders. Bitter intramilitary confrontations between central troops and dissident regional troops as well as intracentral confrontations ensued.

The confusion finally reached a climax during the Wuhan Incident. The military commander of the Wuhan military region, an ultraconservative, arrested a commission of central-radical representatives sent to Wuhan to negotiate a truce between feuding radical and conservative organizations fighting in Wuhan. The Wuhan Incident ended when the central-radicals reestablished their authority and arrested the commander of the Wuhan military region and his high-ranking subordinates. However, the net result of the Wuhan Incident was that it actually signaled the end of the radical phase of the Cultural

Revolution; a military mutiny was a serious affair that could lead to even more serious consequences, such as a military coup d'état.

By late 1967, the growing possibility of additional military mutinies and the increasing threat of anarchy in China soon convinced Mao that, above all, order needed to be restored. Soon after the Wuhan Incident, directives were issued to the central army corps ordering them to stop interfering with the politics of the regional military forces. During the next twelve months revolutionary committees were set up to administer the provinces. These revolutionary committees were dominated by moderate regional military leaders who promptly disbanded the radical mass organizations and restored order. The Cultural Revolution ended officially in 1969. The Communist party had by then been virtually decimated during the Cultural Revolution. The composition of the 1969 9th Party Congress reflected this fact. More military elite members were elected to the Central Committee of the Chinese Communist party than ever before or ever since. The Cultural Revolution clearly had brought about the ascendency of the military--the only structure capable of providing order to a nation torn by three years of bitter conflict.

From 1969 until Mao's death in 1976, the PLA was engaged in a continuous confrontation with the central-radicals. This was especially true after the violent death of Lin Biao in a plane crash in Mongolia in 1971. The radical coalition, known today as the Gang of Four and headed by Mao's wife, Jiang Qing, perceived the PLA as their prime threat to obtaining power. During Mao's final years, the Gang of Four made a concerted effort to tear down the legitimacy of the PLA as a revolutionary structure. The radical Gang of Four called the PLA "bourgeois and unfit for socialism" and depicted the members of the PLA high command as elitists concerned only with high living. There is also evidence that the radicals tried to tamper with the military budgets and planning but had very little success. These acts were met with strong resistance in the PLA, especially in the navy and the air force.[8]

The most serious attempt by the Gang of Four to stop the miliary was its attempt to establish a militia that was not under the command of the PLA. From 1973 to 1976, the Gang of Four repeatedly tried to establish an independent "second armed forces" composed of a peasant militia. The PLA elite opposed such a move vehemently because the militia system always had been an auxiliary branch of the PLA under its direct command.

Mao's death in 1976 quickly put an end to the Gang of Four's feud with the PLA. The Gang was arrested almost immediately after Mao's death, with the PLA's blessing. The ensuing years saw a further purging of the remnants of radical military and party elites in China. Consequently, not since the early 1950s has China seen a more homogeneous moderate elite than today. For the time being the conservative modernizers seem to be in complete control of the Chinese civil-military elite system.

THE CIVIL-MILITARY ELITE SYSTEM OF CHINA

From a historical perspective, the success of the Chinese Communists can be attributed partly to the realization at a very early time that the key to power in China was a successful rural-based political-military uprising. Therefore, the military always has played a special role in the history of the Chinese Communist party. The dual command system of the PLA, on the other hand, always stressed the political presence of the party in the military. Similarly, events during the Cultural Revolution and during the post-Mao period have shown that the party must also have the support of the PLA in order to function properly. Indeed, the military may dominate the civilian in the Chinese political decision-making system when the party itself is weak, as the military did during the post-Cultural Revolution period.

An analysis of the composition of the four Central Committees of the Chinese Communist party from 1945 to 1973 shows that the PLA and civilian elites often shared political power in China. The Central Committee's civil-military distribution pattern through time is a good indicator of the relative power of the civilian and military elites, as almost all of the important decision makers in China are committee members.

We shall now look at the compositions of the various Central Committees. The Seventh Central Committee of 1945 (the last before the Chinese People's Republic was established) had forty-four full members, evenly divided between the military and the civilians. There were twenty-two Central Committee members from the civilian sector and twenty-two from the military sector. The Eighth Central Committee of 1956 saw an increase from forty-four to ninety-one full members. The civilians were the primary benefactor of this increase, occupying fifty-seven seats to only thirty-four for the military. Thus, the civilians held 63 percent of the Eighth Central Committee's seats and the military held only 37 percent. Both civilians and the military enjoyed absolute increases during the Eighth Central Committee. The relative loss of the military can be attributed to the fact that the Eighth Central Committee symbolized the end of the Reconstruction Period, a period when the military provided the only available nationwide organizational structure in China and thus held enormous political power. When this period ended the PLA began to emphasize its role as a professional armed force under Defense Minister Peng. The Korean War also helped to professionalize the PLA during this time. This depoliticization process lasted until Peng was dismissed in 1959 for challenging Mao's radical policies.

The demise of the party and the ascendancy of the military during the Cultural Revolution were reflected in the Ninth Central Committee of 1969, held immediately after the Cultural Revolution. The full membership was entirely due to an increase in military representation. Eighty-seven full members were from the military. The civilian representation to the Ninth Central Committee actually decreased in both absolute and relative terms. Only forty-seven members of the Ninth Central Committee were civilians, an absolute decrease of ten. In percentage, the Ninth Central Committee was almost exactly the reverse of the eighth; the military held 65 percent of the seats and the civilians held 35 percent.

The demise of Lin Biao, the radical defense minister who replaced Peng, reversed the civil-military representation figures again in the Tenth Central Committee of 1973. The Tenth Central Committee saw an absolute and a relative decline in the number of military seats represented in the Central Committee. The Tenth Central Committee had a civilian-military ratio of about two to one in favor of the civilians, roughly the same ratio as the Eighth Central Committee. The military had thirty-two seats and the civilians held sixty-three seats. The same ratio of two to one in favor of the civilians was repeated again in the Eleventh Central Committee in 1977 (twenty-nine military seats and seventy-one civilian seats).[9]

Therefore, from a Central Committee composition perspective, we have provided evidence to show that it is somewhat fruitless to talk about a separate civilian system and a separate military system in China. Rather, the historical development of civil-military relationships in China indicated that it is more appropriate to talk about a civil-military elite system in China that adjusts periodically to systemic imbalances. During crisis periods, especially crisis periods initiated by radicals who wished to telescope time in the process of socialist construction in China, civilian-military and intramilitary conflicts often occurred. During such crises the military sector of the civil-military elite often supported a conservative coalition.

CONCLUSION: MILITARY MODERNIZATION AND MILITARY BUDGET

Systematic purges of radical remnants by moderate in-power elite have produced a more unified Chinese civil-military elite today than at any other time in the past twenty years of Chinese history. This new collective of the moderate Chinese elite, headed by the old "capitalist roader" Deng Xiaoping, have embarked upon an ambitious program of rapid economic development for China. To achieve this goal, one necessary precondition (but not a sufficient condition) is for China to have a politically stable environment. As it has since its inception in 1927, the military will play a crucial role during the 1980s, either ensuring political stability or creating political instability.

The current Chinese civil-military elite has set military modernization as one of four top goals for China.[10] The end of Soviet military aid to China in the late 1950s and the disruption of the development of a modern domestic military technological base during the Cultural Revolution (except for nuclear weapons development) have resulted in a Chinese armed force that is, according to U.S. Defense Secretary Brown, in mobility and fire power about fifteen years behind the United States and the Soviet Union. From the current Chinese civil-military leaders' perspectives, the current weakness of the PLA is a serious shortcoming that needs to be overcome, especially given the Soviet threat to the north and the hostility of the powerful Vietnamese to the south.

How does the PLA compare as a fighting force with that of the Soviet Red Army? During the post-Mao period, China has made a concerted effort to improve its artillery production. China now produces three types of tanks that are about one generation out of date. In total number of tanks the Chinese now have about 13,000 tanks, roughly one-fourth those of the USSR. These tanks, of course, are not as mobile or as powerful as the Soviet tanks. During the past few years China has produced about a thousand tanks annually. The Chinese army is the largest ground force in the world, with approximately 3 million soldiers.

The air and naval forces in China are very weak by superpower standards. The Chinese naval strength lies primarily in its fleet of fast attack crafts used primarily for coastal defense purposes. Among these are over one hundred guided-missile patrol boats, all built by the Chinese, but some designed by the Soviets and some by the Chinese. This fleet of missile-equipped attack craft is cost-efficient for defense purposes, but it is also very vulnerable to an enemy who possesses advanced radar jamming devices that can dramatically lower the missile's accuracy. The Chinese air force numerically is the third largest in the world behind the two superpowers, but its fleet of bombers and jet fighters are obsolete by Soviet standards. The backbone of the Chinese air force is a fleet of an improved domestic version of the Soviet-designed MIG 19. The manufacturing of Chinese MIG 21s have run into numerous technical problems, and they still cannot be mass-produced.

The post-Mao period also has seen an acceleration in the development of the Chinese nuclear strategic forces. The Chinese Second Artillery, in charge of China's nuclear forces, in 1980 successfully tested its first ICBM capable of hitting any region of the Soviet Union. A series of medium-range nuclear-tipped ballistic missiles were perfected in the 1960s, and two types of intermediate-range ballistic missiles were made operational during the early 1970s. The Chinese now have about 350 operational nuclear warheads, up to a range of three to five megatons in explosive power.

It is clear from the above discussion that the push for military modernization in China will probably receive strong support from China's aging military leaders. Military modernization, as I stated earlier, has increasingly received support from the majority of China's military leaders ever since the Korean War, except for a brief period during Lin Biao's tenure as defense minister. Now that the radical opponents of the moderate military elite have been defeated, this push by the military to speed up military modernization can be expected to intensify in the future. Moreover, the military elite will no doubt remind their civilian counterparts about the crucial role that the PLA played in restoring political order and stability after the Cultural Revolution and the post-Mao periods.

This possible push by the Chinese military elite for military modernization may create tensions between military leaders who want a larger military budget and civilian leaders who want to divert scarce Chinese resources away from the military sector to the industrial and agricultural sectors. There are already indications that military needs are now being accorded lower priorities than agricultural and industrial needs in China. For example, the 1980-1981 Chinese military budget is about 4.7 percent less than the 1979-1980 budget, from 17 billion U.S. dollars down to 16.2 billion U.S. dollars. At the same time, investment in the industrial and agricultural sectors is scheduled to increase. Some military officers, especially those involved in such high-investment, high-technology military areas as nuclear weapons research and development, have already complained openly about the impending military budget cut.[11]

This new civil-military tension, unlike the tensions of the past, is not between radicals and moderates; rather it involves policy disagreements between two competing moderate elite groups. Therefore, unlike the past when violent street fightings and purges were used as means of resolving ideological disagreements among China's feuding radical and moderate elites, the current budgetary disagreement may be resolved by bureaucratic bargaining and coalition politics. If bargaining and coalition policies become the dominant modes of decision making in China, then future civil-military conflicts in China could become much less violent. Thus, Chinese civil-military relationships may be entering a new bureaucratic era in the 1980s.

NOTES

1. For an excellent discussion on the history of Chinese civil-military conflicts prior to 1949 see William Whitson, The Chinese High Command (New York: Praeger, 1973).
2. From a causal modeling standpoint, we are theorizing here that there is a direct causal linkage from a Communist army's path to power to its subsequent political influence. Since this book is primarily conceptual, I have not operationalized these concepts, and I have not eliminated other indirect causations.
3. Ying-mao Kau, The People's Liberation Army and China's Nation-Building (White Plains, New York: International Arts and Sciences Press, Inc., 1973), p. 38.
4. For a detailed discussion see Whitson, The Chinese High Command, especially chapters 1 and 2.
5. See William P. Ting, "Coalitional Behavior Among the Chinese Military Elite," American Political Science Review, June 1979, pp. 478-493.
6. John Gittings, The Role of the Chinese Army (London: Oxford University Press, 1967), p. 303.
7. For a detailed discussion on this period read William P. Ting, "A Longitudinal Study of Chinese Military Factionalism," Asian Survey, October 1975, pp. 896-910; Hong Yung Lee, The Politics of the Chinese Cultural Revolution (Berkeley: The University of California Press, 1978), pp. 244-302; and Parris H. Chang, Power and Policy in China (University Park: Pennsylvania State University Press, 1978), pp. 110-166.
8. See Chang, Power and Policy in China, pp. 197-220 for a detailed discussion of this period.
9. The sources for these figures are: Whitson, Chinese High Command, p. 520; Harvey Nelson, The Chinese Military System: An Organizational Study of the Chinese PLA (Boulder: Westview Press, 1977), p. 216; and James Townsend, "Politics in China," in Gabriel Almond and G. Bingham Powell, eds., Comparative Politics Today (Boston: Little, Brown & Co., 1980), p. 264.
10. The four goals of China are: (1) military modernization, (2) scientific modernization, (3) industrial modernization, and (4) agricultural modernization. These four broad goals are called the Four Modernizations Programs.
11. This was reported in the China Daily News (in Chinese), September 4, 1980.

4
The Cuban Army

Jorge I. Domínguez

Scholars have often assumed that there is always a firm distinction between civilians and military, that the two are at least potentially in conflict, that civilians are always capable of governing, and that military activity can be so strictly defined that taking over governments or performing normally civilian functions can readily be identified and analyzed as "unmilitary." Thus arise such terms as "praetorian" polity, a "militarized" society, or a "politicized" army.

The facts in revolutionary Cuba contradict this dichotomy. Cuba has been ruled in large part by military men who govern large segments of both military and civilian life, who are held up as paragons to both soldiers and civilians, who are the bearers of the revolutionary tradition and ideology, who have politicized themselves by absorbing the norms and organization of the Communist party, and who have educated themselves to become professional in political, economic, managerial, engineering, and educational as well as military affairs. Their civilian and their military lives are fused. In this situation, at least until recently, one could not speak of either civilian control over the military or military control over civilians. But in the mid-1970s some new trends have appeared that may herald yet another change in the future.

Although we can identify a ruling elite and some purely civilian leaders, it is not so easy to identify purely military leaders. The vast majority of Cuba's ruling elite have held military rank, and no identifiable purely civilian elite has been available to take their place. There is little evidence of civilian-military conflict. Although the purely civilian share of the elite

---

Abridged by permission of the author and publishers from Cuba: Order and Revolution by Jorge I. Domínguez, Cambridge, Mass.: The Belknap Press of Harvard University Press, 1979 Copyright © 1979 by Jorge I. Domínguez.

has been small, the military's decisive political role has been great and the scope of its legitimate activity not demarcated.

The "civic soldier" has been a key political role in Cuba for a long time. Approximately two-thirds of the high-ranking officials have had civic-soldier careers; most of them learned this role during the uprising against Batista in the 1950s and the suppression of the anti-Communists in the early 1960s. Civil war, more than any other form of conflict, tends to integrate military and political roles. Civic soldiers head both military and civilian agencies in Cuba and, just as military agencies have had civilian tasks, civilian agencies have had military tasks and have used military forms of organization. The civic-soldier role includes not only former soldiers heading government organizations but also soldiers on active duty engaged in political, economic, or other nonmilitary activities.

Because the civilian and military aspects of the civic-soldier role are regarded as equally legitimate, organizations are flexible. The defense budget is not cut when threats to the state decline; rather, it is simply directed to the nondefense aspects of the civic-soldier role. Military elements were stressed again after the intervention in Angola. Since loyalty to the organization will often lead to changes in emphasis for the sake of its survival or growth, the legitimacy of the civic-soldier role has facilitated these shifts.[1]

THE MILITARY MISSION OF THE ARMED FORCES

The military mission of the Cuban armed forces was originally to provide for national defense and to suppress internal challenges to the authority of the government. More recently Cuba's participation in the Angolan civil war has added a third task--overseas combat. Since 1960 the Soviet nuclear shield has been one factor deterring a United States attack on Cuba, somewhat shakily in 1960 and more firmly after 1970. The Cuban armed forces, however, are responsible for their own subnuclear defense. A major challenge thus far was the Bay of Pigs invasion in April 1961. Since then, though with declining frequency, various exile groups have launched hit-and-run attacks on the island or have landed small parties, but they have all been quickly captured.

From 1960 to 1965 counterrevolutionaries rose up against the Cuban government in all six provinces. At one time the country had as many as 179 insurrectionary bands. The revolutionary government estimated the number of armed oppositionists killed or captured at 3,591; about 500 combat deaths in the so-called anti-Bandit Corps--the LCB (League of Cuban Bandits) forces--were reported, apart from deaths from other military actions and terrorism, along with losses of 1 billion pesos from all three.

Antigovernment forces numbered no more than a thousand at their peak strength. The total number of deaths in the 1960s was in the same range--roughly 2,000 to 2,500-- as in the 1950s. The number of regular troops committed by the Cuban government to defending the regime against insurrection was ten times greater under Castro than it had been under Batista; the reserve forces under Castro were ten to fifteen times greater than under Batista; the amount of actual fighting was probably the same. The difference was that Batista's government lost and Castro's won. Revolutionary government in Cuba could not have survived without effective armed forces.[2]

Although Batista had 29,270 regular and 18,542 reserve troops in 1958, Castro's Revolutionary Armed Forces numbered about 300,000 at their peak in the early 1960s. By 1970 they had declined to 250,000, and by late 1974 had declined further to about 100,000. According to Raúl Castro, the Army of Working Youth had another 100,000. A large number of reserve forces were also available at various levels of readiness. The number of civilian workers under direct military command increased 23 percent between 1971 and 1975. Foreign sources have estimated the size of the professional regular Cuban armed forces at approximately 100,000 to 120,000 from the late 1960s on. The Institute for Strategic Studies estimated that Cuba's regular armed forces amounted to 117,000 in 1975, and that the ready reserves, which could be mobilized within a maximum of seventy-two hours, numbered about 90,000 (inactive reserves were not estimated). Therefore, the change in the Cuban armed forces from 1970 to 1974 represents a shift of personnel from semiprofessional, full-time soldiers to reserve status. The size of the truly professional forces has apparently remained constant.

Castro has allocated at least two or three times more expenditures to the armed forces than did Batista. At their peak in the early 1960s Cuban military expenditure totaled nearly 500 million pesos. As counterrevolutionary activity declined and the economy recovered from near-collapse in 1962-63, military spending dropped from 8 percent of GNP in 1962 to 4.8 percent in 1967. This decline was interrupted in 1968. Military expenditure then remained at a constant high level as a result of the expansion of the military into the economic sphere. In addition to Cuba's own resources, the Soviet Union, according to Castro himself, supplied Cuba free of charge with weapons worth several billion pesos between 1960 and 1975.[3]

At the end of 1973 and again at the end of 1976, military ranks and armed-forces hierarchy were reorganized to approximate the system most common in the rest of the world. Until 1973 the highest rank, *comandante*, had no clear equivalent elsewhere. Ranks within the armed forces were poorly differentiated. In 1976 Fidel Castro became commander in chief. A rank below him was Raúl Castro as general of the army. The chiefs of the three main armies became division generals. Everyone along the line received a new rank corresponding to the universal system. Since 1973, former officers in civilian jobs have no longer been addressed by their military titles. Inactive personnel are also discouraged from wearing uniforms and insignia.[4] The change is partly symbolic, but it also serves to draw a clear line between civilian and military roles and provides an incentive for officers attracted to the military life to stay in it and work for promotion there.

The professionalization of the armed forces and the stability of its doctrine and structure are evidence of a high degree of military institutionalization. In fact, the process was well under way even during the 1960s. The long terms of service characteristic of the best officers, the integrated military-school system, and the autonomy of military organizations from civilian organizations for military recruitment have all since added to their stability and ideological coherence and have promoted officer loyalty to the armed forces. These factors would also have led to a military oligarchy had they been left unchecked by the Communist party. Professionalization has increased military autonomy because civilian technicians are less necessary, and it has added to the organizational complexity of the armed forces. The institutionalized armed forces, however, also need a larger share of the national budget. An added cost to civilians--and a gain for the military--was the expansion of military training and military control into the lives of many people. Another trend appeared in the mid-1960s when the armed forces adopted social, economic, and political missions as well as purely military functions. From one point of view civilians were militarized; from another, the military was civilianized. The result was the flourishing of the civic-soldier at least through the mid-1970s.

Cuba's victory in Angola demonstrated the effectiveness of the army and reforms, including war games that stressed long marches, occupation of large areas, and simultaneous deployment of large numbers and varieties of troops. Approximately 20,000 Cuban troops were in Angola at any one time, and the total number involved through troop rotation was probably much larger. The war demonstrated close military ties with the Soviet Union, which provided heavy weapons on the spot. The Angolan operation indicated the organizational versatility of the Cuban armed forces, which was in this case 50 percent black in racial composition, far more blacks than normal. Another organizational accomplishment was the effective dual operation of the army in Angola and in Cuba. There were some costs--demand by the armed forces for more trained military personnel, some limited elite civilian resistance to the war, some insubordination among the troops, widespread unhappiness among the Cuban people concerning compulsory military service, and an increasing gap between military professionals and civilians.[5]

The Angolan war in 1975-1976 demonstrated the improvements in Cuba's armed forces and military reserves, but it also caused a strain in civilian-military relations. If this tension continues in the years ahead, and if the demands for more military professionalization to cope with protracted war in Angola remain pressing, it will spell the demise of the civic soldier. The lines of conflict between civilian and military interests will then be too clearly drawn to permit continuing fusion of those roles.

The redefinition of the military mission of the Cuban armed forces in the mid-1970s was further evident in their active participation in Cuba's foreign-aid program. At the end of 1977, Cuba had about ten foreign military-assistance programs in Africa and the Middle East, of which the one in Angola was by far the largest. In addition, some Cuban military personnel performing civilian tasks were involved in other Cuban foreign-aid programs in another half-dozen countries in Africa, Asia, and Latin America.

THE PRODUCTION MISSION OF THE ARMED FORCES

The military was more successful in expanding its role into economic areas. Even from 1962 to 1964, when their strictly military mission was paramount, LCB units in the Escambray mountains were helping the peasants in the field. This work fit in with their strategy in combatting insurgents who threatened that area and others. But expansion of the military's economic activities came only after foreign and domestic military threats had declined. In 1968, 51,000 soldiers were assigned to the sugar harvest (representing about 46 percent of the regular armed forces and about a fifth of all the armed forces); in 1969, 38,000 were assigned there (35 and 15 percent, respectively); in 1971, 43,000 (39 and 17 percent). In the extraordinary 1970 harvest, however, 70,000 troops were pressed into service, representing about 64 percent of the regular forces and 28 percent of all the armed forces generally.[6]

Unlike Batista's military in the 1930s, which contributed little in terms of technical and managerial skills to economic growth, the Revolutionary Armed Forces in the 1960s took on various nonmilitary technical and managerial jobs to encourage growth. In 1967, the air force operated sixty airplanes used in spraying and fertilizing fields, and the army formed a motorized brigade to run mechanized equipment for tilling new fields for sugar. By the spring of 1969 all farm machinery was under military supervision. Soldiers who had previously served in tank or motorized units were shifted to this new brigade. The Ché Guevara Brigade, organized in the fall of 1968 into thirty-six subunits throughout the six provinces, operated entirely in agriculture. Its commander in chief, Raúl Guerra Bermejo, was also a member of the party's Central Committee. The brigade retained a strict military organization and chain of command. It took over all the machinery formerly administered by the state farms using civilian personnel.

In 1970 the military cut 20 percent of the giant sugarcane harvest. They organized and operated the combines that mechanized cane cutting. They coordinated the cane loading at strategic locations and supervised the transportation of cane for the sugar mills in the eastern provinces. They operated all the tractors and cane lifters. They built roads, railroad tracks, and temporary housing. Members of the Luis Turcios Likma Brigade of the Eastern Army won the coveted title National Heroes of Labor. Harvests in the late 1960s and in 1970 were directed from a national command post linked to the field through provincial, regional, and municipal outposts. The harvest took on all the aspects of a military campaign: It was a battle and a struggle, no less essential to the survival of the revolution than the military engagements of earlier years.[7]

The rest of the world has often put the military to peaceful uses, but rarely on the scale of the Cuban military's involvement in social and economic tasks. Among the other Communist countries, the Soviet armed forces provide the greatest contrast. The Soviet armed forces have stayed strictly with military concerns, arguing that modern technology requires that they give full attention to military pursuits. Even in the early years of the Soviet revolution there was little of the kind of role expansion into nonmilitary employment practiced by the Cuban armed forces, either because of policy or because of military resistance to the idea. The Chinese come closer to Cuban practice. In the People's Republic of China the Great Leap Forward was probably comparable to Cuba'a giant harvest of 1970; soldiers were involved in both. But officers in the Chinese army resisted using the military for social and economic tasks much more strongly than their Cuban counterparts have done, arguing along with their Soviet colleagues that the profession of arms is a full-time occupation.[8]

There is no comparable resistance within the Cuban military. On the contrary, soldiers seem to take on nondefense tasks with a great deal of enthusiasm. Although there may have been some resistance to work in the 1970 harvest, the military's participation was nonetheless extraordinary. Still, the armed forces reverted quickly enough to their "normal" degree of participation, and there are indications that Fidel Castro wanted even more manpower than he got for the harvest. The formation of the Army of Working Youth in 1973 to perform economic tasks and to free the units for pure combat also suggests that some officers preferred specialization in military tasks, and that they

supported creating the Army of Working Youth to free
themselves from production tasks. With these exceptions,
however, the Cuban military seems willingly involved in
social and economic tasks, partly because they have
deliberately set about redesigning their mission so that
it will appear useful to society in order to protect their
budget and partly to promote expansion of military organizations.

THE POLITICAL MISSION OF THE ARMED FORCES

The political mission of the Cuban military has four
aspects. One is the absorption of the structure of the
Communist party, so that the corporate autonomy of the
military institutions is preserved and conflict between the
party and the armed forces minimized. Another is the prevention of the cleavages that plagued the armed forces before the revolution, those between commissioned and noncommissioned officers and between professional and nonprofessional commissioned officers. A third is the political indoctrination of recruits and the weeding out of the
unreliable. A final aspect is the development of cadres
that can be exported to the civilian population, particularly to positions in the civilian elite. It is at this
level that the civilian and military tasks of the soldier
are fused by placing the civic soldier in the position of
highest command in both the party and the military. The
military commander is not merely a technician; he is also
a political officer. A party leader is not only a politician; he is a technician and a manager competent in military as well as civilian tasks.

The Party in the Armed Forces

In 1961-1962 the party's crisis was a result of the
confrontation between Fidel Castro and the prerevolutionary
Communists, not of friction with the military. In those
same years, however, the party sought to control the armed
forces through political instructors who were first trained
at the Osvaldo Sánchez School for the Revolutionary Armed
Forces and then assigned to military units. Because they
were imposed from outside to erode the chain of command,
they were strongly opposed by the professional military
commanders. These early political instructors were simply
copying the experience of political commissars in the
military of other Communist countries. One result of the
massive expulsions from the party in 1962 was the abandonment of that system. Beginning in 1963, students at the
Osvaldo Sánchez School were drawn directly from the military ranks and were usually already officers. The curriculum was revamped so that 40 percent of the program would
be devoted to military topics, reviving the civic-soldier
experience from guerilla days, merging civilian and

military responsibilities.⁹

In contrast to the situation in Cuba in the early 1960s and possibly in other Communist countries, "there is no separation of activity between military and party obligations."¹⁰ Communist party organization parallels the military hierarchy. Criticism of one's superiors is difficult, but possible; innovation remains a prerogative of the top. The party organization in the armed forces is self-contained; nonmilitary party members have no authority over it. Party criticism within the military is criticism within the party, criticism of the military by the party, and criticism of the party by the military, all at the same time, because party and military are often fused.

The formation of the party in the military was complete by the end of 1966. It had moved geographically from the eastern to the western provinces and hierarchically from the bottom up. The last place to organize party cells was the national headquarters of the army chief of staff. By the fall of 1970, 69.6 percent of all officers in the armed forces belonged to either the party or the Communist Youth Union. In the summer of 1973, the proportion rose to 85 percent; in 1976, it was still 86 percent. Since 1970 the fifteen-member advisory commission of party members of the armed forces to the Political Bureau has been composed entirely of commissioned officers, at least half of whom have the highest ranks in the Cuban military in existence at the time. In the fall of 1970, 69 percent of the members of the party in the military were commissioned officers. By mid-1976, 48 percent of the entire western fleet (but 92 percent of its officers) belonged to the party or the youth union. Enlisted soldiers and draftees made up a large, though unspecified, proportion of the membership of the Communist Youth Union.¹¹ The high overlap between the officer corps and party and youth union membership helps fuse political and military authority, though alone it is not sufficient for the task.

In the Soviet Union the proportion of military officers who belong to the party has grown over time: 32 percent in 1924, 65 percent in 1928, 86 percent in 1952, 90 percent in the early 1960s, 93 percent in 1966 (when 80 percent of all Soviet armed forces personnel were either in the party or in the Communist Youth Union, mostly the latter). But this high representation has not prevented repeated conflicts between the party and the military throughout Soviet history. In Cuba the militarization of the political instructors; the willing acceptance of political norms, roles, and structures by military officers; the unified leadership that has preserved a single military chain of command; the self-containment of the party within the military to preserve the institutional autonomy of the armed forces; and the presence of the civic soldiers at the core of the ruling elite in charge of civilian and military organizations have combined to prevent similar conflicts. In the Soviet Union, even when political commissars and military commanders agree on specific issues, the central organizations of the party have little contact with either. In the absence of fusion at the top, conflict between Soviet central civilian and party organizations and military leaders will no doubt continue.

Several problems have troubled the relationship between party and military. The chief problem has been the failure to fulfill political programs in military units. The quality of political work, carried out by political instructors, has been low. Party leaders have complained that political issues were handled as mere administrative matters within the party, that discussions were superficial, that too little time was devoted to political issues, that issues concerning the internal affairs of the party were often ignored, and that ordinary party members did not participate much in discussions. A second problem of the party within the military was a lack of democracy. Officers, accounting for over two-thirds of its membership, monopolized party debate and used military rank to gain party rank. Voting at the cell level by acclamation makes it easy for officers to impose their views on cell members. A final problem is the military party's lack of autonomy from the nonparty military and vice versa, a fact that obscures both the political and the military chain of command. There is no clear boundary between party and technicians.[12]

The proportion of soldiers and noncommissioned officers in the military party--almost one-third--is fairly high, much higher than in the Soviet military, where the proportion of soldiers and noncommissioned officers fell as low as 3 percent of all military party members in the 1940s. The relatively high proportion of soldiers, corporals, and sergeants among party members in Cuba may be explained by the revolution's commitment--qualified, as already noted--to democratic principles even within the armed forces, which is in part a reaction to the cleavage between commissioned and noncommissioned officers in the Cuban military before the revolution. Although this rivalry is at least latent in most military institutions, Cuba is particularly sensitive on the subject because army sergeants and corporals, led by Fulgencio Batista, overthrew the government and the officer corps in 1933. Many officers were arrested or killed. Cuban officers would not like to see another coup like Batista's. The second major cleavage within the military dating from before the revolution is between the professional officers, some trained in Cuba, some abroad, and those who owed their rank to their participation in military coups and shrewd politicking. In the 1950s about one-sixth of the officers were nonprofessionals.[13]

The revolutionary government tried to avoid these rivalries by instituting a new promotion policy. No less than three-quarters and more typically nine-tenths of all professional officers or graduating cadets who are promoted, are members of either the Communist party or the Communist Youth Union. Officers or cadets are now rarely promoted on account of their experience in the rebel army. Although all the first captains and captains promoted in 1968 had served in the rebel army, only a third of the lieutenants promoted had done so; only 1.2 percent of the cadets graduating in March 1969 had ever served in the rebel army. Party membership has become a virtual prerequisite for promotion in the upper ranks and youth union membership a prerequisite for promotion from cadet status to the junior ranks. Even in the reserves, 74 percent of the 5,702 reserve officers promoted in 1975 and 80 percent of the 5,000 promoted in 1976 belonged to either the party or the youth union.[14]

The conflict between party and military in the early 1960s had occurred in part because so few military men were party members. By the 1970s, promotion policies guaranteed almost total overlap of officers and party members. The political deficiencies within the armed forces, especially in the Communist Youth Union, may explain the decline in the proportion of graduating cadets belonging to the party or the youth union from 1973 to 1975. The decline may result in a sharper line being drawn between military professionals and military politicians if the present pattern continues.

Through promotion policies the revolutionary government sought to politicize the officer corps, especially the younger officers who had good professional training but little or no combat experience. It also sought to professionalize and partly to politicize nonprofessional officers with a great deal of practical experience and very little formal training. The common grounds of professionalism and politics, the leaders believed, would reduce the rivalries that had weakened the Cuban military in the past. But resistance to the new policies had become evident by 1975, when fewer graduating cadets joined the party and the youth union, and officers questioned the value of schooling.

Exporting Military Models

Up to now the discussion has focused on political activities within the armed forces. But another, parallel development is the inverse of that endeavor--that is, the export of military models and personnel to the rest of the political system. Party organization in the armed forces by and large ended by 1966; in the civilian central administration, it began mostly in 1967. The party drew on that experience in building the civilian party,

particularly the principle of unified command. As
Armando Hart said, "There cannot be dual leadership in
a central State organization. The maximum authority of the
party, in each branch of the State apparatus, will be that
of the minister or president of the organization, who works
under the direction of the Party Central Committee and
Political Bureau. If in any case this should turn out to
be impossible, we will have to consider the demotion of
the executive."[15]

In the military the party had made it a regular practice to hold assemblies for evaluating its work. They were held virtually every year in every unit at different levels. National meetings were held less regularly, but there was one in 1966 and another in 1970. These, too, became models for the civilian party. Although there had been provincial assemblies in the civilian party since the early days, the military version had a seriousness and regularity that were to be carried over into the civilian party.[16]

The military had also developed cadres for assignment to specifically civilian duties, as the proportion of members of the Central Committee with military backgrounds indicates. This percentage has always been and still is very high, although it reached a peak in 1965. Since 1965, officers whose tasks within the leadership had been strictly military have come to assume new responsibilities in civilian life. This civic-soldier career pattern predominates in all the leading institutions of party and government. Aside from the members of the top elite discussed earlier, there are many examples lower down on the ladder. Rogelio Acevedo, for instance, who headed the militia in 1960, has been a member of the Central Committee since 1965. From 1969 to 1972, he was the Political Bureau's delegate to Camagüey province. He has since returned to the armed forces as a deputy minister.

The 1973 reform of military ranks and titles included the provision that officers on the inactive list could no longer use their military titles. Although the change was primarily symbolic, it did help to distinguish between active and former officers in positions of power, and it may eventually serve to break down the civic-soldier model. When these civilianized officers rejoin the military, however, they immediately recover their titles, so the divorce between the two spheres is by no means complete. The practice of exporting cadres from military to civilian life, begun in the early 1960s, has also been continued. As leaders trained in the military ranks matured, their attention was shifted to civilian tasks. In the central ministries as well as at various levels of the civilian party ranks, one encounters inactive soldiers with great frequency.

The Cuban armed forces differ from the military that performs nonmilitary tasks in non-Communist countries in several ways: The party functions within a military that is thoroughly politicized; the military performs not only managerial and technical but also menial tasks; and there have been no military coups in revolutionary Cuba, as there often have been in other countries where the military element within the government remains strong. The Cuban armed forces differ also from the Soviet armed forces in that they have a much broader perception of their role in society. Unlike the Soviets, they do not retreat behind strict military professionalism to avoid other tasks, and they exercise greater authority in the Central Committee. The Soviet pattern of military membership on the Central Committee--between 7 and 13 percent--was set by the late 1930s. Before that time the military's share of the Central Committee membership was even smaller.

The military in the People's Republic of China more closely resembles the Cuban model, but participation of the armed forces in central decision making is more stable and better institutionalized in Cuba than in China. Moreover, there has been no purge of the Cuban military on the scale of the Lin Biao affair, nor any military coup attempt in Cuba comparable to Lin Biao's. If all Cuban Central Committee members with military titles at the time of their appointments are counted, then the Cuban military share of its party Central Committee easily exceeds that of the Chinese. In 1962, 56 percent of all full members of the Cuban Central Committee held military rank; in 1965, 70 percent held military rank. If only those with full-time military duty are counted, then 28 percent of all Central Committee members in 1962, 58 percent in 1965, and 38 percent in 1975 were career officers on duty.

Professional Chinese officers are known to have resisted becoming involved in nonmilitary tasks even during the Cultural Revolution. The injection of the armed forces into the Cultural Revolution was no military coup. Rather, it was the consequence of a political decision made primarily by leaders outside the armed forces. Cuban officers, in contrast, welcomed role expansion as the vehicle for organizational survival. It is possible that the establishment of the Army of Working Youth was a consequence of professional military resistance to nonmilitary tasks and that the new military specialization thus made possible effective fighting in Angola, but there is little real evidence to support the notion, which is inapplicable to the 1960s in any case. The effect of the reorganization in 1973 was not only to permit military specialization but also to increase military responsibilities over production by absorbing many of the civilian duties of the Communist Youth Union. Both the Cuban and the Chinese military have engaged in role expansion, but Chinese officers resisted it far longer and more strenuously than did their Cuban counterparts. In China the impetus for role expansion came primarily from outside the armed forces, but in Cuba expansion has come about equally as a result of pressures from within and from outside.

Although some Maoists may have had a civic-soldier model in mind, and although they may even have intended to diffuse this role, they did not, in fact, succeed to the degree that the leaders with a similar plan have succeeded in Cuba. Revolutionary Cuba has been governed, in large part, by leaders whose civilian and military roles were fused during the insurgency against Batista, and who have intentionally made the civic soldier the norm for all, even in purely civilian organizations. From the early 1960s to the mid-1970s, no alternative civilian elite capable of governing the country appeared in Cuba. There has also been little evidence of conflict between strictly civilian and strictly military leaders, because both types divide among themselves in disputes.

From 1965 to 1975 the survival and growth of the armed forces were achieved by reemphasizing the continuing legitimacy of old military objectives and expanding the roles of the military beyond defense. Military organizations did not fade away, but organizational boundaries became blurred. At the same time, national-defense strategy came to depend on civilian mobilization rather than on a standing armed force. With their strictly military functions fading in importance, the military took on social, economic, and political tasks.

Conflict between military and civilian agencies was reduced, at first, by the decrease in specialization within the military, so that both kinds of organizations undertook similar tasks in nonmilitary areas. The pressures of conflicting roles felt by civic soldiers serving in civilian agencies may also have diminished. They were no longer obliged to lobby for the reduction in the budgets of their former comrades-in-arms because the military now performed nonmilitary tasks, diverting some military resources to assist civilians. Civilian party members learned from the military how to shape party structures. Civilian party hierarchies filled vacant posts by drawing on civic soldiers.

These changes in the definitions of their roles by the armed forces were generally welcomed by the elite because they reduced disputes within the leadership and made less acute the conflicts felt by civic soldiers administering civilian agencies and by low-ranking personnel in all agencies. However, the new role definitions created new role conflicts within the military. Civilian organizations began to compete with the armed forces for the time and resources of military units, thus creating internal role conflict. Officers and soldiers also experienced role conflict in allocating their own time, exacerbating internal role conflict: Should they emphasize military or other tasks? To cope with these new problems, the Army of Working Youth, which has devoted its energies almost entirely to production, was established in 1973. Military units once again became specialized. Some performed almost exclusively military tasks. Role conflicts were reduced for personnel in units with military specialization, but not for the others, who have continued to experience them.

CONCLUSIONS

What then, is the future of the military in the political and economic life of Cuba? A number of developments in the mid-1970s suggest future trends that may prove to depart sharply from the domination of the civic soldier in the past. First, there is the possibility that military personnel exported to civilian life might at last become totally demilitarized and produce a civilian ruling elite for the first time since the fall of Aníbal Escalante in 1962. During the Angolan war there were already enough influential civilians around to object to the military's demands for personnel and resources. There was also popular dislike of compulsory military service. Instances of insubordination occurred within the ranks; lack of discipline in the Army of Working Youth was a serious problem, and its level of combat preparedness was low; and the usefulness of formal military education--including political education--was being challenged. The military share of the Central Committee membership has declined, as has the proportion of graduating military cadets who belong either to the Communist Youth Union or to the Communist party. The time may have come to separate the military clearly from the civilian, so that the profession of arms in Cuba could be considered a full-time occupation.

On the other side, the expansion of the armed forces' role continues. The draft is used to force civilians to serve the state for three years, in military production or other tasks designated by the government. Efforts to use military methods to educate Cuban young people have been accelerated. The importance of military skills has been reemphasized as a result of the Angolan war. The establishment of the Army of Working Youth is an example of military role expansion, because it absorbed the productive activities of the Communist Youth Union. The change in military doctrine relies on the mobilization of civilians in time of war and on improving the professional military competence of the very large reserve forces in preparation for war. The active reservists who serve as much as three months each year in the military typify the civic soldier, fusing civilian and military life year-round. The militarization of the reserves and the growth of the Army of Working Youth have spread the civic-soldier role to the mass of the population. The military share of the Central Committee, although it may have declined from former days, is nonetheless still the highest in the

Communist world, and the proportion of officers who belong to the party and the youth union exceeds four-fifths of their total. A civilian elite, though it now certainly exists, has not yet been well developed. Although pressures have arisen within the Cuban armed forces to put the civic soldier to rest, to stop using the military for civilian tasks, and to concentrate on military professionalism, they are not yet triumphant.

If the civilian organizations, already strengthened in the first half of the 1970s, can confront the military more effectively in coming years--if they can edge the armed forces out of productive work, find their own leaders, coordinate social services without relying on the draft, and resist military demands for a large share of the national income and the maintenance of a combat-ready reserve--then the day of the civic soldier in Cuba may indeed be near its end. The Angolan war may well have speeded that day.

NOTES

1. H. A. Simon, *Administrative Behavior* (New York: Macmillan Co., 1961), p. 118. P. M. Blau has argued that the attainment of organizational objectives (such as military security) generates a stress on finding new objectives (such as those in the areas of politics or economics). I think it is likely that organizational growth has been a specific goal of the military organizations or, at the very least, that the prevention of organizational decline has been such a goal. The concept of the civic soldier has legitimized shifts in objectives or missions of the military organization as perceived by the entire elite. In turn, the ability to shift objectives, as Samuel Huntington has argued, adds to the organizational age of the military organization, so that it becomes more fully institutionalized. See P. M. Blau, *The Dynamics of Bureaucracy* (Chicago: University of Chicago Press, 1955), p. 195; and Samuel P. Huntington, *Political Order in Changing Societies* (New Haven: Yale University Press, 1968), pp. 13-17. See also W. D. Starbuck, "Organizational Growth and Development," in *Handbook of Organizations*, ed., J. G. March (Chicago: Rand McNally, 1965), pp. 451-533.

2. For a discussion of the various estimates of the numbers of people killed in the 1950s and 1960s see Jorge I. Domínguez, "The Civic Soldier in Cuba," in *Political-Military Systems: Comparative Perspectives*, ed., Catherine M. Kelleher (Beverly Hills, Calif.: Sage Publications, 1974), pp. 216-218. See also Hugh Thomas, *Cuba: The Pursuit of Freedom* (New York: Harper & Row, 1971), pp. 1024-1025, 1042, 1044; Raúl Castro, "Graduación del III curso de la escuela Básica superior 'General Máximo Gómez'," *Ediciones*

al orientador revolucionario, no. 17 (1967): 11; Granma Weekly Review, June 13, 1971, pp. 2-3; ibid., December 12, 1971, p. 6; ibid., January 4, 1976, p. 7; Julio C. Fernandez, "Que fue el bandidismo?," Bohemia 68, no. 23 (June 4, 1976): 44-49. See Carlos Rivero Collado's Los sobrinos del tio Sam (Havana: Instututo Cubano del Libro, 1976) for a fascinating, though obviously partisan, history of Cuban-exile counterrevolutionary activities written by the son of Batista's former prime minister, who became a revolutionary double agent operating in the United States until 1974.

3. See Cuban Economic Research Project, A Study on Cuba (Coral Gables, Fla.: University of Miami Press, 1965), pp. 455, 461, 621; Direccion Central de Estadistica, Compendio estadistico de Cuba, 1966 (Havana: Junta Central de Planificacion, 1966), p. 13; Carmelo Mesa-Lago, "Economic Policies and Growth," in Revolutionary Change in Cuba, ed., Carmelo Mesa-Lago (Pittsburgh: University of Pittsburgh Press, 1971), p. 319; Granma Weekly Review, August 6, 1972, p. 4; Frank Mankiewicz and Kirby Jones, With Fidel (Chicago: Playboy Press, 1975), pp. 118-119; U. S. Arms Control and Disarmament Agency, World Military Expenditures, 1971 (Washington, D.C.: Government Printing Office, 1972), pp. 19-27 (hereafter cited as ACDA); ACDA 1963-1973, p. 28; Boletín 1970, p. 30.

4. Granma Weekly Review, December 16, 1973; Granma, July 12, 1976, p. 4; ibid., July 15, 1976, p. 3; ibid., November 25, 1976, p. 1.

5. For a detailed discussion of these costs, see Jorge I. Domínguez, "The Cuban Operation in Angola: Costs and Benefits for the Cuban Armed Forces," Cuban Studies 8, no. 1 (January 1978). See also Fiscalía Militar de las FAR, "Los estímulos y las correcciones disciplinarias," Verde olivo 17, no. 47 (November 23, 1975): 22-24; idem., "Las reclamaciones en las FAR," ibid. 18, no. 31 (August 1, 1976): 40; "Las resoluciones y acuerdos del primer congreso del partido comunista de Cuba," ibid. no. 18 (May 2, 1976): 30; Barry A. Sklar, "Cuba: Normalization of Relations," Issue Brief no. IB75030, Congressional Research Service, Library of Congress (March 3, 1976): 23.

6. The percentages assume that the size of the military remained stationary in this period at about 110,000 for the regular forces and 250,000 for all forces. The numbers were taken from Granma Weekly Review, July 18, 1971, p. 9. This modifies substantially information in my "Civic Soldier in Cuba," p. 221.

7. Fidel Castro, "Brigada invasora Ché Guevara," Verde olivo 8, no. 44 (November 5, 1967): 6-7; Fidel Vascos, "Brigada invasora Ché Guevara: año 1," ibid. 9, no. 45 (November 10, 1968): 6-7; ibid 10, no. 45 (November 9, 1969): 7-9, 62; ibid. 11, no. 4 (January 25, 1970): 32; "Algunas tareas cumplidas por las FAR en 1970," ibid., no. 52 (December 27, 1970): 14; René Dumont, "The

Militarization of Fidelismo," Dissent (September-October 1970): 417-420; K. S. Karol, Guerrillas in Power (New York: Hill and Wang, 1970), pp. 444-450, 534-544.
    8. John Gittings, The Role of the Chinese Army (New York: Oxford University Press, 1967), pp. 29-32, 176-201; Ellis Joffe, Party and Army: Professionalism and Political Control in the Chinese Officer Corps, 1949-1964 (Cambridge, Mass.: Harvard University, East Asian Research Center, 1965), pp. 80-87.
    9. Verde olivo 4, no. 7 (February 17, 1963): 6-7.
   10. E. Yasells, "Reseña de una asamblea," Verde olivo, no. 51 (December 24, 1967): 11.
   11. Ibid. 7, no. 52 (December 13, 1966): 4; ibid. 8, no. 51 (December 24, 1967): 12; ibid. 11, no. 40 (October 4, 1970): 8, 10; Granma, March 1, 1966, p. 4; ibid., August 4, 1975, p. 3; ibid., June 8, 1976, p. 4; Granma Weekly Review, January 4, 1976, p. 7; ibid., December 12, 1976, p. 12; Bohemia 65, no. 31 (August 3, 1973): 28.
   12. "Indicaciones sobre el processo asambleario," Bohemia 14, no. 42 (October 15, 1972): 55-59.
   13. Jose Suárez Nuñez, El Gran Culpable (Caracas, 1963), pp. 64, 91-92.
   14. Política internacional 6, nos. 22-24 (1968): 93; Granma Weekly Review, March 16, 1969, p. 7; Granma, April 17, 1975, p. 2; Juan Escalona, "Las FAR y los reservistas," Verde olivo 18, no. 17 (April 25, 1976): 17-18.
   15. Granma Weekly Review, May 14, 1967, p. 11.
   16. Granma, May 20, 1966, p. 5; Yasells, "Reseña de una asamblea," pp. 11-12; "Primera asamblea de balance del partido," Verde olivo 8, no. 51 (December 24, 1967): 61; "Sección política de la marina de guerra revolucionaria," ibid. 9, no. 2 (January 14, 1968): 38; "Primera asamblea de balance del partido comunista de Cuba en el cuerpo blindado," ibid., no. 7 (February 18, 1968): 13-15; Gutíerrez, "Segunda asamblea de balance," ibid., pp. 8-12; "Asamblea de balance del partido en el ejército de Oriente," ibid. 10, no. 5 (February 2, 1969): 52-53; "Balance del partido en el cuerpo ejército de Camagüey," ibid., no. 42 (October 19, 1969): 25; "Segunda asamblea de balance del partido comunista de Cuba en una unidad en Matanzas," ibid., no. 43 (October 26, 1969): 28; "Segunda asamblea de balance del partido en el ejército del centro," ibid., no. 44 (November 2, 1969): 58; "Segunda asamblea de balance del partido comunista de Cuba en el estado mayor general," ibid., no. 49 (December 7, 1969): 32-33; "Segunda reunión del partido en las Fuerzas Armadas Revolucionarias," ibid. 11, no. 40 (October 4, 1970): 7-8. Luis Méndez, "La asamblea provincial del PURS en Matanzas," Cuba socialista, no. 31 (March 1964): 134-135.

5
The Vietnamese Army

William Turley

THE PEOPLE'S ARMY OF VIETNAM

The People's Army of Vietnam (PAVN) has been indispensable to the survival and victories of the Vietnamese Communist movement. Army leaders have been legitimate, influential participants in the Communist party's policymaking process ever since the PAVN's founding. Fusion of civilian and military elites existed from the very first moment the party assigned several of its top leaders to organize the armed forces; it was an aspect of revolutionary strategy from the beginning. The road to power then provided favorable circumstances for fusion to persist in spite of rapid growth in the size of forces and specialization of function. It also produced a tradition of consensual decision making that retarded the development of a distinctive military point of view. Party leaders had little need to worry about the loyalty of the military leadership, as this leadership was drawn from the top ranks of the party. The more serious needs were to train illiterate peasants as competent soldiers, to transform petit bourgeois elements into revolutionary cadres, and to maintain close coordination between the army and its highly dispersed civilian support structure. In this setting, the civil-military dichotomy had little validity.

Of all the Communist parties that have won power against more powerful foes, the disparity was sharpest for the Vietnamese. Against the armies of Japan, France, and the United States, the Vietnamese waged a total of nineteen years of war with a comparatively small population base and acutely inferior technology. Ho Chi Minh's aphorism, "Few can defeat many, the weak can defeat the strong," made a virtue of the fact that the Vietnamese had no choice but to compensate for material weakness with political strength. The politico-military doctrine that supported this strategy blurred the distinction between civilian and military responsibilities and legitimized the army's participation in a very broad range of activities.

The underlying cause of the revolution's material disadvantage was Vietnam's very low level of economic development. With the probable exception of the Mongolian People's Republic, the Socialist Republic of Vietnam (SRV) will long remain the least developed nation of those discussed in this volume. This condition perpetuated the PAVN's highly active role. In the absence of significant entrepreneurial classes and adequate political and administrative institutions, the army is the single most important agent for implementation of the regime's ambitious development plan.

Although the PAVN is the most prestigious and effective institution in the SRV today, there is a discernable trend toward gradual reduction of the PAVN's hitherto extensive penetration of civilian society. Professionalization of the officer corps and the rise of leaders in both the party and the army who did not participate in the founding of either organization have established long-term trends toward the separation of civilian and military elites.

ORIGINS

The PAVN can be said with little exaggeration to have originated in the popular uprising precipitated by the Japanese attack on the French outpost at Lang Son in Bac Son district near the Chinese border in late September 1940.[1] Several local party members participated in this uprising on their own initiative, and the Central Committee authorized their activities in November when it recognized the uprising had the potential to be the nucleus of an armed struggle. On February 14, 1941, the committee designated the Army for National Salvation, a group of twenty-four men who had participated with the party in the uprising. Led by members of the Tay and Nung minorities who had been party activists since the early 1930s, one of whom had briefly attended Whampoa and commanded a battalion in China, the Army for National Salvation was the first armed force created under party auspices for the purpose of sustained resistance. The ANS remained a largely minority-based guerrilla movement from its activation until 1944, rising in number up to 400 between the French sweeps that periodically dispersed it.

Shortly after it created the Army for National Salvation, the Central Committee Eighth Plenum in May 1941 established a united front organization (the Viet Minh), ordered the creation of revolutionary base areas in Bac Son and neighboring Cao Bang, and placed Vo Nguyen Giap, a Central Committee member, in charge of military affairs in Cao Bang. This was a fateful assignment. Until then Giap's only military work had been to organize a short training course on politico-military subjects for a small band of party activists in China's Kwangsi province. Giap's assignment in 1941 merely required him to move his training site from Kwangsi into Vietnam and to organize local self-defense forces to assist in the political organization of the Cao Bang base area. Not until July 1944 was he ordered to organize a mobile guerrilla force. The 31 men and 3 women he selected from the 500 militiamen of Cao Bang were designated the Vietnam Propaganda and Liberation Unit on December 22, 1944, the official birthdate of the PAVN.

Giap's unit is officially regarded as the progenitor of the PAVN because it was the first full-time mobile group, or "main force," as distinct from its supporting reserve of part-time local militia and in contrast to the less formally organized guerrilla movement in Bac Son. But it differed from Bac Son's Army for National Salvation in other important ways. The Cao Bang base area from the beginning concentrated on the organization of political support, gradual construction of armed forces in a three-tiered pyramid similar to the Chinese model, and the avoidance of armed conflict so long as the balance of forces on the strategic as well as tactical plane was unfavorable to the revolution. This emphasis reflected the need to build forces where none had existed before and to protect the Central Committee headquarters located in the base area. The Army for National Salvation, by contrast, sprang from a popular uprising, derived much of its support from preexisting family and tribal ties, and was led by local figures who had little responsibility for protecting the party core. These characteristics no doubt had much to do with its propensity to engage in guerrilla skirmishes that provoked French suppression. Both the Vietnam Propaganda and Liberation Unit and the Army for National Salvation relied heavily on the ethnic minorities that populated the mountainous regions along the Chinese border, although Giap's unit, especially at the leadership level, had a distinctly more Vietnamese cast and was more tightly integrated with the party leadership. Leaders almost unanimously perceived the experiences of both units to be proof of the necessity of subordinating armed activities to political mobilization.

Following the Japanese coup against the French in March 1945, the two units merged into a single force dubbed the Vietnam Liberation Army. This force consisted of about a thousand combatants organized into thirteen companies. Almost all of the original members of the Vietnam Propaganda and Liberation Unit and the Army for National Salvation became command cadres in the Liberation Army, which began to recruit peasants in areas only beginning to fall under Viet Minh influence, as well as urban youths anxious to participate in the imminent overthrow of colonial rule. This army and a few thousand semiarmed paramilitary activists scattered throughout the country were the extent

of military or quasi-military formations available to the
party at the time of the August Revolution. Against a
background of raging famine and Japan's collapse, the
movement gained momentum in the countryside and culminated
in a popular uprising in urban centers in which armed force
played a mainly supportive role. One of the important
lessons gained from this experience was that in Vietnam the
revolution should not rely solely on either the cities or
the countryside but on a combination of armed and political struggle in both settings. Neither the Chinese revolution nor the Soviet October Revolution was to be the
exclusive model, at least in doctrine.

The Democratic Republic of Vietnam (DRV), formally
declared on September 2, 1945, was on that date a sovereign
independent state, finally free of French domination, so
far as most Vietnamese were concerned. This fact immeasurably assisted efforts to build an army. Nationalistic city youths flocked to the military banner, and
peasants accepted military service as a legitimate demand
placed on them by the new government. By December 1946,
when fighting broke out over French efforts to reimpose
colonial rule, the DRV had upwards of 100,000 men in
possession of some 80,000 weapons.[2] By mid-1947, the main
force alone of what was then called simply the National
Army numbered 125,000.[3] The growth of forces then tapered
off as the DRV retreated into the countryside, where armed
struggle was carried on by highly dispersed, geographically
isolated units in a guerrilla mode.

Vietnamese forces were making rather slow gains under
difficult conditions when the victory of the Communist
party in China permitted them to break out of their isolation and to gain access to weapons and sanctuary. These
enabled them to improve significantly both the quality and
quantity of their main forces. Between 1949 and 1952 six
divisions, a general staff headquarters, and several front
commands were organized. On the eve of the Dien Bien Phu
battle, PAVN main forces numbered 160,000, supported by
some 70,000 regional forces and 100,000 local guerrillas,
and possessed substantial quantities of artillery and
other equipment.[4] Thus Chinese assistance was crucial
in helping to develop conventional capability. But in
the same period the United States supplied the French with
roughly ten times the quantity of much more sophisticated
weaponry. The DRV armed forces were much inferior in both
numbers and weaponry to the 420,000 man French Union forces,
which at war's end were falling back to protect coastal
enclaves.

The Military Elite

The first generation of Vietnamese Communist military
leaders without exception were high-ranking party leaders
or at least party members, long before the Eighth Plenum

launched armed struggle in May 1941. Between 1941 and 1945, almost all of the top-ranked party leaders worked on some aspect of military affairs, including the future premier, Pham Van Dong, who had attended the Whampoa Academy. Except for a handful of men who had passed through Guomindang military academies or the Chinese Red Army, members of this generation were military amateurs. Coincidentally, the highest-ranking party members who did have some formal training and who were given military responsibilities in 1941 died before 1945, leaving Giap, a former history teacher, and men like longtime chief-of-staff Van Tien Dung (now minister of defense), who had only fifteen days of military training prior to 1954, a clear field. These men were primarily political organizers similar to the super commissars of the Soviet Red Army, who became tracked into military careers when the Central Committee assigned responsibilities at the outset of armed struggle. Few were "mandarin revolutionaries," like some of the party's most prominent members, as they came mainly from poor and middle peasant or urban petit bourgeois backgrounds. However, their common experience in political agitation prior to 1941, their relative lack of military training, and the shared hardship of 1941-1945 unified them with other party leaders. Unlike the Chinese Communists whose military leadership included such disparate elements as former warlord generals and Moscow-trained specialists, or the Soviets who absorbed former officers of the czar's imperial army, the Vietnamese party relied almost exclusively on its own quite homogeneous ranks for early military leadership.

The August Revolution was a watershed in the development of this elite. The frenzied construction of a national army that followed the uprising created a demand for officers that could be met only by promoting those in the ranks who had even minimal military training or basic literacy. Since the number of cadres available from the Cao Bang-Bac Son movements and the number of Vietnamese who had received officer training in French forces were small (and only a minority of these joined the Viet Minh anyway), the party had no choice but to recruit educated youths, mostly from petit bourgeois or rural upper-class backgrounds, if only because they could read orders. This, the second generation of PAVN officers, experienced very rapid advancement during the war of resistance. Because of the priority given to the anticolonial struggle and to recruiting literate cadres--priorities that required downplaying class-based political qualifications--the better-educated and usually middle-class elements within this generation were actually favored for admission to the first officer training schools established during the war. A large proportion of these men were still students or barely beyond high school when they joined the revolution, and unlike the first generation of leaders, they had experienced neither party membership nor political activity before they were catapulted to officer rank. Their adult lives began with military service, and they were therefore much more inclined than their superiors to acquire professional values and orientations. With the introduction of land reform and the upgrading of the "antifeudal" struggle in 1953, many of these officers were frozen in rank or were denied the choicest opportunities for career development (training abroad, for example) to which they believed their service and abilities entitled them. Although the subsequent "reform" of the officer ranks was mild in comparison with that which occurred among civilian party and state cadres, it left a residue of tensions that tended to divide generations on the issue of the relative merits of political or professional qualifications. The senior leadership usually held political and professional qualifications to be not only reconcilable but complementary; pressures for professionalization were stronger at lower levels.

The Party and The Army

As mentioned above, the army's loyalty to the party was above question in the beginning because its top leaders were ranking leaders of the party. The military elite, moreover, lacked a distinctive point of view that might have pitted it against civilians within the party. The distinction between military and civilian roles before 1945 was extremely blurred, if it can be said to have existed at all. The conditions that justified an elaborate system of control and surveillance in the Soviet Red Army at its birth, and to a lesser extent in the Chinese PLA, did not exist in Vietnam. The Vietnamese did create a party organization within the armed forces and appointed political officers in accordance with established Communist procedure when they first organized units in Bac Son and Cao Bang. But this political apparatus was created primarily for the purpose of indoctrinating peasant recruits and for recruiting new party members, not for guaranteeing the loyalty of military commanders. The latter consequently had a free hand with military affairs and tended to look upon political officers as assistants rather than as intrusive competitors for authority.

Following the August Revolution, the overnight creation of officers from nonparty sources called for closer supervision of military commanders. A decision was made to strengthen the party and political work system in the army and to insist on the countersignature of military orders by political officers. Because political cadres were in even shorter supply than military ones this decision did not begin to have much practical effect until the late 1940s. In 1946, the first year for which such figures are available, fully 40 percent of all party

members were in the army, but these members accounted for
only 9.4 percent of the men in arms. It took until late
1949, during which time the party as a whole grew twenty-
five-fold while the army barely doubled in size, for the
proportion of party members in the army to rise to a
satisfactory 28.6 percent. (The military proportion of
total party membership declined to 8 percent.)[5]

When political officers began to be trained in large
numbers, they tended to be drawn from the same urban petit
bourgeois and middle peasant backgrounds as their military
counterparts, and for the same reasons. Their control
function still was secondary to educational and liaison
functions. The new military commanders were regarded as
trustworthy so long as the emphasis on anticolonialism
made patriotism, rather than social class or ideological
formation, the primary measure of political reliability.

A major overhaul of the political organization in
the army began in 1949-1950, when steps were taken to
organize main-force divisions and to attract poor peasant
support with greater emphasis on social reforms. Initiated in anticipation of discipline and morale problems
connected with both of these steps, the overhaul precipitated the first dispute over the role and authority of
political work in the army. The Central Committee began
the overhaul in late 1948 by abolishing the party committee
system at regiment level and above and replacing this
system with delegated political officers under the direction of General Giap, who was elected general political
delegate to the army. This move, though intended to
strengthen party authority in the army, concentrated unprecedented power over the military in the hands of Giap
and his chief political assistant, Van Tien Dung. It also
opened the way for the military component of the party
leadership to control its own political organization in the
army. These trends went against the grain of doctrine and
predisposition.

Following the reorganization of the Ministry of Defense and General Staff in 1950, power in the military was
deconcentrated. The office of general political delegate
quietly disappeared and the formerly weak Army Political
Department was upgraded to the General Political Directorate
(GPD), one of three directorates in the ministry. The
Central Committee selected the chief officers of the GPD
from its own membership and appointed Nguyen Chi Thanh,
a party leader from central Vietnam who had no debt or
even prior working association with Giap, as the directorate's first head. Giap remained minister of defense and
head of the Central Military Party Committee, but the
CMPC was detached from the Central Committee and given
only consultative duties under the supervision of the GPD.
These moves appear to be designed to curb Giap's personal
power in the army and to establish a conventional Marxist-
Leninist political work system under Central Committee,

not military, control. The reform process was completed in July 1952 with the reinstatement of the party committee system from the top down to the company level on the principle of collective decision making and individual responsibility.

There is no evidence that Giap ever objected to strengthening the party organization in the army, an organization he had helped to create. If he had objections, they most likely were to the appointment of Nguyen Chi Thanh to head the GPD. Personal frictions tended to count more than and to cut across institutional rivalries, for leaders were still politico-military generalists before they were functional specialists with particular organizational loyalties.

POST-RESISTANCE PRIORITIES AND THE PAVN'S MISSIONS

From 1954 to 1975 the principal policy issue for the DRV was what balance to strike between development in the North and reunification with the South. The balance between these priorities was debated constantly within the party. The military had a stake in this debate not only because of the established roles of the top military leaders in the political process, but also because whatever balance was struck would have important implications for the PAVN's mission. Development of the North was a requisite of military modernization, whereas reunification held potential for drawing the PAVN into combat again, either in the South or in defense of the North or both. A unified institutional point of view was slow to evolve, however, partly because of the durable fusion of civilian and military leadership at the top and partly because of conflicts unleashed by postwar reorganization and development within the army itself.

The first priority as resistance ended--recovery and reconstruction in the North--involved the PAVN deeply in essential economic and administrative work. Economic conditions required the concentration of all available resources on these tasks. The PAVN was the regime's largest single reservoir of the critical resources. It virtually monopolized transportation, communications, and construction, and it contained a majority of the DRV's experienced administrators. Moreover, the resistance experience, particularly the guerrilla aspects of it, had blurred the distinction between military and civilian roles, making it easy for military personnel to adapt working styles to nominally civilian duties. (The most important problem of adaption was not from military to civilian styles but from rural to urban ones, and this problem afflicted party and state organs as much as the army.) Veterans were demobilized specifically to strengthen village governments, and a number of officers moved semipermanently into state technical or administrative services. Military leaders accepted this mission without complaint because they had been socialized into the fused role of civic soldier and because the PAVN so clearly needed to help stabilize its own economic base before a military building program could begin.

In late 1957 the PAVN embarked on a program of regularization and modernization to reverse the military deterioration that had set in while land reform and economic recovery were under way. More important, the program sought to transform what was still a rather loosely led "people's army" into a centralized, hierarchically organized, conventional armed force. Whereas in the resistance the main forces and guerrillas had mostly waged a war of movement against the enemy's fixed positions, henceforward there was to be a clearer demarcation of function. The main forces were to defend fixed positions by conventional, high-technology means, while popular militia and regional forces were to provide defense-in-depth if this became necessary. This transformation was strongly advocated by top military leaders and supported by the party leadership in the belief that the PAVN's primary mission in the future would be the territorial defense of the DRV. It also had strong support from second-generation officers who saw themselves as military specialists and who recognized that the program would open new career opportunities. There was some skepticism, however, among southern returnee officers who feared that the emphasis on defense of the DRV meant indefinite postponement of reunification, and there was opposition among older guerrilla cadres who saw no future for themselves in the new army.

Regularization and modernization almost immediately altered officer behavior in ways that clashed with the values of the senior military and political leadership. The introduction of formal ranks, increased emphasis on hierarchy and centralization, and intensified instruction in modern military science produced inegalitarian attitudes and disrespect for received doctrine. In late 1958 General Giap publicly expressed shock at the disrespect of junior officers for resistance military doctrine,[6] and Nguyen Chi Thanh railed at the erosion of political values and the declining effectiveness of the GPD.[7] Despite their differences, the two men jointly expressed the leadership's wish to preserve the PAVN's popular and revolutionary character by enhancing political instruction, involving the army more actively in economic production, and in various ways curbing the tendency of the army to remove itself from society and of professional officers to separate themselves from the men.[8] The top leadership wanted a modern professional army but would not tolerate the organizational autonomy and counterrevolutionary values that such an army tended to produce.

General staff officers, however, were quickly coming

to agree with younger officers just emerging from the new military academy or returning from training in the Soviet Union and Eastern Europe. They believed that more attention to professional and technical training, instead of political activities, was necessary if the PAVN was to make effective use of the more sophisticated equipment it was beginning to receive from the USSR. They also were aware that the military's share of the state budget had declined every year since 1955, and that the party was under increasing pressure from its southern branch to authorize armed struggle in the South. Nguyen Chi Thanh, who was to leave the GPD in 1961 to take charge of reunification planning, had found it expedient to argue that the reunification struggle could be begun and possibly won by forces indigenous to the South. However, he and other advocates of forcible reunification had to admit there would be risk to the North and need of northern support if the United States intervened. In this context, the PAVN high command could make a very persuasive argument for raising the priority of developing the DRV's conventional defense, and this is exactly the decision that General Giap revealed at the 3rd Party Congress in 1960.[9]

At this congress PAVN officers almost doubled their representation among the full members of the Central Committee (from 14 to 26 percent) and significantly increased their representation among the alternates. The new military members were either general staff officers with strong ties to General Giap or officers with southern experience who were to be assigned to a southern command. The general staff probably exchanged its endorsement of the plan to seek reunification through armed struggle using southern forces for greater emphasis on building conventional capabilities in the North. From then until 1964, time spent on training in military subjects increased and time spent on political subjects declined. Although the general staff apparently acted as an integrated political unit to win these concessions, it is important to note that a lively debate over whether political or material factors were decisive in warfare continued as the party weighed the risks of provoking the United States.

The emphasis on professionalism and conventional capability lasted as long as it was assumed the PAVN's mission would be confined to defending the North. This assumption was invalidated in December 1963 when the Central Committee, recognizing that a strategy relying mainly on southern resources and political struggle was unlikely to succeed, authorized planning for increased northern participation contingent upon further American intervention. In the spring of 1964, as some PAVN units began to train for infiltration into the South, both officer and troop training programs were revised to enhance instruction in political subjects (emphasizing the primacy of political over material factors and therefore the vincibility of the U.S. Army) and guerrilla tactics. Facing the probability that the United States would introduce large numbers of ground troops and a much more sophisticated form of high technology warfare than the PAVN could ever hope to match, PAVN leaders felt they had no choice but to resort, at least in the short term, to these methods. Debate continued over details of strategy and tactics, pitting advocates of protracted, low-risk, small-unit guerrilla warfare against advocates of more daring main-force assault, but this division cut across all levels of party and army alike and soon was overtaken by battlefield exigencies.

IMPACT OF THE SECOND INDOCHINA WAR

The most important effect of the Second Indochina War for civil-military relations in the DRV, at least up to 1968, was to revive the esprit, solidarity, and doctrine of the resistance. The North became the rear base for the southern revolutionary movement, and the PAVN once again became a people's army fighting a more powerful adversary. Strategic doctrine emphasized balanced use of regular, regional, and local guerrilla forces, interdependence of political and armed struggle, and coordination of movements in both urban and rural areas. The revolution, in effect, reverted to its prestate condition. Though it had established a state structure over half the country in 1954, from 1964 onward it acted as the insurgent party in a civil and revolutionary conflict that the party defined as a struggle for national unity and independence.

Space does not permit recounting the highly complex debate over strategy and tactics, and particularly over the role to be played by regular forces, following the entry of the first whole PAVN unit into the South in December 1964.[10] It suffices to note that although debate was sharp, it was conducted within a stable consensus on basic principles and ultimate objectives. But the substance of debate and the influence of different participants shifted in response to battlefield events.

There can be no doubt as to the effectiveness of the PAVN in this war. In both numerical and material terms, the disparity between itself (plus local southern forces) and the combined Saigon-U.S. forces was even greater than the disparity between the PAVN and the French had been during the resistance. By late 1966, according to American estimates, PAVN regulars in the South numbered about 46,000, complemented by 68,000 troops of the People's Liberation Armed Force (PLAF--locally recruited main forces) and 112,000 guerrillas for a total of 225,000.[11] Well-armed with light weapons but lacking mechanized transport, tanks, heavy artillery, or air support, these forces faced over a million men including 385,000 Americans armed with everything the PAVN and its associated forces lacked. The numbers and equipment of both sides increased over the next couple of years, but the disparity was not significantly reduced until the bulk of American forces had withdrawn. Nonetheless, Communist forces were able to stalemate their opponents and, in early 1968, to launch the coordinated attacks on remote outposts and urban centers remembered as the Tet Offensive. PAVN main forces engaged the Americans in the highlands, and local irregulars, many of them very recently recruited in lowland provinces, were the mainstay of the attacks on the cities. Conventionally regarded as a political victory but military defeat for the Communists, the Tet Offensive ended with the PAVN still effective and in better condition than its auxiliaries, as it had been used selectively and not committed to the cities.

The cost of preserving stalemate was high for the PAVN, however, and this cost was cited in support of arguments both for partial return to guerrilla warfare and for accelerated main-force modernization. During 1969, the PAVN generally did commit smaller units to battle than in 1968, but three factors made adoption of the latter course inevitable. First, the sheer intensity of the fighting, the shift of population from the countryside to the cities, and an aggressive pacification program eroded the political base needed to wage a resistance-style people's war. Second, the phased withdrawal announced in September 1969 meant that it would be increasingly feasible to engage the enemy that remained in a conventional, frontal mode. And third, the PAVN had been steadily upgrading its weaponry, equipment, and command structures and soon would have resources and combat capabilities to rival those of the enemy. Together, these factors justified ever-larger combined operations by main-force units. The high command strongly supported measures to induce the United States to cease bombing the North, as economic recovery was needed to sustain the more capital intensive form of warfare that would be needed in the end to defeat the Army of the Republic of Vietnam.

The PAVN, of course, had been steadily if rather gradually enhancing its ability to wage this kind of war for years, but the pace of development now quickened. The spring offensive of 1972 relied mainly on PAVN divisions accompanied for the first time in the South by medium tanks, 122mm and 130mm field artillery, and SAM-7 missiles. The use of armor and attempts at combined tank-infantry-artillery operations, however, revealed the PAVN's lack of prior experience and inadequate training in this type of combat. But rather than revert to earlier, more familiar forms of warfare, the PAVN learned from its mistakes and in the spring of 1975 mounted the more competently executed operations that ended the war.

The PAVN at war's end could be characterized as a hybrid force. It possessed an institutional memory of guerrilla skills: Units could still move long distances on foot undetected with remarkable speed. Strategic doctrine still echoed with the concepts of coordinated struggle and subordination of military action to political objectives. But the PAVN also possessed the material assets of a modern conventional army, able to sustain combat with its own internal logistical system. It was led by a professional corps of officers. Moreover, for a decade its sole mission of consequence had been to wage war. A different army than it had been in 1954, it could not be expected to play the same political role it had then.

POSTWAR MISSIONS AND POSTWAR WARS

As the Second Indochina War came to a close, SRV military leaders tended to advocate continued emphasis on professionalism and on the military mission. Leaders who had helped to expedite the Soviet military assistance program especially feared that if the PAVN were diverted on a large scale into economic or administrative work, professional and technical competence would decline. They attempted to forestall this by offering to trade size for quality. If the PAVN were made smaller, more compact, further upgraded its weaponry, and recruited more selectively from large reserves, they reasoned, it could actually improve combat effectiveness without increasing the burden on resources needed for development.[12] This reasoning did not prevail, however.

Because of the devastation left by war, the weakness of state structures relative to their tasks, and the absence of alternative agents of development, the regime had no choice but to rely heavily on the army as it had in 1954. The problems were compounded by the need to integrate the South, where local party as well as state cadres were sorely lacking. Party membership in the South at war's end was not over 200,000 and had risen to only 273,000 or 1.3 percent of the South's population by mid-1978 when party membership in the North was about 6.3 percent of the regional population.[13] Only the army had the resources-in-place to supervise recovery and administration of the South in 1975-1976.

In the North, the shift of some PAVN units to reconstruction work began as early as 1973, and in early 1974 a special unit was created to assist in recovery work in Hanoi. The massive assignment of the military to economic tasks nationwide was signaled in October 1976 by the establishment of a General Directorate for Economic Development in the Ministry of National Defense. The purpose of this directorate was to coordinate the PAVN's rapidly growing contribution to the building of roads, canals, and bridges, to construction of hydroelectric projects, to land reclamation, and to virtually anything else that required sizable technical, transportation, construction, or organized labor forces. Army officers were appointed to head the Ministry of Supply, the Ministry of Oil and Natural Gas, the Ministry of Contruction, and the Ministry of Marine Products. Cadre training programs continued to produce twice as many military cadres as civilian ones, partly to meet the needs of state administration and economic management.[14] In the first nine months of 1977, 10,000 officers and NCOs were specially trained for reassignment to district-level administrative organs.[15] Force levels were raised rather than reduced in order to increase the number of laborers available for work under military discipline on construction projects. The PAVN, it was hoped, would become the SRV's largest "school of socialism," in which rural youths would acquire work habits needed in the industrial society of the future, and southern city youths would acquire the political values needed in the future socialist society.

Thus, following the Second Indochina War, military and civilian roles were reintegrated on a large scale. This occurred at the behest of civilian planners with the concurrence, if not the enthusiasm, of the most senior military leaders.[16] But officers at lower levels complained that the army's economic mission reduced combat readiness, eroded discipline, and retarded modernization.[17] General Giap himself, no doubt reflecting the mixed feelings of the general staff, appears to have accepted a major role for the army in economic construction partly because he believed this was the only way the industrial base needed to improve the SRV's military self-sufficiency could be quickly built. Many officers, more at lower than at top levels, positively resisted return to civic-soldier roles because these diverted them from purely military duties.

The opportunity to withdraw from economic work arose in the form of a dual threat from China and Kampuchea. So long as these threats did not include large-scale cross-border attacks, they were met by local auxiliary and reserve forces, and the country continued to concentrate on recovery and construction. But the invasion of Kampuchea by 150,000 Vietnamese troops (subsequently 220,000) in December 1978 and of Vietnam by a comparable number of Chinese troops in February 1979 required the SRV to return to a war footing. The question was what kind of war footing should this be: one that took earlier resistance wars as the model, or one that combined a permanent high state of preparedness with continued socialist development? If the latter, how was this to be organized?

The SRV faced several dilemmas in attempting to reconcile its economic difficulties with its military involvements. Some PAVN units had to be reassigned from economic to combat duties, but the PAVN could not be withdrawn completely from economic work without sacrificing projects on which recovery and development, and ultimately defense, depended. At the same time, with almost one-third of the PAVN in Kampuchea and some units still engaged in economic construction, defense needs could be met only by radically expanding and strengthening local self-defense forces. Public statements by PAVN leaders about the Chinese attack revealed that they drew two major lessons from the experience: First, they still lacked experience in defending fixed points and needed to strengthen PAVN main forces for this purpose, and second, the SRV still needed to mobilize civilians on a mass basis for defense. In combination, these responses to the Third Indochina War left the PAVN with broadened rather than narrowed responsibilities. It remained an important resource in heavy capital construction; it was in charge of the occupation of Kampuchea; it had to backstop frontier forces against China; and it was responsible for implementing the March 5, 1979, general mobilization order that decreed two hours of training and guard duty daily for all males aged eighteen through forty-five and females aged eighteen through thirty-five. Henceforth the PAVN not only would have heavier conventional military missions but also would retain an important role in civil construction and administration while organizing, in General Giap's words, "fifty million compatriots nationwide into combat units made up of fifty million valiant warriors."[18]

THE PAVN'S CONTEMPORARY POLITICAL ROLE

Since the end of the Second Indochina War, the PAVN's political role has been complicated by several conflicting trends. Internally, the growth of professionalism in the officer corps and the imperatives of conventional, high-technology warfare have created pressures to demarcate military and civilian functions more clearly and to withdraw the military from the latter. The intensity of these pressures has varied according to rank and assignment, however. In general, the topmost military leadership, although sharing the concerns of professional officers, is still largely composed of first-generation leaders who were party organizers before they donned a uniform. Though increasingly inclined to articulate institutional points of view, particularly on economic questions affecting defense strategy,[19] they remain legitimate and cooperative participants in policymaking on a very broad range of issues. General Giap has made more public statements since 1975 on scientific and technological development than he has on military affairs and has led several diplomatic missions abroad. When he stepped down as defense minister in February 1980 he remained a vice-premier. Indicative of the long-range trend, however, is that the new chief of staff, Le Trong Tan (replacing Van Tien Dung who replaced Giap as minister of defense), is a Soviet and East European-trained officer whose career has concentrated almost exclusively on professional training and main-forces command. If internal forces were the sole factor in the PAVN's development, generational differences over the proper role of officers would decline as senior leaders retire or die and are replaced by younger professionals.

Externally, however, circumstances have militated against any abandonment of the civic-soldier role or significant reduction of the military penetration of society. Following the Second Indochina War, state and party deficiencies, not to mention the unique burdens posed by the South, made dependence on the military for a full range of logistical and administrative services unavoidable. Ambitious development plans in the absence of significant alternative means sharpened the need for the army to participate in economic construction. Although in the aftermath of the Third Indochina War the PAVN was able to increase attention to its conventional combat mission, chronic shortcomings in the state sector and a revival of popular defense doctrine maintained and in some ways probably expanded its duties outside this mission. Since a high state of international tension is built into the SRV's geostrategic position, the fusion of civilian and military life is likely to persist, with significant elements inside the military pressuring for separation of the two.

The consequences for party-army relations of a highly professional but politically active officer corps emerging in the context of the above conditions can only be guessed. The immediate effect appears to be to forestall the reduction of army representation in high party organs and probably to increase it. At the 4th Party Congress in December 1976 the number of active duty officers holding full membership in the Central Committee increased, but their proportion in the total actually declined about three points to 23 percent (23 out of 101). The military probably was able to maintain this large representation only because during the war years it had been a major source of new party members, as befit the priorities of the time, and therefore was entitled to elect a large number of delegates. In 1979 the army increased in size, and a major party-building program aimed at recruiting youth from the most modern and politically reliable organizations had a built-in bias for the military. In the first quarter of 1980 upwards of 70 percent of all new party members in some regions were from the army.[20] Such heavy dependence on the military for the recruitment of new party members can only increase the overlap between the two organizations and the representation of the military in the next Central Committee. It is not impossible that a new generation of civic soldiers could emerge to take the places of those who inevitably must depart in the next few years, and that this generation could constitute a substantial proportion of party membership as well as military leadership.

The preservation of the PAVN's political role would only have reflected the prevailing economic and security conditions if the 4th Party Congress had not also decided to replace collective leadership in military units with the "one-person command system." This decision, which was not widely implemented until the outbreak of the conflicts with China and Kampuchea, in combination with the continuing high level of party-army interpenetration, may enhance both the professional autonomy and political influence of PAVN military commanders. Whereas the collective leadership principle unified authority in unit party committees and divided responsibility for execution between military commanders and political officers, one-person command concentrates executive responsibility, including responsibility for political work, in the hands of each unit's highest-ranking individual (who almost invariably is the military commander) but limits party committees to policy transmission and consultation. The ostensible reason for adopting this principle was that the growing complexity of the PAVN's military mission required quicker command reflexes and tighter vertical integration than was possible with collective leadership. Continuing improvement of the PAVN's technical capabilities also was seen as justification for expanding the management prerogatives of the technically qualified military professionals. This change has been resisted by individuals who have feared it would erode the authority of the party organization and of political officers in the army.[21] Certainly it does hold some potential for releasing military commanders from direct supervision by party committees.

These developments suggest that PAVN officers could in the future develop and advance more distinctly professional views on strategic and foreign policy. They could, for example, observe the corrosive effects of counterinsurgency in Kampuchea on PAVN discipline and morale, negatively assess the affect of an interminable occupation in both Laos and Kampuchea on the PAVN's ability to defend more important terrain from more powerful enemies, and become a focal point of opposition to party policy. Against this line of thinking, however, it must be reemphasized that the effect of post-Second Indochina War developments on the PAVN has been to intensify cross-pressures between civic-soldier and professional roles, preventing the emergence of a unified military point of view or the delimitation of the military mission. Even the occupation of Kampuchea and defense against China create opportunities for the civic soldier as well as for conventional combat leadership, since in both instances the PAVN must perform political, administrative, and economic functions where civilian organization is weak or lacking. No doubt some officers fit only one model or the other, whereas others combine elements of both. Differences of role within the PAVN, and role conflict within individuals, may continue for some time to be more politically significant than the presumptive division between party and army.

NOTES

    1. This paper is drawn from a much longer work in progress tentatively titled The People's Army of Vietnam in War, Peace, and Politics, which for sources relies primarily on Vietnamese publications, captured documents, and interviews with former PAVN officers conducted in Saigon in 1972-1973 under the auspices of the Ford Foundation.
    2. John T. McAlister, Jr., Viet-Nam: The Origins of Revolution (New York: Alfred A. Knopf, 1969), pp. 246-247, 250-251.
    3. Ban nghien cuu lich su quan doi [Army Historical Research Committee], Lich su Quan doi nhan dan Viet-Nam [History of the People's Army of Vietnam], vol. 1 (Hanoi: NXB Quan doi nhan dan, 1974), pp. 235, 308.
    4. House Committee on Armed Services, Department of Defense, United States-Vietnam Relations, 1945-1967 (Washington, D.C.: Government Printing Office, 1971), Book 1, IV.A.2, face 6, citing Rand Corporation translation RM-5271-PR, May 1967.
    5. Lich su Quan doi nhan dan Viet-Nam, pp. 231, 235, 308, 311, 381, and Central Committee report on party expansion dated 1948 in U.S. Department of State, Working Paper on North Vietnamese Role in the War in South Viet-Nam: Captured Documents and Interrogation Reports (Washington, D.C., May 1968), Item 1.
    6. Vo Nguyen Giap, "Tich cuc phan dau de hoan thanh thang loi nhiem vu nam nay cua quan doi" [Struggle enthusiastically to achieve victory in the army's mission this year], Quan doi nhan dan [People's Army Newspaper]. March 14, 1958, pp. 1, 6.
    7. "Y kien phat bieu cua dong chi Nguyen Chi Thanh trong cuoc hoi nghi chinh uy toan quan ngay 10-3-1958" [Opinions expressed by Comrad Nguyen Chi Thanh at All-Army Political Delegates' Conference, March 10, 1958], Quan doi nhan dan, March 18, 1958, p. 1.
    8. Vo Nguyen Giap and Nguyen Chi Thanh, "Duong loi quan su Mac-xit la ngon co chien thang cua quan doi ta" [The party's Marxist military line is the banner of victory of our army], Quan doi nhan dan, December 22-23, 1958.
    9. Vo Nguyen Giap, "Cong tac cung co quoc phong, xay dung luc luong vu trang nhan dan" [The task of consolidating national defense and building the people's armed

forces], <u>Quan doi nhan dan</u>, September 10, 1960, p. 4.

10. See Patrick J. McGarvey, ed., <u>Visions of Victory: Selected Vietnamese Communist Military Writings, 1964-1968</u> (Stanford, Calif.: Hoover Institution on War, Revolution, and Peace, 1969); and Thomas K. Latimer, "Hanoi's Leaders and Their South Vietnam Policies: 1954-1968" (Ph.D. diss., Georgetown University, 1972), pp. 112-347.

11. Communist internal sources gave much larger estimates for guerrillas and popular self-defense forces, but even the most inflated estimates showed the total of revolutionary armed forces to be a fraction as large as that of the Saigon-U.S. side. All of these forces were ultimately under the direction of the party Central Committee in Hanoi, either through a direct chain of command as in the case of some PAVN units or through the Central Committee Directorate located in the South that comprised, besides a detachment of Central Committee and Political Bureau members charged with supervising the southern revolutionary movement, a military command composed of PAVN officers who oversaw the PLAF and provided theater coordination. The distinction between PAVN and PLAF units was largely vitiated in the late 1960s when northern regulars began to be used in large numbers to replenish the latter. The term "Viet Cong," a contraction meaning Vietnamese Communist that was used on the Saigon-U.S. side to refer variously to the enemy as a whole, indigenous southern forces, or guerrillas, is not the proper name of any Vietnamese Communist military organization, lacks precise meaning, and is purposely avoided in this work.

12. Tran Sam, "Nang cao trinh do khoa hoc--ky thuat cua can bo, gop phan tang cuong suc manh chien dau cua quan doi ta" [Raise the scientific and technical level of cadres, contribute to the combat strength of our army], <u>Tap chi Quan doi nhan dan</u> [People's Army Journal], February 1974, pp. 1-18; and Nguyen Ngoc, "Tim hieu not so tu tuong tien bo trong xay dung quan doi cua to tien ta" [Seek progressive ideas in our ancestors' army building], <u>Tap chi Quan doi nhan dan</u>, January 1974, pp. 67-73.

13. Alexander Casella, <u>Foreign Policy</u>, no. 28, Spring 1978, p. 72; <u>Los Angeles Times</u>, October 18, 1978; Speech by Le Duc Tho at 4th Party Congress, Hanoi Radio broadcast, December 17, 1976, in Foreign Broadcast Information Service, <u>Daily Report: Asia and Pacific</u> (hereafter FBIS-APA), December 23, 1976.

14. Che Viet Tan, <u>Nhan dan</u> [The People], December 7, 1976, in FBIS-APA, December 13, 1976.

15. Vietnam News Agency, October 10, 1977, in FBIS-APA, October 13, 1977.

16. Vo Nguyen Giap, talk to a class in economic management for high and middle-level army cadres, <u>Tap Chi Quan doi nhan dan</u>, November 1976, in FBIS-APA, November 30,

1976.

17. General Giap attacked these complaints in "Xay dung nen quoc phong toan dan vung manh, bao ve To quoc Viet-nam xa hoi chua nghia" [Build the foundations of a solid all-people national defense, protect the socialist Vietnamese father-land], <u>Hoc Tap</u> (Study and Practice], May 1976, pp. 13-45.

18. "People's War for National Defense in the New Era," <u>Tap chi Cong san</u> [Review of Communism], May 1979, in FBIS-APA, May 24, 1979.

19. General Giap has done so explicitly: "Facts in our country and especially in the Soviet Union permit us to conclude that the superiority of the socialist regime can enable us not only to meet the very high and urgent requirements of consolidating national defense and defending the fatherland, but also to vigorously develop the economy of a large-scale socialist production in order to gradually build a highly developed and heavy engineering industry." Speech to the National Assembly, May 28, 1979, in FBIS-APA, supplement, June 5, 1979. These remarks are not inconsistent with the party's established economic policy, but Giap is the only leader to have publicly drawn a comparison with the Soviet Union as a model for linking industrial development with defense needs.

20. Hanoi Radio broadcast, May 5, 1980, in FBIS-APA, May 6, 1980.

21. Bui Bien Tuhy, "Dealing with the Initial Experiences Gained by a Number of Units that Have Successfully Carried Out the One-Person Command System," <u>Tap chi Quan doi nhan dan</u>, Hanoi radio broadcast, October 26, 1980, in FBIS-APA, October 28, 1980.

6
The Yugoslav Army

Robert W. Dean

It is our general thesis that within the framework of efforts to strengthen central authority in the early and mid-1970s, the Yugoslav army's political role evolved to the point where military support became and remains central to the preservation and extension of that authority. The civilian leadership after the 1970 nationalist crisis in Croatia has relied on the military as a guarantee of Yugoslavia's political system and stability. The political influence that has been gained by the military institution is likely to continue in the foreseeable future. In the post-Tito era, assuming the military's continued respect for civilian institutions, its role within them is likely to grow. In no other European Communist state does the military play as integral a part in political affairs. It is the uniqueness of the army-party relationship in Yugoslavia--the army's legitimacy, as much as its capacities as an institution; its skills and resources-- that have accounted for the army being drawn into efforts to counteract the sociopolitical fragmentation of recent years. The army has been the source of top political leadership. Military officials have been incorporated into the political leadership most prominently, though by no means exclusively, in the area of internal security. They have been drawn further into the political mainstream via expanded participation in leading party bodies as well as in lower levels of party and state organization. The military has also assumed greater ideological-educational functions.

The catalyst of some of these politico-organizational changes, both in the body politic and in the military, was the succession problem. The expansion of military responsibility in the country's political life was a consequence both of efforts to fashion a unified leadership in anticipation of Tito's departure and to insure the loyalty of the military. The process was a reciprocal one. The army's expanded political involvement called forth efforts to alter the character of the military itself

to insure its subscription to party hegemony and its
adherence to civilian institutions. Changes were implemented in defense policies, the system of party control,
the army's ethnic composition, and in a renewed emphasis
on ideology in military training.

DISARRAY AND CONSOLIDATION

   In 1971 Yugoslavia faced its gravest political crisis
since Tito's 1948 confrontation with Stalin. Long-dormant
ethnocentric attitudes surfaced in Croatia over opposition
to siphoning off its foreign exchange earnings to less-
developed republics and raised anew the question of the
viability of an integral, multinational Yugoslav state.
In November 1971 a student strike in Zagreb, the Croatian
capital, threatened to mature rapidly into an outright
popular and official challenge to federal authority. At
this critical point Tito forced the resignation of leading
figures in the Croatian leadership. This outburst of
Croatian nationalism was the culmination of a process of
decentralization of federal authority set in motion by
economic reforms in 1965 and accelerated after the 1966
political defeat of the centralist party secretary,
Aleksander Rankovic.[1]
   A concept of loose federalism reinforced by the doctrine of self-management was well ensconced when, in mid-
1970, the Yugoslav leadership began preparation for the
post-Tito era. In June 1971 a series of constitutional
amendments transferred to the republics comprehensive powers
previously held by the federal government in Belgrade--
except responsibility for defense, foreign policy, and
broad economic policy. A twenty-three member Collective
State Presidency grouped together representatives of the
republics and provinces and performed the often conflicting functions of policymaking and arbitration. No less
the product of regional forces, the party, the League of
Communists of Yugoslavia (LCY), had also become a federal
body. In effect the country had six or more parties.[2]
   The aim of political reform since 1972 has been to
reconstitute a central authority fragmented by the earlier
transfer of powers to republic and provincial leaderships.
Federal principles have been maintained in state and government organizations, albeit in a more restrained form. In
contrast, the party has been returned to the principle of
democratic centralism so that it can serve, in Tito's
words, as "the connective tissue which binds multinational
Yugoslavia together."[3] Nevertheless, although the essence
of this political consolidation could fairly be termed
recentralization, Yugoslavia remains very much a federal
state. Federal power is still bound to respect particular
republican interests.

THE POLITICAL METAMORPHOSIS OF THE MILITARY

As the social and political stability of the multinational state has proved vulnerable, and the credibility of newly buttressed federal institutions remained untried, the Yugoslav military, consisting of 250,000 men, came to occupy a position of major importance for the country's political future.

The relationship of party to army has never been simply that of two distinct, highly disciplined rival institutions. Indeed, in contrast to most Communist states (with China the most notable exception), the institutional roots of party and army are the same: They grew together out of the partisan struggle and in that formative period were highly integrated organizationally and ideologically. The institutional identity of the military became quite distinct over time. Today its formal institutional boundaries and professional interests and attitudes are well established. But the fact that Yugoslav military and political elite emerged from the same mold means that, in comparison to other East European states, institutional boundaries have been more permeable. Generals assigned to civilian leadership positions operate according to a complex code of military and party loyalites that tend to combine, rather than exclude, one another. While institutional conflict or competition may exist, at the same time a respect for civilian institutions is evident.

The scope of civil-military relations is broader and more complex than the simple elite army-party nexus. One must take account of the military's penetration of the party and other civilian organizations, as well as the entire military and quasi-military establishment. This includes the Yugoslavian People's Army (YPA) party organization, the 1.5-million-man veterans' and reserve officers' organizations, and potential civilian constituencies whose conservative leanings might cause them to gravitate politically toward the army.

The weakness of the central political authority has pushed the military into a greater political role over the past few years. Although Tito's parting may eventually accelerate this process, the military has not sought to alter its subordinate place in the Yugoslav political system. Unquestionably, a strong sense of custodianship is to be found in the YPA that could provide both a political license and an impulse toward autonomous political behavior, especially in situations of stress or crisis. Under Yugoslav conditions the party has the disadvantage of being a political coalition. By virtue of its organization and discipline, the army is less subject to the nationality conflict and other disputes that have rent the party. The army, at the same time, is based on hierarchy, discipline, and responsiveness to command, all antithetical to compromise and negotiation. The army as the only "all-Yugoslav" institution is not and cannot be a political coalition. Although the army may be able to transcend nationality or ethnic quarrels within its own ranks, it is ill suited to achieve this in society at large.

Thus, the army is not a convincing alternative to the party in the preservation and extension of domestic integration, although it may serve as an instrument of such policies. It is the party's overarching political and ideological claims that have made it the legitimate embodiment of an integral Yugoslavia. The military's recognition of this has served and will continue to serve as a strong restraint against an interventionist role-- once again, short of a situation of extreme instability.

But if the YPA is to function along traditional and unambiguously subordinate lines, that is, solely as the instrument of the party, the latter must present a strong, stable, and convincing center of power. A divided and undisciplined party cannot hope to maintain clear control of the army. Military loyalty to the principle of subordination is also conditional upon the ability of the party to preserve the integral Yugoslav state. Should that leadership or its resolve be seriously weakened, the army could assume a more direct political role as arbiter, factional ally, or challenger.

A main question and concern for Tito's successors will be the party's success in asserting and insuring its control over the army. During the 1970s, the army party organization was reorganized and revitalized, and the military leadership was integrated to an unprecedented extent into leading positions in both party and government. There is now a group of high-level officers, "political generals," whose responsibilities extend beyond the scope of their professional competence to the political process, and who have been active in shaping and implementing LCY policy. This is a species of public official that was virtually unknown in Yugoslavia in the 1960s. The integrity of the civilian position has been blurred and compromised in some cases, and the identity of party with military policies and responsibilities has been increased, with a view to precluding the development of a gap between party and army. Senior officers have not encroached upon civilian prerogative in nonsecurity areas, nor has there been evidence of military pressures--other than conservative rhetoric-- to push the party in directions it might otherwise choose not to go. This suggests that they have been <u>coopted</u> into the political process, rather than having <u>insinuated</u> themselves into it, with a view to narrowing the margin for disagreement between army and party.

Tito's unassailable personal prestige was a central factor insuring the subordination of the military and eliciting its support and/or acquiescence for party-

defined policies. In the event of future high-level
political rivalry and disagreement the army is sure to
become more of an autonomous political actor. This need
not be inconsistent with civilian political supremacy but
certainly will alter the shape of institutional or leadership politics in Yugoslavia.

THE YPA AND TERRITORIAL DEFENSE

Subsequent to the August 1968 Soviet invasion of
Czechoslovakia, Yugoslavia undertook a radical reorganization of its national defense that established total popular
mobilization against an invasion from the east. This
revival of the partisan war concept, which also exploited
ethnic identification in military activity, dictated an
emphasis on command flexibility, and thereby on republican
and communal organization and operational prerogatives at
the expense, inevitably, of federal central command authority. The system of All Peoples' Defense (APD) established
territorial defense organizations within each republic in
1969.

In addition to the threat of a Soviet invasion,
domestic motives were important in the creation of APD.
As the decentralization of party and state authority
proceeded in the late 1960s, the army remained something
of an institutional anomaly--monolithic, hierarchical,
centralized--immured against reforms associated with self-
management, federalization, and the general devolution of
political authority. The centralized, all-Yugoslav YPA
seemed a threat to the rights of Yugoslavia's constituent
republics. APD neatly embraced an effort in existence
since 1967 to reduce the exclusivist character of the YPA
and to enhance greater republican influence in military
affairs.[4]

Territorial defense threatened the professional and
institutional integrity of the YPA by subjecting the army
to pressures for republican control and internal reforms
to accommodate a pervasive federalization. Two early
signs of this were increased pressures for posting by
nationality and use of multiple command languages. Some
Croats insisted that republican officials be given wider
and more explicit authority in military matters, the
"sharpest opposition to attempts to separate the concept
of nationwide defense from that of the self-managed
society, and to the view that the self-management system
is unsuitable for effective conduct of nationwide
resistance."[5] The territorial defense units under republic
defense staffs were not subordinated to the YPA, perhaps
the most direct alteration of army authority. The February
1969 law extended to every "social-political unit" (a
rubric that included republic, communal, and lower echelon
bodies) the obligation and responsibility "to organize
total national defense and to command the battle directly."[6]

With the alarm of the 1971 Croatian nationalist crisis, the slide toward greater republican power was reversed and with it the attrition of YPA authority. The YPA successfully lobbied for a redefinition of territorial defense that would restore its authority and central role, and developments since then bear the imprint of these efforts. A 1974 new law on national defense limited republican-level authority and control by withdrawing the comprehensive grant of authority to lower-echelon commands contained in the 1969 law. Local command authority was confined to instances of foreign aggression. The YPA emerged in a strengthened and preeminent position in what was understood as a "unified defense system." Previously the YPA's role was prescribed as a holding action that would blunt and delay the invader's attack, thus buying time for the mobilization of the countrywide territorial organization. It was also to serve as the basis for mobilization by providing the nucleus for wartime units. In its reevaluated role the YPA was viewed more as a force in being, the main striking element and core of the combined defense forces, to be organized and ready for its wartime role. Now the system concentrated on the reequipping and training of the territorial defense units with gradual integration into the overall system, thus excluding any notion of a two-tiered system of defense or republican armies. All military training in peacetime is by permanent YPA officers, and emphasis was placed on training territorial units in conjunction with regular YPA units. The process of integration into a unified defense structure with the YPA in the operational command will no doubt continue.[7]

The program of territorial defense has a political rationale as a vehicle for encouraging Yugoslav unity. Broad popular participation in defense training and organization provide a framework for socialization in the values of cohesive Yugoslavism and self-management, for the sublimation of national and ethnic differences, and for reinvigoration of sociopolitical organizations. One such program is the adoption of compulsory premilitary training in the country's universities, originated and supervised by YPA officers. It accorded the military a place in the universities and authorized a system of centralized premilitary training under army control.[8]

As it has come to be interpreted, the doctrine of territorial defense has reinforced the central importance of the YPA. Territorial armies and republican authority in military affairs have been removed as a threat to the YPA. These revisions cannot, however, be construed as the direct result of military influence or pressure. Obviously, the political logic of Yugoslavia's development in recent years, above all the need to restrain "republicanism," to restore meaningful authority to the federal level, and to anticipate instability, dictated such change.

THE MILITARY AND THE 1971 CROATIAN CRISIS

Before 1971 the trend toward decentralization threatened to encroach upon the army's integrity, cohesion, and capacity to act as an all-Yugoslav force in the event of internal crisis. Out of an urge toward institutional preservation, the army leadership participated in the debate over what form Yugoslav federalism was to take. Earlier attempts to seal off the YPA from these decentralizing pressures by stressing its institutional exclusiveness were no longer viable because of the gathering strength of republicanism and the reorientation of defense policy to the doctrine of All Peoples' Defense.

As the portents of nationalism in Croatia grew more ominous in the spring of 1971, it became obvious that a defense policy that stressed the devolution of military authority threatened to compromise Belgrade's ability to utilize the military in dealing effectively with domestic strife or with an insubordinate republican leadership. The military leadership stressed that the army must not become subject to the conditional agreement of republican authority. The military clearly felt its priority was the possibility of domestic strife rather than foreign aggression. In one opinion poll a large majority of officers and NCOs singled out nationalism and chauvinism as the main dangers to the country. Only 12 percent thought foreign aggression the most likely source of conflict.[9]

During the pre-December 1971 period, military leaders became increasingly visible as spokesmen on internal affairs. Rumor abounded that a military putsch had either been attempted or was being planned. Statements appeared of the army's qualified willingness to intervene, registering the military's alarm. The army was both prodding the civilian leadership and preparing to contribute to internal stabilization in Croatia if necessary.[10]

It does not appear, however, that Yugoslav military leaders actually took an independent stand in the Croatian crisis, confronting Tito with an ultimatum to oust the errant Croatian leadership faction. But, as the atmosphere of crisis mounted in December 1971, their entreaty was an important factor in precipitating his intervention in Croatia. In the wake of that December confrontation much media output was given over to explicit denials that the army had forced Tito's hand. Vladimir Bakaric, a Croatian leader, insisted "that the Army has never exerted political pressure of any kind or threatened Tito with a coup." Bakaric did acknowledge a "certain potential danger" from the army but concluded that "the Army does not serve to keep order in the country; its only task is to protect the Yugoslav borders from external enemies."[11] However, Tito overruled Bakaric and asserted that he would call upon the army, the "ultimate means," to establish order. However, he was eager not to bring the army directly to bear for fear of forfeiting a measure of his political control over both it and the situation.

Following the ouster of the discredited Croat leadership, the army adopted a more assertive political posture. The military criticized openly those nonmilitary aspects of the country's life about which it was alarmed. The tone was loyalist, but avuncular. Such criticism was wide-ranging, extending to culture and the economy, but it tended to focus on the preservation of civil peace and military preparedness and the restoration of discipline in party life. The unusual exceptional prominence of the military in the political debate was regarded by one Yugoslav observer as a public signal of its potentially "decisive political influence [in] decision-making and perhaps even leadership."[12] This appraisal, though extravagant, did correctly interpret clear support from the military as conditional upon the success of the party's efforts to consolidate itself and the country as a whole.

YUGOSLAVIA'S VETERANS: STEWARDS OF THE REVOLUTION

Throughout 1971 and 1972 Yugoslavia's powerful veterans' groups (SUBNOR) were a prominent part of the conservative groundswell that were the first to rally against national activity in Croatia the political insubordination of the liberal Serbian leadership, and the general trend toward decentralization of political authority. The veterans, possibly in response to army influence,[13] showed themselves capable of acting independently of republican party organizations.

The strength of the veterans and their determination lay in the fact that they are a well-organized group whose cohesion is the product of a shared wartime experience and, more immediately, of the common attitudes and ideological rectitude of a politically déclassé social stratum. Having once occupied a favored place in society, they grew disaffected during the mid-1960s as a result of personnel policies that sought to minimize participation in the partisan war as the criterion for political and social mobility. The vanguard of the revolution found itself "driven out of public and political life in various ways: [veterans] had been pensioned off or proclaimed conservative or too old."[14] The Croatian crisis seemed to vindicate their widely held resentments and held out the prospect that lost privilege and status might be regained.

Between 1947 and his forced resignation in 1966 the interior minister and heir-apparent to Tito, Aleksander Rankovic, headed the veterans' union. It became the pool from which the party, army, state, and economic cadres were recruited. The ouster of Rankovic signaled the beginning of the collapse of the veterans' powerful political-bureaucratic position. The 1965 economic reform put a

premium on technical and managerial skills rather than
political loyalty. Politically disenfranchised, veterans
not only lost their unique accessibility to the political
administrative leadership but were gradually replaced in
favor of younger men distinguished by their education or
professional expertise.[15]

In the wake of the Croatian leadership purge the
veterans' and reserve army officers' associations emerged
as a source of orthodox pressures. In open disagreement
with the moderation and relative caution being shown by
the LCY, and acting for the most part not through their
national leadership but rather from communal-level associations, they charged that extirpation of nationalist and
liberalist sentiments was not thoroughgoing enough and
punishment of its proponents insufficient. They criticized
LCY attitudes in dealing decisively with such phenomena
as the growth of excessive social differences, the accumu-
lation of wealth, and artistic dissidence--trends that in
their view amounted to the political and moral deterioration
of Yugoslav society. SUBNOR's secretary general warned
that an irresolute response by the LCY to continuing
political deviation left veterans the choice of remaining
silent or "independently taking political initiative."
The attempt was made, in effect, to supersede the political
authority of the party.[16]

Tito and the party leadership showed an ambivalent
attitude toward the veterans, carefully admonishing them
for their conservative zeal and at the same time currying
their support. "Apart from the Communist Party and the
Socialist Alliance," said Tito, "our most important organization is the Veterans' Federation....There are perhaps
still some unsolved problems... but in the past the Veterans'
Federation was always a powerful pillar of our socialist
society."[17] Addressing veterans on July 4, 1972, Veterans'
Day, Edvard Kardelj lauded them, but he cautioned them not
to be manipulated by "ideological and political protagonists of bureaucratic dogmatic socialism."[18] Another party
leader attacked them as a "neo-Stalinist revanche."[19] Such
public remonstrances apparently had little effect on cur-
tailing such veterans' activities. A political consolidation stretching to Serbia and the Vojvodina province in
late 1972, the veterans again surfaced as the sponsors
of a more radical purge.

The veterans remain a powerful conservative and quasi-
independent force, which the party, cognizant of the importance of their support as well as their ties with the YPA,
has been unwilling (or unable) to bridle completely. They
now have a political mandate that extends well beyond the
protection and pursuit of immediate interests, such as
pensions. They claim the distinction of being able "more
than anybody else [to] feel and identify the activities
of class enemies."[20] Furthermore, although the veterans'
republican and federal leaderships have made an effort to

eliminate indiscipline in lower-level organizations, these organizations continue to exercise a political influence in accord with this mandate in areas of culture and the economy.

POLITICAL CONTROL AND INSTITUTIONAL STABILITY:
THE ARMY PARTY ORGANIZATION

In the wake of the Croatian events, and given the uncertainties of succession, the military and its loyalty to the party and fidelity to its political direction assumed a crucial importance. The party felt that the more the army existed as a well-defined exclusive professional institution separate and apart from society, the less subject it was to routine political control and the more capable of autonomous political and military behavior, especially in time of crisis or near-crisis.

Although Tito claimed that the army firmly supported the party leadership in its rout of the dissident Croatian faction and purge of other republican leaderships, subsequent events suggest otherwise. In October 1972 the army party organization had 80,000 members. By January 1973 the figure had been reduced to 66,475.[21]

An effort was made to strengthen the role of the army party organization and insure it closer access to regular military activities such as promotion. The number of basic organizations was at least doubled and their membership halved. They were established on the battalion instead of the regimental level, and emphasis was placed on recruiting workers. The army party organization was more closely integrated with the League of Communist Party (LCP). Indoctrination and socialization efforts were re-emphasized, and ideology was presented as the determining factor in enabling "all cadres to increase the duties efficiently."[22]

An additional change in its status in relation to the regional party organizations has transformed the army party organization--and through it the army itself--into a potential counterweight to republican and provincial regional parties. Previously, the increasingly independent republican parties tended to dominate the respective army party organizations to insure that their activities and positions did not conflict with the republic autonomy. New party statutes in 1974 freed the army party organizations from supervision by the republican parties and established a coequal status. The army party organization was made responsible and responsive to the central LCY. The new statutes also made the army party organization responsible for implementing LCY policies. These horizontal links to other party bodies have a statutory and political significance previously denied the army party organization, even if they are not likely to dominate the political process.

The extension of party authority in the army has not met with uncritical acceptance in the professional officer corps. There is evidence that it fostered differences over the basic issue of professional military authority, as well as over priorities in allocations of manpower and resources, training time, and other issues. Army-party differences revolve most around the extent of political-ideological work: Many professional officers are skeptical of the utility of such work. Criticism of lagging interest by officers reflects the resistance with which the ideological campaign was greeted, even within the army party organization. A November 1973 study of the problem revealed that one-third of the army's party members had not involved themselves sufficiently.[23] The aim of these accelerated indoctrination efforts is to mobilize opinion and attitudes in support of civil institutions in the armed forces and reflects a genuine concern over the cohesion of the officer corps.

TOWARD A NATIONAL BALANCE IN THE OFFICER CORPS

The image of the YPA as an instrument of Serb hegemony, inherently hostile and uncompromising toward Croatian interests, accounted for the deep mistrust with which Croatian politicians viewed the YPA in 1971, as well as for their predisposition for national or territorial armies. The incubus of a Serb-dominated military has plagued efforts to overcome national resentments in Yugoslavia. Although an approximate national balance exists in the uppermost level of the military hierarchy, the officer corps as a whole is composed of a disproportionate number of Serbs. In the mid-1970s, Serbs represented 39.7 percent of the population but comprised 60 to 70 percent of the officer corps (46 percent of the general officer corps). Croats, comprising 22 percent of the population, accounted for only 14 percent of the officer corps (19 percent of the general officer corps).[24]

The effort to establish a genuinely proportional representation in the officer corps, already under way in 1970, was begun again in earnest following the Croatian crisis, spurred by a new sense of urgency to transform the YPA into an all-Yugoslav organization. A greater number of career alternatives in economically more advanced Croatia and Slovenia and Croatian distrust of a Serbian-dominated army have traditionally hindered recruitment.

To remedy the imbalance a new national defense law provided for compensatory education and accelerated promotion for noncommissioned officers and for special schooling in two-year university-level military schools. Promotion policy is also weighted toward rectifying the national imbalance. The most active officer recruitment efforts were undertaken in Slovenia, apparently without sufficient response. Postings for Slovenese in Slovenia became common policy. By 1974 an adequate national representation of students in nearly all officers' schools and among officers in reserve units had been achieved.[25]

PROFESSIONAL GRIEVANCES

Consistent with the YPA's greater political importance in recent years, a good deal of attention has been given to improving the professional status and emoluments of officers. Many professionally related reforms predated the Croatian events, but were accelerated in its wake.

Reforms provided greater job security, more apartments, better jobs for dependents, increased salaries, and training in military schools to ease the transition of retirees into civilian life. A new military pension system provided guarantees against involuntary retirement. The institution of a system of early promotion helped promote non-Serbian officers and rejuvenate the higher levels of the officer corps. Lower age limits were fixed for promotion to general rank, and the emphasis on participation in the partisan war has been dropped. The title "noncommissioned officer" was changed to "junior officer," and such individuals became eligible for additional education and subsequent promotion through the rank of lieutenant colonel. New laws also prevented the emigration of skilled workers and reserve officers and allowed extended terms of duty on a contract basis.[26]

LESSONS FROM THE MISKOVIC CASE

The military was drawn into the political process in the early 1970s because of the heightened concern over internal security. In general, military leaders may have sought to make their voices heard in private on military and security-related issues, but have not openly challenged the authority of political officials either to make decisions or to implement those policies once made. The army has remained subordinate to the party.

Such a statement, however, must not obscure the increase in the political relevance of the military or its ability to influence the politics of crucial--and in some future scenario, possibly paramount--security decisions. The one apparent example of an untoward expansion of military influence was the unique and short-lived rise to prominence of Col. Gen. Ivan Miscovic. In October-November 1971 Miskovic became Tito's chief security adviser, evidently in preparation for Tito's assault against the insubordinate elements in the Croatian leadership. In January 1972 he gained further state duties and resigned as chief of military counterintelligence (KOS). As KOS chief since May 1963, he had been instrumental in the rout of Rankovic and his minions in the security apparatus. From November 1971 through April 1973 he probably retained effective supervision over the entire military and civilian apparatus of internal security. As Tito's adviser during the purges, Miskovic held a position of extraordinary influence and importance.

In March 1973 the general assumed an unprecedented public posture. In the army paper, Front, he vigorously attacked the West, alleged that the Voice of America had permitted hostile emigres to broadcast calls for demonstrations and terrorist acts in Yugoslavia, and singled out liberal dissidents Milovan Djilas and Mihajlo Mihajlov as traitors. Miskovic portrayed the army by implication as the most capable instrument to pursue subversive elements, vindicated by its success in the Rankovic episode. He also made a plea for expanding the purview of organs against "counterrevolutionary aspirations" in the economy.[27] Such outspoken and alarmist treatment of Yugoslavia's security concerns raised questions of professional impropriety. Miskovic clearly overextended his mandate as the country's chief security officer. Although Miskovic made no observable departures from the Tito line, he chose to associate himself with the more conservative interpretation still permitted by that centrist position.

The general's demise was more sudden than his elevation. In April 1973 he was removed as Tito's special adviser on security affairs. In June the Executive Bureau of the LCY Presidium, including Tito, met in an enlarged extraordinary session and no doubt sealed Miskovic's fate. The relative ease with which he was ousted and the evident absence of more far-reaching personnel repercussions in the wake of his departure suggest that no military conspiracy existed and that in any case he lacked a base of institutional support.[28]

His summary elimination probably was part of a general effort to reemphasize the subordination of the military and attenuate the prominence of a number of military leaders who had publicly overstepped their proper responsibilities. The reorganization of the security adviser position was meant to prohibit the kind of monopoly Miskovic had fashioned and the distortions it had evidently made possible. Miskovic's removal marked the end of a phase in party-military relations during which, as a result of Tito's reliance on the military and its importance in buttressing party consolidation efforts, the military gained inordinate political influence in a period of political realignments and uncertainty. The ultimate and almost only check on Miskovic's political engagement was Tito's personal authority.[29]

MILITARY DOMINATION OF CIVILIAN SECURITY ORGANS?

Miskovic's ouster did little to alter the trend toward

an integral, centralized internal-security system or the
expansion of the military's role in it. The most visible
aspect of the military's central role in the system of
internal security was the May 1974 appointment of two
Croatian army generals to the two federal internal security
posts: Col. Gen. Franjo Herljevic replaced Yugoslavia's
civilian minister of internal affairs, and Maj. Gen. Vuko
Gozze-Gucetic occupied the public prosecutorship, the
highest civilian judicial office. Both organizations were
badly shaken, especially at the republican level, by the
disintegrative pressures associated with the political
disruptions of 1971-1972. The appointments were an unprecedented effort to strengthen these key civilian
offices by placing them in the hands of military officers.
They illustrate Tito's conviction that the army, because
of its disposition, loyalties, and institutional strengths,
was better equipped to insure continuity and guarantee
stability. The changes therefore encouraged the coordination of military and state security activities at every
level and provided the means of overseeing the republican
security services.

As a result of the discovery by KOS of the 1966
Rankovic conspiracy against Tito, KOS's role in his ouster,
and its success in preventing the penetration of the army
by the conspiracy, the responsibilities of military counterintelligence for internal security were greatly expanded.
The ouster of Rankovic both decimated and discredited the
state security apparatus; some 20,000 individuals were
expelled from its ranks after 1966. KOS was vindicated
once again, and its authority further enhanced, by the
inadequate response of the Croatian and Serbian security
services during the 1971 and 1972 political crises. The
Rankovic episode demonstrated the importance of the army
in any political struggle or bid for power, as well as the
importance of its loyalty to the ruling group. KOS therefore becomes an extremely important factor in insuring
this loyalty; it is in a sense, the kingpin of the army's
political role, and this would be so especially in circumstances where a military putsch might be planned. Indeed, the de facto jurisdiction of KOS probably extends
well beyond military ranks.

Although the role of the military in the domestic
security system has been enhanced, it is by no means an
exclusive one. The LCY has also sought to monitor the
security apparatus through party organs. As in its
approach to the YPA, the party leadership has emphasized
the need to curtail the institutional separateness of the
security service with a view toward eliminating any scope
for autonomous action.

THE INTERNAL ROLE OF THE MILITARY REDEFINED

The expanded presence of military officials in party

and state executive organs is the most visible sign of the
enhanced political role of the military, reflecting both
the growth in military influence and the conscious premise
that the military institution imparts a measure of its own
stability and strength to governmental institutions and
processes. The May 1974 LCY Party Congress named an active-
duty general, Ivan Kukoc, to the twelve-member Executive
Committee, the LCY's highest executive body. Two generals,
Defense Minister Nikola Ljubicic, and the secretary of the
army party organization, Dzemil Sarac, retained their
positions on the thirty-nine-member LCY Presidium. The
army had 12 percent of the Central Committee seats. At
the LCY Party Congress in June 1978, the Presidium was
reduced to twenty-five members--with one from the army.
By contrast, at the 9th Party Congress in 1969 only two
army representatives were on the Central Committee, and
at the 8th Party Congress in 1964 ten military delegates
comprised 6 percent of the total.

Thus, the army assumed a status within the party
formally somewhat akin to that of a province. Military
positions on the Central Committee grouped together the
most important military leaders and integrated them in an
unprecedented way in Central Committee policymaking,
enhancing their motive to identify with the established
political process. At a minimum, the secretary of defense, the assistant secretary of defense responsible for
political administration, the chief of staff, and the
commander of the most important army districts--Belgrade,
Zagreb, Ljubljana, and Split--seem, by virtue of their
positions, to have been assured places on the Central
Committee. The secretary of the army party organization
has specifically been designated as a Central Committee
member ex officio.

The constitutional control of the military was also
altered to favor its more efficient and timely use.
Procedures for activating the YPA were centralized and the
number of participants involved in the decision and implementation process reduced. The ambiguity surrounding the
delimiting of republican and federal authority in defense
and military matters were eliminated; the state presidency
now directs and commands the Yugoslav armed force in peace
and war. The command of the armed forces can now be
delegated to the defense minister alone, thus strenghening
his personal role and authority, removing opportunity or
latitude for delay, and rendering less complicated the
procedures for the activization of the army, either for
internal or external purposes.

Until Tito's death in May 1980 the legitimacy of
political institutions in Yugoslavia derived in large
measure from a highly personalist and therefore transcen-
dent sense of loyalty to Tito. It is uncertain to what
extent party and state institutions will command or elicit
this loyalty over time, deprived of the politically binding

force of Tito's charisma. The deference that the military showed for political and civil institutions during this period, therefore, flowed at least in part from Tito's presence.

It will be recalled that after the Croatian crisis (especially between January and June 1972) it became a fixture in the public statements of military leaders that domestic stability was the sine qua non of a successful defense policy against foreign aggression and the precondition for the successful implementation of All Peoples' Defense. The October 1972 "Tito Letter," which demanded an end to the desultory and disorganized pace of consolidation within the party and the economy, was greeted by the military with uncommon enthusiasm, accompanied by simultaneous denials of any independent interest in it, apart from accelerating efforts to restore the vigorous leading role of the party. The army depicted itself as cooperating in the political realm, not through "its status as an armed force, but primarily through its sociopolitical activity and the behavior of Communists and members of the Army." The army thus professed not to wish to engage in "some kind of interference in internal life." But it did insist upon its right of participation in the discussion and resolution of major social and political questions as entirely appropriate.[30]

The equating of domestic consolidation with the country's defense capacity has served as the platform from which the army has prodded and criticized the party. Similarly, the rationale for urging the active involvement of army personnel in extramilitary affairs is that "the penetration of technocratism and liberalism, the activity of nationalists and of bureaucratic and other anti-self-management forces, the underestimating of the League of Communists' role in society, the alienation of a considerable part of surplus value from the working class [are] directed against the defense efforts of our society as a whole....The LCY requires of Communists and other members of the YPA that they be active in political life...."[31] The military, in short, has the right and obligation to voice its views and assert its influence in areas that lie outside its formal responsibilities.

Such criticisms and the strong corporate support that the military gave to Tito's consolidationist course of the mid-1970s bespeak the generally conservative political attitudes harbored by the officer corps and the military leadership. Of rank-and-file attitudes, little is known except that an army of conscripts is probably a muted reflection of the trends and divisions of the society from which it is drawn. It has been openly acknowledged that the army was "infected" or "penetrated" by the same divisions that overtook society, but to nowhere near the same extent. Such pressures within the army are more easily contained. The party leadership passed through various stages of disarray, but the army leadership remained essentially unified. Had the application of force tested YPA cohesion in the 1971-1973 Croatian confrontation, division and disagreement might have surfaced within the military itself. Indeed, this prospect must have served as a powerful restraint on the use of the army in any domestic dispute. There are, however, no indications that the party leadership would not feel confident in using the army to maintain or restore domestic order, or in the army's ability to cope with any dissension that might be provoked as a result.

In Yugoslavia there is no evidence that major attitudinal differences exist that derive from relative positions in the military hierarchy. Yet because the officer cadre below general rank is so predominantly Serbian, its approach to any future crisis involving nationality disputes could prove to be a partisan one. Middle-level officers might take on an independent importance in other ways. They could provide a source of pressure on that leadership for outright intervention in a politically unstable situation. This possibility renders the party's indoctrination and control function within the YPA all the more crucial.

The military's foreign political attitudes could also be crucial in the post-Tito setting. There seems little reason to doubt the army's ability to act with decision and unity should Yugoslavia face an attack or heavy diplomatic pressure from the Soviet Union. The loyalties of the officer corps and the military leadership seemingly remain firmly behind the principle of Yugoslav federation and the determination to defend it. In all probability, however, the situation will be less dramatic and more complex.

NOTES

1. Rankovic, a Serb, captained a conspiracy in 1965-1966 designed to put him in a position to succeed Tito and possibly even to challenge his leadership. Centered in the State Security Service, especially in Serbia, its goal was to reverse the liberal trend in the country encouraged by the economic reforms and to restore greater centralism.
2. Following Rankovic's expulsion, the central LCY secretariat had been abolished; many of its powers subsequently were distributed to republican parties. A radical move was the elimination of the Central Committee's department of organizational and cadre affairs, which traditionally exercises the central party leadership's control over the nomenklatura system, the right to appoint all leaders in the party and state apparatus.
3. Interview in Vjesnik, October 1972.

4. Ross Johnson, <u>The Yugoslav Doctrine of Total National Defense</u> (Santa Monica: Rand Study, April 1971), pp. 4, 23-27.
5. See Mladen Pave, "What Sort of Law on Defense?," <u>Vsenarodna Obrana</u>, 1 (Zagreb, 1971).
6. Johnson, <u>The Yugoslav Doctrine</u>, pp. 4-5.
7. Defense Minister Ljubicic described the YPA as "a framework of the entire system of All Peoples' Defense under all conditions of aggression," <u>Borba</u>, November 6, 1974. Speech by CGS Col. Gen. Stane Potocar to officers of the Belgrade Garrison, Narodna Armija, January 31, 1974.
8. <u>Tanjug Domestic</u>, April 26, 1974, December 12, 1974.
9. See RFE Research Report, June 9, 1971; <u>Nin</u>, June 20, 1971.
10. Lt. Gen. Djoko Jovanic, commander of the Zagreb military district, told his officers that the YPA had "a clearly defined role; to fight foreign enemies. Therefore, there is no real danger that the Army could become an instrument in the solution of internal difficulties, <u>except in the case where constitutional order is threatened</u>" (emphasis added). <u>Vjesnik</u>, April 28, 1971.
11. Interview with <u>Frankfurter Rundschau</u>, December 17, 1972.
12. Primoz Zagarj, "The Politicization of the Army or a Deliberation about the Future," <u>Problemi</u>, 108 (January 1972).
13. SUBNOR was founded in 1947 and comprised over 800,000 Communist partisans. The party itself numbered 260,000 at the time and its leadership and that of the veterans' union were identical. Today SUBNOR numbers some 1,350,000 and is closely associated with over 400,000 members of the Federation of Reserve Officers and Noncommissioned Officers (1969 figures). RFE Research Report, April 10, 1973. (See also Stane Dolanc, address to Federal Committee of the Federation of Reserve Officers and Noncommissioned Officers of Yugoslavia, March 29, 1974. <u>Tanjug Domestic</u>, April 1, 1974.)
14. <u>Tanjug Domestic</u>, April 16, 1974.
15. In 1971 the average age of retired officers was forty-four years. A survey in the same year of the elite group of veterans, who joined the partisan effort in 1941, revealed that half had been retired from their functions before pension age, 27 percent had an income below the established minimum, and that despite this, they complained most of the lack of prestige, their social isolation, and inactivity. RFE Research Report, April 10, 1973; Radio Belgrade, February 19, 1973.
16. <u>Tanjug</u>, January 7, 1972, January 18, 1972; and Frane Barbieri, editorial, "Offers and Applause," <u>Nin</u>, February 6, 1972.
17. Speech at Prijedor, September 10, 1972. New LCY status has specifically included the "veterans' organizations" as the coequal of the trade unions and SAWPY

(Soviet Armed Workers Party of Yugoslavia) in the overall system of social self-management and governmental authority.
18. Tanjug, July 4, 1972.
19. By Stane Dolanc, secretary of the LCY Presidium's Executive Bureau, speaking at the January 1972 LCY Conference.
20. Belgrade Domestic Service, March 23, 1973.
21. Kommunist, November 12, 1973.
22. Tanjug Domestic, November 18, 1973; Narodna Armija, April 18, 1974, March 29, 1973.
23. Tanjug Domestic, November 18, 1973.
24. 1971 figures. RFE Research Report, April 12, 1973; and the interview with Vladimir Bakaric in Frankfurter Rundschau, December 17, 1971. Montenegrins, 2.5 percent of the population, are also overrepresented; they comprise 8 percent of the officer corps and 19 percent of the general officer corps.
25. Narodna Armija, according to Tanjug, April 24, 1974, commended Slovenian efforts as exemplary and called for more vigorous efforts in other republics, Mladina, December 11, 1973, Tanjug Domestic, November 19, 1973, and June 24, 1974.
26. Ljubicic has stressed that "we are rejuvenating our forces according to age--not according to participation or non-participation in the war." Tanjug Domestic, December 15, 1972.
27. "Both sides of the Enemies of Our Country," Front, March 16 and 23, 1973, Viesnik u Srijedu, April 5, 12, 19, 1972.
28. Borba, June 13, 1973.
29. Juza Vlahovic, "Colonels as Watchmen," Vjesnik u Srijedu, October 13, 1971. Presidency of the Soviet of Federal Republics of Yugoslavia (SFRY), Belgrade Domestic Service, May 15, 1974. See the speech by Mitja Ribicic, vice-president of presidency of SFRY, Belgrade Domestic Service, May 15, 1974.
30. Col. Vasilije Cerovic, military commentary, "The Strengthening of Defense," Politika, October 22, 1972; cf. also, editorial, "Preparations for the Tenth LCY Congress: The Tasks of the Army," Narodna Armija, February 8, 1973.
31. Lt. Col. Gen. Dzemal Sarac, secretary of the army party organization, in an interview with Kommunist, December 17, 1973.

7
The Polish Army

Andrzej Korbonski

This chapter has two major objectives: first, to fill some gaps in our knowledge of the early stages in the development of the armed forces in Communist Poland; and second, to test in a preliminary fashion the historical developmental model, postulated by the editor of this volume in order to provide an underpinning for a theory of civil-military relations in Communist societies.[1]

Until relatively recently, the Polish military and its role in politics has not been a favorite topic of research among Western scholars. There were two main reasons for that neglect: the infatuation with the totalitarian model according to which armed forces in Communist systems had no independent identity of their own and were totally penetrated by and subjugated to the ruling party; moreover, for reasons I will discuss below, there was considerable dearth of information about the Polish military itself and about its origin and development.

The situation began to improve in the course of the 1960s. On the one hand, there was a growing disenchantment among the students of Communist societies with the value of the totalitarian model as an explanatory and predictive device. The seminal work of Roman Kolkowicz, regardless of later criticism of his work, has shown conclusively the limited applicability of the totalitarian model in the case of party-military relations in the Soviet Union.[2] On the other hand, the process of destalinization in Poland has not only demonstrated the bankruptcy of the Stalinist model but also was accompanied by a veritable outpouring of studies and monographs dealing with the formative period in the history of what came to be known as the Polish People's Army.[3] Furthermore, the posture and behavior of the Polish army in October 1956 at the time of a direct confrontation with the units of the Soviet army advancing on Warsaw, and the attitude and behavior of the military during various domestic political crises in June and October 1956, December 1970, June 1976, and August-September 1980, suggested that contrary to some earlier assumptions, the Polish army has either maintained or achieved a political and professional identity of its own. Faced with a political emergency, it was able and willing to assert its independence vis-à-vis the ruling party.

All these factors combined to make the Polish military a much more interesting object of study. The last decade or so witnessed the appearance of a growing body of literature on the subject, associated mostly with the names of Jerzy Wiatr and Dale Herspring.[4] Pioneering as their work was, it was focused primarily on the recent and contemporary developments in the Polish armed forces, neglecting to a large extent the early developmental period that, for all practical purposes, remained a tabula rasa until today.

The great virtue of the above-mentioned historical developmental model is that in order to test its validity, we were forced to take a look at and reexamine the role of the military in the process of the Communist takeover of Poland. We shall see whether the model has any applicability to the Polish case; but even if it has not, or even if it provides only a partial explanation of the state of civil-military relations in today's Poland, its major accomplishment was to provide an incentive to fill some empty boxes, thus making a contribution to our knowledge not only of recent Polish history but also of civil-military relations in general.

The growth over time of the role of the military in Polish politics may be analyzed with the help of a framework that distinguishes four separate stages in the military's development: cooptation, subordination, accommodation, and participation.[5] In Poland, each of these changes in the military's role coincided with major phases in the process of the country's political development: nation- and state-building, participation, and subsystem autonomy. The analysis that follows will be focused on the stages of cooptation and subordination, the remaining two phases to be examined in lesser detail.[6]

THE POLISH ARMED FORCES ON THE EVE OF
THE COMMUNIST TAKEOVER

Following Poland's defeat by Germany and the occupation of the country's eastern provinces by the Soviet army in September 1939, the Polish armed forces, practically speaking, ceased to exist. Some 350,000 officers and men found themselves in the German prisoner-of-war camps, and 181,000 ended up in Soviet captivity.[7]

Already the first few weeks following the fall of Warsaw, which marked the beginning of the German occupation, witnessed the founding of the Polish underground movement with its civilian and military branches remaining loyal to the government-in-exile in London. The military resistance that eventually acquired the name of Home Army (<u>Armia Krajowa</u>, or AK), attracted considerable support, especially among the Polish youth. By the end of 1943, on the eve of the Soviet army's entry into prewar Polish territory, it numbered a total of about 380,000 men and women.[8]

Following the outbreak of the German-Soviet war in June 1941, diplomatic relations between the Polish government-in-exile in London and the Soviet government were established at the urging of Great Britain. One concrete result was the agreement by the Kremlin to create a Polish army on Soviet territory, composed of former prisoners of war and more recent deportees from eastern Poland.[9] It was initially assumed that the newly formed army would be ultimately deployed on Soviet soil fighting the Germans alongside the units of the Red Army. The original plan went astray, and instead of remaining in the USSR, a large part of what came to be known as the Anders Army was evacuated to Iran and ultimately deployed in Italy where it remained fighting until VE Day.

At this stage a word should be said about an actor that so far has been absent from the scene. The missing actor was the Polish Communist party, which was forcibly dissolved on Stalin's orders on the eve of the war in circumstances that remain largely obscure to this day.[10] With all the top leaders executed, the party practically disintegrated. In the wake of Poland's defeat in September 1939 some members of the rank and file remained in the German-occupation zone while others escaped eastward reaching ultimately the safety of Soviet territory. With few exceptions, as members of the dissolved party the Polish Communists were viewed with considerable suspicion by Soviet authorities, who treated them almost as harshly as they did the masses of Polish citizens deported as slave laborers from eastern Poland in 1940-1941.

The situation of the Polish Communists improved drastically in the aftermath of the German invasion of the Soviet Union in June 1941. Even though the Kremlin agreed to recognize the government-in-exile in London as the sole legitimate government of Poland, it also decided at roughly the same time to resurrect the defunct Polish Communist party. Subsequently, a small group of specially chosen organizers were parachuted into Poland in late December 1941. In January 1942, the Kremlin announced the formation of the Polish Workers' party (<u>Polska Partia Robotnicza</u>, or PPR).[11] In due course, the new party created a military organization of its own that eventually came to be known as the People's Army (<u>Armia Ludowa</u>, or AL).

In the meantime, relations between Moscow and the government-in-exile in London continued to deteriorate and were ultimately broken off in the wake of the German announcement of the discovery of the graves of thousands of Polish officers at Katyn in April 1943. There was unmistakable evidence that the mass killing of the officers, captured by the Red Army in Poland in September 1939, was conducted by the NKVD (Soviet secret police), most likely in the summer of 1940.[12] The break-off in diplomatic relations between the Kremlin and the London exiles apparently removed the last remaining obstacles to the creation of a new Polish army on Soviet territory. This was announced in July 1943.

The history of the new army, known as the Berling Army after its first commander, Gen. Zygmunt Berling, is not well known in the West, for a number of reasons.[13] Apart from the fact that for many years its origin and early formative period have been kept under a rather surprising veil of official secrecy, conventional wisdom in the West perceived the Berling Army as a Moscow puppet, totally controlled by the Soviet political and military authorities with the help of trusted Polish Communists who occupied key positions, especially in the political apparatus. In other words, the Berling Army was viewed as having no identity of its own. Both its contribution to the anti-German war effort and its rather heavy battle losses have been invariably ignored or slighted by Polish exile scholars, who instead have sung paeans about the accomplishments of the Anders Army in the West (in Italy) and of the non-Communist and anti-German resistance inside Poland.

Space limitations preclude a fuller treatment of the growth and accomplishments of the Berling Army, but in light of the relative lack of knowledge about it among students of the East European military a few comments are in order.[14] The one single fact that has been constantly used by the critics of the Berling Army to underplay its importance was the overwhelming presence of Red Army officers in nearly all the commanding positions. Undoubtedly, this was true for one very good reason: namely, the dearth of qualified Polish officers in the Soviet Union at that time. Of those who found themselves on Soviet soil in September 1939, most were murdered at Katyn and the rest were evacuated to the Middle East, leaving few if any senior and middle-ranking officers available for duty. Consequently, more than 10,000 Red Army officers, most of them with only a rudimentary knowledge of the Polish language, were transferred to the Berling Army between its formation in July 1943 and the end of 1944.[15]

There is little doubt that both the Soviet leadership, which allowed the creation of the army for its own political purposes, as well as the Polish Communists in the USSR, who provided the political and ideological guidance, were painfully aware of the sharp dichotomy between the Soviet officer corps and the Polish noncommissioned officers and enlisted men. They tried to compensate for it by emphasizing the traditional symbolic Polish military

trappings--uniforms, banners, distinctions, and even
martial music. Nonetheless, it was not until the establishment of the precursor of the future Communist government, the so-called Polish Committee of National Liberation in the city of Lublin in July 1944, that several
thousand Polish officers were recruited into the Berling
Army, reducing somewhat the predominant position of the
Red Army officers who, however, continued to hold most of
the leading commands, at least till the end of hostilities.[16] On the other hand, the NCOs and enlisted men were
almost entirely Polish.

As suggested earlier, the posts of political commissars were invariably held either by the prewar Polish
Communists or by fellow travelers of various kinds.[17] In
that capacity they were faced with at least two major
problems. The first one concerned the overall ideological
thrust to be imparted to the troops under their command.
On the one hand, their major task was to emphasize the
inherently Polish character of the new army, over and above
the symbolic trappings referred to earlier, and on the
other, to maintain a certain ideological profile. As was
to be expected, the former line stressed above all patriotism and the historic struggle against the Germans, showing the Berling Army as the continuator of Polish military
traditions.

The ideological line was, if anything, more complicated. It was relatively easy to criticize and condemn the
interwar Polish state of "landlords and capitalists," but
it was much more difficult to explain the Communist party's
agreement to surrender to the USSR the eastern provinces
that accounted for about 40 percent of the territory of
prewar Poland. To offset its negative impact, much
emphasis was put on Poland receiving territorial compensation in the west, at the expense of Germany.

One of the most fascinating internal debates within
the hard core of the military-political apparat in the
Berling Army concerned the blueprint for the sociopolitical
character of the new Communist Poland.[18] It appears that
one school of thought favored the immediate creation of a
Soviet-type Polish republic with all the standard institutional arrangements, without even bothering with the
preliminaries of a popular or united front, coalition
government, and parliamentary elections.[19] By hindsight
it was clear that these ideas had been proclaimed without
Soviet imprimatur: By 1943, even before the official
dissolution of the Comintern, the official Soviet policy,
binding on all Communist parties engaged in anti-German
resistance, was to favor the formation of the broadest
possible united front including both Communists and non-Communists. In light of this policy, another group
within the apparat criticized the sectarian approach of
their opponents, calling for the creation of a truly
"democratic" Poland with all the standard institutional

trappings. Eventually the latter concept prevailed, but the sharp differences of opinion between the two factions were not forgotten. They were resurrected some twenty-five years later in the heat of the 1968 anti-Semitic campaign: As it happened, the chief protagonists on both sides of the 1943 dispute were of Jewish origin.

The other problem facing the Communist leadership in the Berling Army was its relationship with their ideological brethren in Poland. Although the newly recreated Communist party, the PPR, was initially organized by individuals selected by the Comintern and, therefore, presumably acceptable and loyal to Moscow, by the end of 1943 most of them had been either killed or imprisoned by the Germans. The new PPR leadership consisted of persons who were largely unknown to the Soviet leaders. This was even more true for the Communist military resistance composed, by and large, of volunteers whose links to Moscow and to the Polish Communists in the USSR were at best tenuous. Moreover, radio communication between the Communist underground and the Comintern headquarters was interrupted for several months, which meant that there was no contact between the two groups. Consequently, neither side knew what the other one was doing.[20]

Communication between the two groups was finally reestablished in May 1944 when a delegation from the Communist underground crossed the front line and met with their counterpart in the Berling Army. As a result of the meeting, and presumably on the advice of Stalin who personally received the delegation, the Berling Army formally subordinated itself to PPR in Poland and accepted its program. In this way a political conflict between the two Communist factions--the "Moscovites" and the "natives"--was avoided, at least for the time being, only to be resumed some four years later.

THE COMMUNIST TAKEOVER--OR, WAS THERE A CIVIL WAR IN POLAND?

After more than thirty-five years, the history of the Communist seizure of power in Poland still needs to be told. Available accounts of the takeover published either in Poland or in the West suffer from a variety of biases and are not entirely reliable.[21] Few of them discuss the participation of the Polish military in the seizure of power by the Communists, and it is rather difficult, therefore, to pinpoint the exact role of the Polish armed forces in aiding in the actual seizure of the commanding heights in the country.

The first step in the Communist takeover was the announcement on July 22, 1944, of the formation of the Polish Committee of National Liberation in the city of Lublin, which was the first major Polish city liberated by the Red Army. Insofar as the military affairs were concerned, several key measures were undertaken by the committee. To begin with, a merger was ordered between the Berling Army and the Armia Ludowa, creating a single armed force to be called the Polish Armed Forces (Wojsko Polskie). By that time General Berling, the first commander of the army created in the USSR, was gradually falling into disgrace and was eventually purged in October 1944. The new commander in chief was Gen. Michal Rola-Zymierski, who was the last commanding officer of Armia Ludowa prior to the merger.[22]

Second, the committee ordered the call-up of men born between 1921 and 1924 to serve in the rapidly expanding army.[23] Special emphasis was laid on the recruitment of officers, not only to man the newly formed divisions and regiments but also to increase the percentage of Polish officers in the officer corps, which was still heavily dominated by former Red Army officers.

Third, the second half of 1944 witnessed the rapid buildup of police and internal security forces, recruited mostly from lumpenproletariat and other marginal elements, for the purpose of eliminating anti-Communist resistance, thus freeing regular military units for combat duty. By the end of the year, the civil and military resistance units loyal to the London government-in-exile were either destroyed or forced again into hiding.

The situation was much more complex in the German-occupied part of Poland centered around the capital city of Warsaw, where the non-Communist underground, spearheaded by its military wing, the Armia Krajowa, ruled supreme with the Communist resistance barely surviving. In a desperate attempt to assert the authority of the London government vis-à-vis the Lublin committee, the Armia Krajowa staged an uprising in Warsaw on August 1, 1944, which eventually collapsed after sixty-three days of fighting. The defeat of the uprising meant for all practical purposes the end of organized non-Communist resistance, even though a fairly large number of small units continued guerrilla warfare against the German occupation forces until the January 1945 Soviet offensive that in a matter of days liberated the remainder of the Polish territory. With the end of the war in sight, the London government formally dissolved Armia Krajowa in January 1945, which marked the official end of organized non-Communist military resistance in the country.

Following the end of hostilities in May 1945, the Polish Communists had to face the task of consolidating their authority at home by eliminating the existing opposition. There was little doubt that the new army was to play a role in that process. Nevertheless, before deploying the armed forces to combat internal opposition, the Communist leadership had to solve a number of problems affecting the military. One unique feature of the new Polish army that to a large extent distinguished it from the other Communist-led armies in Eastern Europe was its highly complex composition. In the early postwar period, which coincided with the beginning of the second and last stage in the takeover, one could distinguish, especially in the officer corps, the following major groupings that eventually had to be forged into a more or less integrated military force:

- the Soviet-led Polish army formed in the USSR (the Berling Army);
- the Communist armed underground, the People's Army (Armia Ludowa);
- the non-Communist armed underground, the Home Army (Armia Krajowa);
- the members of the prewar Polish army released from the German prisoner-of-war camps;
- the officers and men of the Polish army in the West (the Anders Army) who decided to return to Poland after the war.

The existence of these five highly disparate component parts succeeded in sowing seeds of discord and conflict that influenced the civil-military relations in Poland for years to come. In a sense history was repeating itself. The situation in Poland at the end of World War I had also witnessed the presence of several "armies" most of which had little if anything in common with each other and soon found themselves struggling for power in the newly independent country.

Each of the post-World War II groups deserves a separate discussion but because of space limitations only some general comments are in order. Insofar as the Communist takeover was concerned, the Soviet-led Polish army formed in the USSR played the most important role. Apart from its sheer size, its leadership and especially its political officer cadre included most of the members of the top Communist elite that ultimately proved not only largely responsible for the takeover but also for the ensuing sovietization of Polish society.[24] Nearly all of them occupied key positions at various levels of the political-military apparatus. In that capacity, they were entrusted with fostering if not the revolutionary zeal then at least the political neutrality of the officer corps as well as of the noncommissioned officers and enlisted men. There is no doubt that they must have managed to reach the latter objective, as there is little evidence of specific cases of mass desertion or disobedience.

A good case may be made to show that the military did not get actively involved in the takeover until the cessation of hostilities in May 1945. Until then the army was engaged in heavy fighting against the retreating Germans. By that time it had also reached an impressive strength of close to 400,000 men that, together with the Polish units in the West, made the Polish Armed Forces the fourth strongest force in the Allied camp after the United States, the Soviet, and the British forces.

Between July 1944 and VE Day in May 1945, the takeover was conducted essentially by the newly formed security organs--the militia (police), the secret police, and the special internal security detachments--often supported by the armed Communist underground that would surface to coincide with the arrival of the Red Army.[25] This meant that by the time the armed forces became available for domestic peacetime duties, the Polish Communists had largely succeeded in establishing themselves in power, at least in the urban areas, and the need for the military's active involvement in the process of takeover became much less intense.[26]

Still, there remained large areas of the country where the Communist writ did not reach very far. These regions tended to be controlled and occasionally even terrorized by clandestine armed groups of all hues-- various remnants of the by-then formally dissolved Armia Krajowa, relics of the strongly anti-Communist nationalist underground (NSZ), detachments of the Ukrainian Insurgent Army (UPA), and some conventional gangs--all of which conducted fierce and often desperate resistance against the Communists. The true size and real strength of the anti-Communist resistance in the early postwar period cannot readily be ascertained. A good case may be made that both the Polish Communist and anti-Communist historians at varying times tended either to underplay or exaggerate the strength of the resistance for their own purposes. Initially, at least, the official line tended to downgrade the armed resistance in order to show that the Communist takeover was not resisted by the overwhelming majority of the Polish population, while at the same time the opposition claimed that the reverse was true. In the course of the 1960s the official attitude changed in the direction of possibly exaggerating the strength of the resistance in order to glorify the role of the military and of the security organs in the period 1944-1948, thus creating a necessary legend around both of them as conquerors of foreign and domestic enemies.

Some idea of the real strength of the armed opposition to the Communist takeover may be gathered from data published in official Polish sources.[27] As a result of two amnesties proclaimed by the government in August 1945 and February 1947, some 97,000 former members of Armia Krajowa and other resistance groups decided to lay down their weapons and cease armed resistance.[28] Nonetheless, the hard-core anti-Communist partisan units continued fighting at least until early 1948. Between 1944 and 1948, their strength was estimated at about 100,000.[29] Total losses suffered by the resistance in the period 1945-1948 was 7,400; the comparable figures for both military and civilian casualties suffered by the regime in the same period were calculated at 13,400.[30] Some of the fiercest fighting took place in the southeastern part of the country against the Ukrainian insurgents who operated also on Soviet and Czechoslovak territory. In the absence of an objective yardstick, it is difficult to say whether the relatively heavy losses were high enough to justify calling the struggle a civil war. Nevertheless, with the possible exception of wartime Yugoslavia, no East European country experienced this kind of internecine warfare. There is little doubt that this fact had some impact on the future development of People's Poland.[31]

As the military was not needed in the final stages of the takeover, its leaders turned to the very important task of creating a unified armed force out of the five component parts listed earlier. By late 1947, a date that marks the end of the process of Communist takeover, the difficult task of forging the new military establishment had been essentially completed.[32] What was not clear at that time, however, was the role to be played by that establishment in People's Poland. Part of the reason was the considerable uncertainty surrounding the future of the country itself: Even top party leaders appeared to believe sincerely that Poland would not necessarily have to imitate the Soviet experience and that it could follow its own road to socialism.[33] If this were to be true then the part played by the military in Communist Poland might conceivably represent a synthesis of the old and the new, in line with other institutional arrangements so characteristic of the initial version of the concept of a people's democracy.

Insofar as the military's relations with the political leadership were concerned, it may be argued that they were characterized by partial cooptation rather than by accommodation or participation. It may be speculated that the ruling oligarchy viewed the military as a key component of the new political and socioeconomic order that, in time, might be given considerable professional autonomy in return for its commitment to support and defend the new system. At that time the Polish Communist leadership seemed not to be overly concerned with the specter of Bonapartism that historically tended to influence if not dominate the Communist attitude vis-à-vis the military in the Soviet Union.

In other words, it may be hypothesized that the new rulers of Poland did not view the military as a serious potential threat to their monopoly of power. One of the more interesting consequences of World War II in Poland was a subtle change in the popular attitude toward the military. Before the war both the elite and the mass political culture had emphasized the military ethos and historical support for the military leaders who had always guided the fate of the Polish nation. The war brought heavy human and material losses to Poland, and this suffering apparently succeeded in raising serious doubts in people's minds about the historic role of the military as national leaders responsible for the country's destiny. The traditional feeling of respect for, even adulation of, the military, often bordering on blind obedience and subservience, had in a relatively short time given way if not to outright hostility then to nearly total indifference. It seemed that in the minds of a large majority of the Polish people the military ceased to be a major and prestigious actor in the domestic political arena.

The decline in the military's prestige could also most likely be traced to at least three additional considerations: the popular perception of the Polish military as being essentially impotent; as representing an alien order about to be imposed on the country; and as being composed, especially at the officer level, of the "lower" social classes--peasants and workers--viewed as the forerunners of the new social order that the majority of the Polish people probably found objectionable.

THE FALL AND RISE OF THE POLISH MILITARY

The period 1948-1953 coincided with the process of sovietization and subjugation of the Polish military that followed roughly the conventional Stalinist pattern also imposed on the other satellite countries. The process of stalinization of the armed forces had several major consequences: subordination to the Soviet Union as the hegemonial power in the bloc; thorough penetration of the military by the Communist party and secret police; and the sharp decline in the political role of the military. Although the general pattern of the sovietization of the armed forces in Poland showed essentially the same characteristic features as elsewhere in Eastern Europe, there were some interesting departures from the model.

Undoubtedly, the most important was the appointment of the Soviet Marshal Konstantine Rokossovsky as the minister of defense and commander in chief of the Polish Armed Forces, replacing Marshal Rola-Zymierski, who was sent into oblivion. The nomination, announced in November 1949, made Poland a very uncommon example of total domination by the Soviet Union. Even today it is difficult to explain the rationale behind this Soviet move that was not paralleled elsewhere in Eastern Europe. There was no evidence that either the Polish party or the military appeared disloyal toward Moscow, or that they harbored stronger Titoist sympathies than their counterparts in the other satellites. To be sure, the party's Secretary General Gomulka was purged together with a handful of the senior party leaders, but the purge was probably less extensive in Poland than in the rest of the region. As will be seen, the same was true for the purges in the military. Another possible explanation might have been

Stalin's desire to humiliate the country as a proof of its total subjugation to Soviet control. Although not entirely credible, the idea cannot be totally dismissed as irrational; after all, only a decade earlier Stalin forcibly dissolved the Communist party of Poland for reasons that remain as obscure today as they were in 1938.

Rokossovsky's appointment was followed by mass purges in the military. The purges in the army were directed primarily against the officer corps. Among the victims of the purge were not only many of the former officers of the Anders Army, the <u>Armia Krajowa</u> officers, former German prisoners of war and officers of the Communist military resistance, but also members of the Berling Army and <u>Armia Ludowa</u>. Most of them were arrested, tried, and given long prison terms. Only relatively few were executed, especially when compared with similar executions in Czechoslovakia and Hungary.[34]

The purges of the military marked the simultaneous ascendance of the secret police and internal security forces. As elsewhere in the bloc, the military in Poland after the purges became further penetrated by the secret police. Moreover, the creation of a separate, fully equipped internal security command represented additional weakening of the military's monopoly of armed power and provided further proof of the Stalinist party's lack of confidence in the army's reliability as loyal supporter of the regime.

Thus the military together with the other elements of the Polish polity and society were brought under the control of the Stalinist faction in the party in the true totalitarian fashion. Among the consequences of this particular process was the further alienation of the armed forces from the rest of Polish society, which viewed the military establishment headed by Rokossovsky and other Soviet generals as one of the major instruments of Moscow's control over its satrapy. The estrangement continued the process of a significant change in Poland's traditional political cultural development that began in the aftermath of World War II.

The partial recovery of the military's standing and prestige that reached its peak in October 1956 was an integral part of the process of destalinization that in Poland appeared to have started later than in the rest of the Soviet bloc. However, once under way the disintegration of the Stalinist system did go deeper and farther than elsewhere in the region except for Hungary. The process of destalinization in Poland has been fairly well described and analyzed in the literature and there is no need to repeat the major arguments.[35] Insofar as the role of the military was concerned, the salient stages in the process included the following:

1. The downgrading of the secret-police apparatus

that in the Polish context resulted not only from Beria's demise but also from the highly publicized defection and public revelations of a high-ranking secret-police official;[36]

2. The gradual release of political prisoners, including a number of generals and other high-ranking officers, most of whom were subsequently rehabilitated and readmitted into the army. Among them the most prominent was Gen. Marian Spychalski, a veteran of the Communist underground who occupied a number of important military posts in the early postwar period;[37]

3. Escalating criticism of Stalinist practices in all walks of public life, especially after the 20th Party Congress of the Soviet Communist party. This included condemnation of the official policy toward the former members of Armia Krajowa, the non-Communist military resistance organization that for many years was accused of outright collaboration with the Germans.

The watershed event was clearly the workers demonstration in the city of Poznan in June 1956 that necessitated the use of troops. There was conflicting evidence as to whether the soldiers had actually fired at the demonstrators; even if they had, it became fairly obvious to the regime that the military could not be fully trusted in the event of a similar future demonstration.[38] There is little doubt that this awareness contributed to the escalation of the split within the party hierarchy and to the increasing demands for a drastic change in the top leadership.

The events of October 1956 are well known and will not be discussed here.[39] The crucial factors were, of course, the overwhelming support of the military for Gomulka and the new leadership and the determination of the Polish military to resist Soviet intervention aimed at stopping or slowing down the process of liberalization. The immediate result of the changeover was the departure of Marshal Rokossovsky and his replacement in the Ministry of Defense by the previously mentioned General Spychalski, a close confidant of Gomulka with whom he was accused of "rightist-nationalist deviation" in 1949.

The direct involvement of the military in the process of destalinization and liberalization, and especially the army's willingness to fight if necessary in order to defend the new regime, appeared to stop, at least for a while, the growing alienation of the society from the military. The degree of alienation and indifference vis-à-vis the army was too high, however, to reverse the trend, but for a few months in late 1956 and early 1957 one could witness almost a return to the traditional "organic unity" between the Polish people and their army. Once the threat of Soviet intervention began to wane, however, the old distrust of the military reappeared, although clearly not as sharply as in the preceding period. Hence it may be speculated that the popular attitude of indifference toward or even contempt for the military had become one of the more interesting permanent features of the Polish political culture, although some interesting changes in that respect could be detected in the 1970s.[40]

Obviously, one of the more important reasons for the rapprochement between the military on the one hand and both the regime and the rest of society on the other was the reemergence of powerful nationalist sentiments within both the military and society at large. In the military this was primarily reflected in the early return to the USSR of those Soviet officers who had occupied leading positions in the Polish army, often for more than a decade.[41] Their places were filled by their Polish counterparts chosen by the new regime that in this way laid the foundations for a party-military coalition that survived more or less intact for the next twenty-five years or so.

THE MILITARY SINCE 1956: PARTNER OR COMPETITOR?

The developments within the Polish military since 1956 have been recently analyzed in considerable detail. A brief summary of the main conclusions of this study[42] follows.

As suggested earlier, the ouster of Marshal Rokossovsky and the Soviet advisers was followed by the creation of what initially appeared to be a strong alliance between the party and the military. In fact, the relationship was anything but close and smooth, as indicated by the events of 1967-1968, 1970, 1976, and 1980, which demonstrated that continuing attempts at closing the gap between the military and the ruling party have been largely unsuccessful.

In its early stage, however, the alliance seemed close. The minister of defense, General Spychalski, was made a member of the Central Committee and together with a few other veterans of the wartime Communist underground formed the core of the Gomulka regime. Other key positions in the military were also occupied by members of the wartime Communist resistance and Polish army in the Soviet Union who filled the slots left vacant by the departing Soviet advisers.[43] The closer relationship between the party and the military was also reflected in the growth of party membership within the officer corps, which increased from 40 percent in 1949 to about 67 percent in 1958.[44] In the early postwar years class origin had served as the main criterion for officer recruitment. Beginning in the mid-1950s, however, the level of educational achievement became the main condition for entry into the Polish army officer corps.[45]

The process of apparent accommodation between the party and the military did not get very far, and the next decade witnessed a gradual erosion of the party-military alliance, culminating in the major purge of the officer corps in 1967-1968 that was closely linked with the anti-Semitic campaign of the same period. The inability to solve the country's basic economic problems resulted in a rapid decline of popular support for Gomulka, who by 1967 found himself under severe attack from various directions within and outside the party. Among the former, the most significant was the so-called partisan faction that soon made a fairly obvious bid for power.

The opportunity for the partisans to expand their influence, especially in the Polish military establishment, arose in 1967 in connection with the Six-Day War in the Middle East. The overwhelming Israeli victory was openly applauded by a number of high-ranking officers who were soon given discharges as the first victims in the ensuing vicious struggle for power between Gomulka and the partisans.[46] Gomulka was saved at the last minute by Brezhnev, who was facing the Czechoslovak crisis of 1968 and who was clearly reluctant to face another emergency in Poland. The Polish leader managed to survive for more than two years before he was forced out and replaced by Gierek in the wake of the Baltic Coast riots in December 1970.

The part played by the military in the factional struggle is not easily reconstructed. It may be assumed that although the nominal head of the Polish Armed Forces, Marshal Spychalski, was a loyal supporter of Gomulka, some segments of the military sympathized with the partisans with whom they shared traditions of nationalism and anti-Semitism. Hence, there is no evidence of any mass resentment of, or resistance to, the purging of officers of Jewish background in 1967 and after, which illustrated rather well the weakness of professional pride and military esprit de corps when faced with an attack from the outside.[47] On the contrary, one might speculate that the purge was widely applauded as creating room at the top for partisan followers.

Nevertheless, the partisans' hopes of capturing the high command of the armed forces were dashed in April 1968 by the appointment of General Jaruzelski as minister of defense, replacing Spychalski who was elevated to the largely ceremonial chairmanship of the State Council, the collective presidency of the country. In the context of civil-military relations in Poland, Jaruzelski's appointment was an important turning point in that it symbolized the emergence in its own right of the professional officer corps. Thus, it may be argued that it was only in 1968 that accommodation became a truly relevant and accurate description of the political-military relationship in Poland.

In light of this, it is really not surprising that the Polish military did not support Gomulka in his hour of need in December 1970. On the contrary, there is some circumstantial evidence suggesting that the military high command favored Gomulka's ouster and Gierek's succession; and the fact that the minister of defense, Jaruzelski, not only retained his post in the cabinet but also his seat in the new Politburo speaks for itself. It was clearly the reward for the military's refusal to prevent the changeover.[48]

It may be taken for granted that, together with the rest of Polish society, the military could not help being impressed with the initial record and performance of the Gierek team. The relations between the new regime and the military seemed relatively close, at least on the surface, and Gierek's dismissal of his erstwhile supporter and latter competitor, Moczar, identified as the leader of the partisan faction, was apparently not opposed by the military.[49]

There has been no evidence of any deterioration in the party-military relationship in the mid-1970s when the Polish economy began to slow down following a spectacular growth period earlier in the decade and when, in late 1975, the announcement of constitutional revisions resulted in the emergence of a first serious dissident movement. The concessions granted the opposition by the Gierek regime must have had the approval of the military. The military, one may guess, was probably less than happy with the original revisions emphasizing the leading role of the Soviet Union in the socialist camp and stressing the special exalted position of the Communist party at home.

The first serious confrontation between the party and the military took place in the course of 1976. By that time it was common knowledge that the Polish economy had been in serious difficulties that, among other things, were reflected in growing shortages of certain foodstuffs and consumer goods that, in turn, resulted in increasing popular dissatisfaction. One of the suggested remedies was a comprehensive reform of retail prices that was intended to raise the general price level of goods to bring demand closer to supply and make the whole price structure at the retail level more rational.

The announcement in June 1976 of a sharp and largely uncompensated increase in retail prices of meat and other foodstuffs resulted in violent strikes in several key industrial cities, forcing the regime in less than twenty-four hours to cancel the price reform. Little is known of what transpired in those twenty-four hours, but it may be assumed that the top party leadership found itself under strong pressure to surrender to the workers' demands and acknowledge defeat. It appears that at the crucial meeting of the Politburo called in the wake of the strikes, the minister of defense moved to call off the rise declaring that "the Polish soldiers would not shoot at the Polish workers."[50] Thus in June 1976, the Polish military reemerged as a critical political actor whose position could be decisive in resolving the crisis. However, the real test of strength between the party and the military took place four years later, in August and September 1980, in the course of mass strikes by Polish industrial workers demanding the establishment of free and independent trade unions.

Many details of the party-military confrontation in the critical days of August 1980 are still not well known. There is no doubt, however, that Gierek's reluctant agreement to the workers' demands was largely if not solely the result of the military's refusal to use force to bring the workers to heel. There is considerable evidence suggesting that both Defense Minister Jaruzelski and the secretary of the Central Committee, Kania, who was in charge of military and security affairs, from the very beginning have steadfastly favored a peaceful, "political" solution of the crisis. At the plenary session of the party's Central Committee on August 31, called to ratify the Gdansk agreement that opened the way to the establishment of free labor unions in Poland, the commander in chief of the navy made an impassioned speech pleading for the approval of the agreement and suggesting that the Polish navy would only most reluctantly obey the orders of the party leadership to seize the Gdansk shipyard. It may be taken for granted that Gierek's ouster in early September and his replacement by Kania received a warm blessing from the military.

Thus, in the summer and fall of 1980 the Polish military once again reasserted its position as the key actor in the domestic political arena whose veto or approval has ultimately proved decisive in time of emergency. At least three times in ten years the military forced the party leadership to grant significant concessions to the population, and three times the armed forces and the industrial working class found themselves on the same side of the barricade in the conflict with the ruling oligarchy--thus duplicating the situation of October 1956 when the Warsaw workers and soldiers were ready to resist Soviet forces advancing toward the Polish capital.

CONCLUSION

A good case may be made for the position that party-military relations in Poland since the end of World War II have by and large conformed to the pattern suggested at the outset. Hence, the period of Communist takeover was reflected in the process of cooptation of the military into political decision-making structures. This was followed by the subordination of the armed forces to both the Soviet Union and to the Stalinist party faction at home. The period after 1956 witnessed mutual accommodation between the military and civilian leaderships. Finally, the last decade or so mirrored the growing participation of the military in the Polish political system.

In light of the above, the first question to be raised is whether the Polish military has behaved in the past twenty-five years as a pressure group, voicing and protecting its own particular interests. The answer to this is inconclusive. It may be hypothesized that in the aftermath of the October 1956 crisis the military acquired its own professional identity, especially vis-à-vis the other important components--the party, the police, and the internal security force. However, as there is no evidence that any of these tried in the past two decades or so to reduce the authority of the military, there really has not been any need for the armed forces to act as a typical interest group competing with others for power, influence, and human and material resources.

Although one may hesitate to call the Polish military a typical pressure group, one would most certainly view it as a "veto group" without whose approval no major political decision was likely to be made in the country. This does not mean that the military is or has been consulted at every step in the process of decision making: It simply suggests that faced with a deadlock situation, which has become endemic in Polish domestic politics, the military tends to be called upon to pass judgment in its role as the supreme arbiter, a situation acceptable to the various contending factions within the party and the government.

Could the Polish military be viewed as an agent of modernization and political change? Here, it may be argued that this particular role has not been very significant, especially when contrasted with the interwar period when the Polish Armed Forces performed a series of functions as an important agent of state- and nation-building, of socialization, and of political participation. After World War II this role has been diminished, although not entirely eliminated. The military not only played a role in the actual Communist power seizure but was also instrumental in the campaign to reintegrate the newly acquired former German territories with the rest of the country, a process that might be viewed as falling under the rubric of nation- and state-building. After the hiatus caused by the process of subordination to the ruling party, one could again view the Polish People's Army as becoming involved in the process of modernization, but even here that role tended to be passive rather than active. In other words, there is no evidence of the military initiating a process of change, just as there is no indication of its opposing programs of political and economic modernization, especially those inaugurated in the decade of the 1970s.

Finally, does the Polish case validate or falsify the historical developmental model suggested in the introductory chapter of this volume? The model in question claims that the reason, in such countries as Poland, for the "minimal political influence exerted by the army... has been deeply rooted in the path to power and external Soviet role." Unlike Yugoslavia, where "the party created its first legitimate and effective institution--the army"--which also generated "a core of experienced Communist government bureaucrats who would help run the government after victory was obtained," the situation in Poland and the other East European countries was quite different. There, according to the proposed model, "power was handed to the local Communists in the wake of the Red Army occupation of Eastern Europe in the closing phases of World War II." Because the various armies that fought alongside the Soviet forces were numerically insignificant, "the creation of a legitimate and effective army in <u>any East European country</u> [my emphasis]" would have been a lengthy and difficult process. The conclusion that emerges is that "under these conditions the armies of Eastern Europe have tended to remain peripheral and limited actors in policymaking."[51]

It may be argued that as is the case with many other models, paradigms, and typologies, Poland does not fit neatly in this particular scheme. Thus, although it is true that the presence of the incoming Red Army was instrumental in helping the Polish Communists in seizing power in the aftermath of the war, this is not tantamount to having the power simply handed over to them by the Soviets. As discussed in the early part of this essay, it took the Communists more than three years to consolidate their power in the country, and the process itself proved to be quite costly in human and material terms. Moreover, the Polish army at that time was not weak--on the contrary, it was a rather impressive and experienced fighting force. Finally, the army also provided a large number of future political leaders who eventually came to occupy leading positions in the Communist regime.

There is no doubt that the process of creating a popularly accepted army took a long time, but this was primarily due to the relatively oppressive period of sovietization that affected the image of the Polish military much more strongly than its counterparts in the other East European countries, except for Yugoslavia. However, it may be shown that in the roughly thirty years since the imposition of the Stalinist model, the character and role of the Polish army has been transformed rather drastically, and that as a result the military today is an active and respected participant in the political management of the country.

Thus, on balance, it appears that the historical developmental model is not fully applicable to Poland. Poland seems to fit best somewhere halfway between the Chinese-Yugoslav and East European subspecies. This does not mean, however, that the model has only limited applicability and utility. On the contrary, as suggested at the beginning of this chapter, its great merit lies in forcing us to reexamine the largely neglected role of the military in the initial period of Communist rule in Eastern Europe and this alone makes it an important contribution to knowledge.

NOTES

Research for this paper was aided by a grant from the UCLA Center for International and Strategic Affairs, the support of which is gratefully acknowledged.

1. See Jonathan R. Adelman, "Toward a Typology of Communist Civil-Military Relations," Chapter 1 in this volume.
2. Roman Kolkowicz, <u>The Soviet Military and the Communist Party</u> (Princeton, N.J.: Princeton University Press, 1967).
3. For example, J. Margules, ed., <u>Z zagadnien rozwoju Ludowego Wojska Polskiego</u> (Warsaw: Wydawnictwo MON, 1964); S. Komornicki, ed., <u>Regularne jednostki Ludowego Wojska Polskiego</u> (Warsaw: Wydawnictwo MON, 1965); W. Jurgielewicz et al., eds., <u>Ludowe Wojsko Polskie 1943-1973</u> (Warsaw: Wydawnictwo MON, 1973); K. Frontczak, ed., <u>Sily zbrojne Polski Ludowej</u> (Warsaw: Wydawnictwo MON, 1974); M. Plikus, ed., <u>Mala Kronika Ludowego Wojska Polskiego 1943-1973</u> (Warsaw: Wydawnictwo MON, 1975); and M. Anusiewicz and I. Ruszkiewicz, <u>Tarcza socjalistycznej ojczyzny</u> (Warsaw: Wydawnictwo MON, 1979).
4. Jerzy J. Wiatr, "Social Prestige of the Military," in Jacques van Doorn, ed., <u>Military Profession and Military Regimes</u> (The Hague and Paris: Mouton, 1969), pp. 82-93; "The Public Image of the Polish Military: Past and Present," in Catherine M. Kelleher, ed., <u>Political-Military Systems</u> (Beverly Hills, Calif.: Sage Publications, 1974), pp. 199-205; Dale R. Herspring, "Technology and the Changing Political Officer in the Armed Forces: The Polish and East German Cases," <u>Studies in Comparative Communism</u> 10, no. 4 (Winter 1977): 370-393; and "Poland and East Germany: The External Factor," in ibid 11, no. 3 (Autumn 1978): 225-236.
5. This typology is a modification of that developed by Roman Kolkowicz in his "Civil-Military Relations in Communist Systems: The Case of the Soviet Union" (Paper presented at the Conference of the Inter-University Seminar on Armed Forces and Society, SUNY Buffalo, October 1974).
6. For an analysis of the latter two stages--accommodation and participation--see Andrzej Korbonski and Sarah M. Terry, "The Military as a Political Actor in Poland," in Roman Kolkowicz and Andrzej Korbonski, eds., <u>Soldiers, Peasants and Bureaucrats</u> (Allen & Unwin,

forthcoming).

7. The figure for Germany comes from Tadeusz Rawski et al., eds., Wojna wyzwolencza narodu polskiego w latch 1939-1945 (Warsaw: Wydawnictwo MON, 1966), p. 179. The estimate for the Soviet Union is from Stanislaw Kot, Rozmowy z Kremlem (London: Jutro Polski, 1959), p. 79, citing Krasnaia Zvezda of September 17, 1940.

8. Komisja Historyczna Polskiego Sztabu Glownego w Londynie, Polskie Sily Zbrojne w Drugiej Wojnie Swiatowej, vol. 3, Armia Krajowa (London: Instytut Historyczny im. Generala Sikorskiego, 1950), p. 124.

9. The estimates of the number of deportees vary, reaching the highest figure of 1.7 million persons. General Sikorski Historical Institute, Documents on Polish Soviet Relations 1939-1945, vol. 1 (London: Heineman, 1961), pp. 573-574.

10. For details see Andrzej Korbonski, "The Polish Communist Party 1938-1942," Slavic Review 26, no. 3 (September 1967): 430-444.

11. For an extensive treatment see Marian Malinowski, Geneza PPR (Warsaw: Ksiazka i Wiedza, 1975).

12. For details see J. K. Zawodny, Death in the Forest (Notre Dame, Ind.: Notre Dame University Press, 1962).

13. General Berling, who died in Poland in July 1980 at the age of 83, had an interesting military career in interwar Poland. Some of the key details in his wartime experiences are still shrouded in secrecy. See Jan Nowak, "Sprawa generala Berlinga," Zeszyty Historyczne (Paris), no. 37 (1976): 39-60, and the correspondence generated by this article in subsequent issues of this journal.

14. The standard account can be found in Fryderyk Zbiniewicz, Armia Polska w ZSRR (Warsaw: Wydawnictwo MON, 1963).

15. As of October 25, 1944, some 11,500 Soviet officers were transferred to the Polish army. Jan Zamojski, "Sily Zbrojne Polski Ludowej w walkach o wyzwolenie ojczyzny," in W. Gora and J. Golebiowski, eds., Z Dziejow Polski Ludowej (Warsaw: PZWS, 1966), p. 78. In addition, as of January 1, 1945, there were close to 16,000 Soviet NCOs and enlisted men attached to the Polish army, accounting for about 6 percent of its strength. The percentage of Soviet officers was close to 40 percent. Ignacy Blum, "Rola partii w organizacji i ksztaltowaniu ludowego charakteru Wojska Polskiego," Wojskowy Przeglad Historyczny 7, no. 22 (January 1962): 86.

16. Apparently as a result of the mobilization ordered in August 1944 only some 4,200 Polish officers entered the expanding army. Zamojski, "Sily Zbrojne Polski Ludowej," p. 78.

17. For a detailed list of individual officers and their functions see Ignacy Blum, Z dziejow aparatu politycznego Wojska Polskiego (Warsaw: Wydawnictwo MON,

1957), pp. 273-296.

18. For an account by a participant see Roman Zambrowski, "Wspomnienia czy fikcja literacka," Zeszyty Historyczne (Paris), no. 22 (1972): 153-160.

19. General Berling himself asserted in November 1956 that members of this group were also opposed to the formation of a Polish army in the USSR. Nowak, "Sprawa Generala Berlinga," p. 42.

20. This was due to the arrest in November 1943 of the secretary general of the PPR, Pawel Finder, and his aide, who were the only ones to know the secret radio code that was used in communicating with Moscow. Contact was reestablished when an agent with a new code was parachuted into Poland in the spring of 1944.

21. For a recent serious effort see Susanne S. Lotarski, "The Communist Takeover in Poland," in Thomas T. Hammond, ed., The Anatomy of Communist Takeovers (New Haven and London: Yale University Press, 1975), pp. 339-367.

22. For a brief biographical sketch of Rola-Zymierski see M. K. Dziewanowski, The Communist Party of Poland, second edition (Cambridge, Mass.: Harvard University Press, 1976), p. 386.

23. Krystyna Kersten, Polski Komitet Wyzwolenia Narodowego (Lublin: Wydawnictwo Lubelski, 1965), p. 98.

24. Apparently at the end of August 1944, the Politburo came out against the notion of an apolitical military as being harmful to both Polish national interests and the military itself. A special military section was established in the Central Committee under direct control of Secretary General Gomulka. Plikus, Mala kronika, p. 145.

25. This was true even after VE Day. For example, in order to ensure a "peaceful" conduct of the plebiscite (referendum) in January 1946, the government mobilized about 54,000 policemen, over 11,000 members of the secret police, 8,400 members of the special internal security forces, and 36,000 regular army soldiers. Plikus, Mala kronika, p. 202.

26. Yet, on the eve of the January 1947 parliamentary elections, over 2,600 special "Protection-Propaganda Brigades," composed of some 56,000 officers and men, were formed for the obvious purpose of preparing the ground for Communist victory. Lotarski, "The Communist Takeover in Poland," p. 353.

27. Among the two most interesting studies are Maria Turlejska, ed., Z walk przeciwko zbrojnemu podziemiu 1944-1947 (Warsaw: Wydawnictwo MON, 1966) and Tadeusz Walichnowski, U zrodel walk z podziemiem reakcyjnym w Polsce (Warszawa: Ksiazka i Wiedza, 1975).

28. Leszek Grot, "Dzialania Ludowego Wojska Polskiego przeciwko zbrojnemu podziemiu w latach 1944-1947," Wojskowy Przeglad Historyczny 18, no. 3 (July-September 1973): 476, 495.

29. Walichnowski, U zrodel walk, pp. 285 and 332. The strength of government forces earmarked for combatting the anti-Communist resistance was estimated at about 250,000. Anusiewicz and Ruszkiewicz, Tarcza socjalistycznej ojczyzny, p. 168. This figure included the regular army, internal security forces, and police.

30. Grot, "Dzialania Ludowego Wojska Polskiego," p. 496. In addition, some 71,400 suspected resistance members were arrested by the authorities, of whom 22,800 were tried and sentenced by military tribunals.

31. As of July 1, 1945, 16,400 officers out of the total of 40,000 officers in the Polish army were former Soviet army officers. Blum, "Rola partii w organizacji i ksztaltowaniu ludowego charakteru Wojska Polskiego," p. 91.

32. The professional origin of the officer cadre in 1948 was estimated as follows: Polish People's Army--63.2 percent; prewar Polish army--28.7 percent; Soviet advisers--7.7 percent; and others--0.4 percent. Jozef Graczyk, Problemy socjologiczne Ludowego Wojska Polskiego (Warsaw: Wydawnictwo MON, 1972), p. 73.

33. For a good example see Wladyslaw Gomulka, "O uchwalach Plenum Majowego," Ksztaltowanie sie podstaw programowych Polskiej Partii Robotniczej (Warsaw: Ksiazka i Wiedza, 1958), pp. 386-387.

34. In 1956, nineteen high-ranking officers were posthumously rehabilitated in Poland. They had been shot in 1952 on trumped-up charges. Zbigniew Brzezinski, The Soviet Bloc, revised and enlarged edition (Cambridge, Mass.: Harvard University Press, 1967), p. 526.

35. For example, in ibid., pp. 230-268.

36. The Ministry of Public Security was abolished in 1954, and its functions were taken over partly by the Ministry of the Interior and partly by a newly formed Committee on Public Security. For details of the defection see Jozef Swiatlo, Za kulisami bezpieki i partii (n.p. and n.d.), an English version of which may be found in News from Behind the Iron Curtain 4, no. 3 (March 1955): 3-86.

37. Spychalski, who was one of the earliest organizers of the Communist military resistance, occupied high positions in both the party and the military between 1944 and 1948. Accused of "rightist-nationalist deviation" in 1949, he was subsequently arrested, imprisoned, and even tortured. Released in the mid-1950s, he was subsequently rehabilitated and restored to his party and military positions in October 1956. His career went into decline in the second half of the 1960s. He died in Poland in June 1980.

38. Apparently "the soldiers of the Poznan garrison remained passive and in some cases willingly handed over their weapons to the crowd." Dziewanowki, The Communist Party of Poland, p. 265.

39. For an interesting recent summary see George Sakwa, "The Polish 'October': A Re-appraisal Through Historiography," The Polish Review 23, no. 3 (1978): 62-78.

40. According to a comprehensive analysis of occupational prestige in Poland in 1958, the inhabitants of Warsaw ranked army officers twentieth out of twenty-seven occupations; inhabitants of rural areas gave them a higher ranking, ninth out of twenty-one occupations. In 1975, the inhabitants of Warsaw ranked army officers thirteenth out of twenty-seven occupations; the inhabitants of rural areas ranked them tenth out of twenty-one occupations. In comparison with 1958, the officers' prestige improved in the eyes of Warsaw citizens but remained essentially unchanged in the rural areas. The aggregate ranking put officers as eleventh out of thirty occupations. Michal Pohoski, Kazimierz M. Slomczynski, and Wlodzimierz Wesolowski, "Occupational Prestige in Poland," Polish Sociological Bulletin, no. 4 (1976): 70-71, 75.

41. According to a Polish source, the percentage of Soviet officers in the Polish army declined from 3.6 percent in 1950 to 0.4 percent in 1955. Tadeusz Konecki, "Zawodowe szkolnictwo Ludowego Wojska Polskiego w pierwszym powojennyn dziesiecioleciu," Wojskowy Przeglad Historyczny 19, no. 2 (April-June 1974): 358.

42. For an extended treatment see Korbonski and Terry, "The Military as a Political Actor in Poland." Most of this section is based on this particular work. See also A. Ross Johnson, Robert W. Dean, and Alexander Alexiev, East European Military Establishments: The Warsaw Pact Northern Tier (Santa Monica, Calif.: RAND Corporation Report R-2417/1-AF/FF, December 1980), pp. 19-73.

43. For details see Michal Checinski, "'Ludowe Wojsko Polskie' przed i po Marcu 1968," Zeszyty Historyczne, no. 44 (1978): 16-19.

44. Dale R. Herspring, "The Changing Role of the Party-Political Apparatus in the Polish and East German Armed Forces," (Paper presented at the National Convention of the American Association for the Advancement of Slavic Studies, St. Louis, Missouri, October 1976).

45. For a discussion of this problem see J. Graczyk, "Problems of Recruitment and Selection in the Polish People's Armed Forces," in Morris Janowitz and Jacques van Doorn, eds., On Military Ideology (Rotterdam: Rotterdam University Press, 1971), pp. 199-208; and "Social Promotion in the Polish People's Army," in Jacques van Doorn, ed., Military Profession and Military Regimes, (The Hague and Paris: Mouton, 1969), pp. 73-81. See also Laszlo Revesz, "Die Polnische Volksarmee," in Peter Gosztony, ed., Zur Geschichte der europaischen Volksarmeen (Bonn-Bad Godesberg: Hohwacht, 1976), p. 34.

46. Dziewanowski, The Communist Party of Poland, pp. 296-301; and Joachim Georg Gorlich, "Tendenzen und Stromungen innerhalb der polnischen militarischen Fuhrung,"

Wehrwissenschaftliche Rundschau 18, no. 7 (1968).
  47. Checinski, "Ludowe Wojsko Polskie," pp. 24-30. See also "USSR and the Politics of Polish Antisemitism 1956-68," Soviet Jewish Affairs, no. 1 (June 1971): 33-38; and Harald Laeuen, "Die Marzunruhen in Polen and ihre Folgen: (II) Partisanen gegen Zionisten," Osteuropa 19, no. 2 (February 1969): 110-124.
  48. Jaruzelski discussed the behavior of the Polish military during the December 1970 crisis at the Eighth Plenary Meeting of the Central Committee of the Polish Communist party on February 6-7, 1971. Radio Free Europe Research, Polish Press Survey, no. 2317, August 10, 1971. For an extensive discussion of the military's behavior in December 1970 see Michael Costello, "The Party and Military in Poland," Radio Free Europe Research, Poland/12, April 26, 1971.
  49. Apparently one of the chief leaders of the "Partisans," General Korczynski, who was also commander in chief of the Territorial Defense Forces, was accused of ordering his troops to fire at the Baltic Coast strikers. Harold Laeuen, "Moczar's Entmachtung," Osteuropa 27, no. 1 (January 1972): 37-38. See also Michael Costello, "The Political Fortunes of Mieczyslaw Moczar," Radio Free Europe Research, Poland/15, June 2, 1971. It is interesting to note that Moczar was returned to the Politburo in the critical days of November 1980.
  50. Personal interviews, Warsaw, June 1976.
  51. See Chapter 1 in this volume.

8
The Czechoslovak Army

Jiri Valenta
Condoleezza Rice

The development of the Czechoslovak People's Army (Československá Lidová Armadá, or ČLA) is at once strikingly similar and fundamentally different from that of other Communist armies. By design, the ČLA organizationally and administratively copies the Soviet army. Like its East European counterparts, however, the client-state status of Czechoslovakia is a pervasive influence and has fostered a military establishment that differs substantially from that of the Soviet armed forces. In particular, a markedly different relationship between party and military exists in the client states in which the professional military has been largely isolated from the political process.

Important political, cultural, and economic features further distinguish the history of the ČLA and make it quite unique among client militaries. Of prime importance is that the early developmental stage of the present Czechoslovak armed forces took place during an era of "true coalition," a period in which the Communist party was not fully in control. A second related feature is the absence of Soviet troops on Czechoslovak soil from 1945-1968. In accordance with an agreement, American and Soviet troops departed from Czechoslovakia in 1945. The Soviet army was thus not present during the critical period of development and there were fewer Soviet military advisers at the disposal of the Communist party of Czechoslovakia than in other East European states.[1] A third factor is the existence of a prewar military establishment that was virtually intact at the end of World War II. The association with fascism that compromised so many officers in Romania, Bulgaria, and Hungary was far less pervasive in the Czech lands. Many Czech officers fled the protectorate, fighting in the USSR. This was not the case in Slovakia where an army was created in Joseph Tiso's puppet "Slovak Republic" compromising numerous Slovak officers. The Czechoslovak officer corps was heavily Czech, however, and most senior officers were able to return to the homeland and pursue military posts after the war. Nor was the Czechoslovak officer corps involved in a war with Germany or in an experience comparable to that of the mass killing of Polish officers at Katyn, which helped to dismantle the Polish prewar elite. The role of these returning officers in the postwar Czechoslovak forces is instructive.

Moreover, Czechoslovakia is a political and cultural anomaly in Eastern Europe, and its military and political heritage is marked by contradiction. Unique because of its cultural identification with the West, Czechoslovakia fostered both the only democratic interwar regime in Eastern Europe and the only legitimate and viable indigenous Communist party. Furthermore, in spite of cultural sympathies with the West, Czechoslovakia's geographic location forced the newly independent state to undertake a tenuous political position between West and East. The tensions between geographical necessity and cultural kinship have persisted throughout the history of the Czechoslovak state.

The military tradition of Czechoslovakia also manifests interesting contradictions. It is said that the Czechoslovaks are simply antimilitary, that the use of force runs contrary to the state's cultural values. Yet a proud military tradition, dating to the exploits of the Czechoslovak Legion in World War I, does exist. It is worth noting that the Czechoslovak nation owes a considerable debt in the attainment of independence to the performance and the fine reputation of these first autonomous military units. In addition, the interwar military was one of the finest in East Central Europe, and Czechoslovak soldiers, as individuals, fought valiantly on both fronts in the Allied effort in World War II. But ironically, the Czechoslovak military has never lifted a hand to defend the homeland from attack. Twice, in 1938 and 1968, under different forms of government, the Czechoslovak armed forces remained confined to barracks during the invasion of Czechoslovak lands. Furthermore, the military remained neutral in the political crisis that led to the February takeover. Curiously, high officers of this same Czechoslovak military have been implicated in political meddling at least three times. Though the existence of such political interference has never been conclusively proven, it is interesting that this otherwise politically inactive group has been suspect in times of political crisis.

In spite of these peculiarities, Czechoslovakia is a very critical case. The state is a central cog in the Soviet security system. Czechoslovakia is one of the most industrialized states in the Eastern bloc and possesses, as a member of the Warsaw Pact's northern tier group, one of the most modern and technologically advanced militaries of the Soviet alliance. Czechoslovakia is also a client state with a mature and historically active domestic arms industry and is an important supplier to the Soviet allies and "progressive" Third World countries. Perhaps a greater interest for our purposes, however, is the fact that this advanced and strategically important military was subjected to an extended period of tension during the crisis of 1968. Unparalleled in the annals of Communist military history, the behavior of the Czechoslovak military in 1968 is one of the most important cases for study in the analysis of Communist military development.

This study will proceed through a discussion of five major periods in the development of the ČLA. The essay focuses on three periods: the developmental and gestation period under coalition rule from 1945-1948, the immediate postrevolution era from 1948-1956, and the remarkable developments of the 1968 crisis. It is the authors' belief that these periods most clearly demonstrate the tensions and difficulties of Communist military development under the peculiar conditions of clientship and the unique circumstances of Czechoslovak history.

THE DEVELOPMENT OF "THE NEW ARMED FORCES": 1945-1948

Although Communist histories distinguish between military development during the period of coalition and under the Communist regime of 1948, it was during the three-year period of Edward Beneš's presidency that the framework for the communization of the military was achieved. Postwar cooperation with the Soviet Union was long a cornerstone of the wartime policy of Beneš. In 1940, with the Soviet Union still allied with Germany, Beneš explained that Central European postwar security rested in alliance with Moscow. The 1945 governmental blueprint for the postwar Czechoslovak state known as the Košice Program reflected this philosophy. The military plank of the Košice accords is indeed remarkable. Pledging absolute coordination with the Red Army and promising to copy the Soviet example faithfully,[2] the accords afforded the Soviet Union and the Communist party of Czechoslovakia considerable leverage in shaping the postwar armed forces.

In spite of the promises at Košice, however, non-Communist members of the coalition tried to balance Communist influence in the military by insisting that pro-Western military men hold important positions. The primary difficulty in the early years was thus the development of officer corps acceptable to both Beneš and the Communists. There were four sources available to the leadership in the reconstitution of the military elite: the First Army Corps on the territory of the USSR; the London-based officers, including the air force and the Czechoslovak Defense Brigade fighting in France; the resistance fighters; and the partisans. Apparently the few prisoners taken from the Slovak army were largely repatriated before the end of the war and enlisted in the forces forming in Moscow. Several important clarifications on the use of these officers in the postwar army appeared in the Košice accords and merit consideration. First, the Košice Program clearly states that special consideration should be given to the officers and soldiers of the Czechoslovak First Army Corps formed on Soviet territory. By virtue of their role in the liberation of Czechoslovak territory, the First Army Corps gained considerable justification for dominance in the postwar army. Perhaps of greater symbolic value was the liberation of Prague by Soviet and First Army Corps troops; a feat accomplished because of an Allied decision leaving the liberation of the capital to the East. But much to the chagrin of the Communist leadership, the pro-Western officers had a counter-claim. The officers of the Moscow-influenced corps were inexperienced and had held no elite positions prior to the war. It is here that the use of the modifier "new" in Košice references to the army takes on considerable significance. The "new army" implies a complete break with the past.[3] In order to penetrate the upper echelons, it was necessary to find justification for starting all officers out on equal footing. The concept of a new armed forces deprived the pro-Western officers of their prewar positions and allowed the reconstitution process to begin with the slate clean and the heroic effort in the liberation of the homeland as the primary criterion for postwar promotion.

A second clarification is the distinction between resistance fighters in the Slovak national uprising and partisan fighters. There were, according to Košice, "<u>slovenští a čestí partyzáni</u>," or partisan fighters, and "<u>povstalecká jojska na Slovensku</u>," or fighters in the Slovak uprising.[4] Partisan movements were stronger in Slovakia than in the Czech lands, but still dwarfed by comparison with the efforts in countries such as Poland and Yugoslavia. The movements that did exist were heavily infiltrated by Communist party members. In most cases only the Communist party retained its structure and was able to proselytize among partisan fighters and the population. The resistance fighters of the Slovak national uprising were quite another matter. Although the resistance fighters probably numbered Communists among them, the Soviet Union was ambivalent about the uprising, and the distinction in Košice reflects this attitude. Although later histories herald the aid that the Soviet Union afforded the Slovaks, it is a fact that Red Army assistance was minimal. As in the Polish uprising at Warsaw, Stalin apparently allowed the Slovak uprising of 1944 to fail, insuring Soviet dominance of the liberation process.

The officer corps that was selected as a result of

these complicated criteria was extremely heterogeneous. Communist sources lamented the bourgeois nature of the new officer cadre. In 1945, only 605 members of the corps were Communist.[5] This meager Communist representation was a source of consternation for the party. One Soviet writer noted that "Beneš used his office to secure in the army the most reactionary bourgeois officers who worked in the time of occupation as functionaries in the control organs, served in the 'Slovak army'...and themselves were accomplices of fascism."[6]

At the insistence of the party's military soviets (formed in 1945), the officer corps was reviewed by a commission in 1946. Applications were taken from all officers who "had not compromised themselves."[7] Of the 11,000 applications received, only a handful were rejected.[8] Even in Slovakia, where the army collaborated, only 87 of 1,530 applications were turned down.[9] Dissatisfied with the work of the commission, the Communists took steps to change the composition of the officer corps over time. Communist party chief and Prime Minister Klement Gottwald personally appealed to sons of working-class or peasant families to enroll in reserve officer training.[10] Twenty new military and premilitary training schools were then opened, of which eight were officer training academies.[11] The results were impressive. By 1947 there were 5,350 students in these schools.[12] Soviet instructors staffed most of the institutions.

Another step that the Communists took to change the complexion of the officer corps was the initiation of an exchange program between Soviet and Czechoslovak officers. In 1947, twenty-five young officers of Svoboda's corps were sent to the Soviet Union for advanced study.[13] Finally, steps were taken to dilute the air force, a pro-Western stronghold. Officers of air and air-support units of the First Army Corps were brought en masse into the air force. Although the First Army Corps air units were quite underdeveloped, officers of this background progressed rapidly, thanks to the expenditure of immense resources on air-operations training. The steps succeeded in laying the foundation for a loyal cadre. Party accounts proudly state that there were 3,000 new Communist party members in the officer ranks by 1947.[14] The accounts also claim that by the time of the 1948 revolution, there had been a turnover of about one-third of the officers reinstated in 1945.

In conjunction with these changes in the middle and junior ranks, the party was able to secure several elite positions. The minister of defense, deputy minister of defense, and chief of the general staff of the military-in-exile were all dismissed. Beneš's request to name wartime Minister of Defense Gen. Sergei Ingr to that postwar position was vetoed, and Gen. Ludvik Svoboda, the commander of the First Army Corps, was installed. The position of chief of the general staff of the army was given to Bohumil Boček, another officer who had been in Moscow, rather than to Beneš's candidate, Alois Liška, the commander of the Czechoslovak armored brigade in Great Britain. Two of the highest elite positions remained in pro-Western hands, however. Gen. K. Janoušek retained his position as commander in chief of the air force for a short time, and Gen. Karel Klapek remained commander in chief of the ground forces of the Czechoslovak army. Thus, although the junior grades were being steadily transformed, the highest and most visible elite positions were divided between Westerners and Muscovites.

The effort to gradually shift the officer corps balance was aided by other policy initiatives. The installation of Communist educational programs in the military was one such policy. The Košice Program provided for the establishment of a cadre of "<u>osyetoví dvstojníci</u>," or "enlightenment officers," and for a political education department within the Ministry of Defense.[15] This department was the predecessor of the Main Political Administration. Charged with proper education of the military, the department was headed by Col. Gen. Jaroslav Prochazka, political commissar to the First Army Corps during the war. Under Prochazka, "enlightenment officers" were placed in each unit but were subordinate directly to Prochazka's department, not to the unit command.[16] Apparently there were not enough trustworthy officers, and Prochazka's network was somewhat incomplete. Nevertheless, non-Communist officers expressed concern about usurping of command functions and especially about disciplinary problems caused by enlightenment officers' exhortations to young soldiers to challenge the political and moral positions of their officers.

As efforts like the enlightenment program took hold and with the institution of party cells within each unit, Communist influence on young officers grew. Party work in the army was curtailed somewhat by laws that prohibited party politics during regular army training periods. Though often ignored, the laws did provide a legal basis for commander complaints against proselytizing. Ironically, the same laws restricted the available literature on military bases to the "press of friendly nations." The friendly status was to be determined by the Defense Ministry.[17]

Although these efforts were successful, the communization of the armed forces was in no way completed during this period. The heralded training and coordination with the Red Army lagged. Training was beset by many difficulties, but most crippling was a lack of small arms and equipment. The USSR was unable to meet its commitments to Czechoslovakia, and Svoboda was reduced to begging for surplus war materials in the West. The British welcomed the opportunity, hoping to maintain contacts with the

pro-Western air force. The Americans, however, insisted
that the Soviet Union was to be Czechoslovakia's primary
supplier and feared a barrage of similar requests from the
rest of Eastern Europe. The supply problem was exacerbated
by severe disagreements between members of the coalition
on the fate of Czechoslovak armaments industries. The
Communists favored total coordination with the USSR or
integration of Czechoslovak industries with the Soviet
arms production effort.[18] The non-Communists insisted on
maintaining the integrity of domestic arms production.
This debate effectively paralyzed the once-prolific armaments sector. Interestingly, much of what was produced
during this period was sold on the black market rather
than put into domestic use. Czechoslovak equipment surfaced in many areas of the Third World.

Before leaving the discussion of this early period,
it is important to mention the reconstitution of the intelligence network. The postwar intelligence establishment was several times larger than it had been before the
war. In the military, Col. Gen. Bedřich Reicin's <u>Obranne
Bezepečnostní Zpravodajství</u> (OBZ), the Defense Security
Intelligence Unit, was especially powerful. Reicin's
group is said to have been active down to the unit level,
and the trustee was often unknown to the commanding
officer.[19] Late in 1946 the OBZ was becoming so powerful
that non-Communist parties were asking for its abolition.
Reicin's group was not disbanded and continued to grow in
influence. Considerable rivalry surfaced between the
different police arms and the regular military. Reicin's
group, which was supposedly subordinate to the Ministry
of Defense, was accused of operating quite independently.

In sum, the state of the military under the coalition
government was part of the struggle for power. At the
time of the 1948 February Revolution, the army was
Communist in form and organization. However, pro-Western
officers still controlled many elite positions. The military was called upon by neither side in the crisis and remained confined to barracks. It is believed, however,
that Svoboda and other pro-Communist generals might have
pressured Beneš to accept the results of the February
takeover.[20]

THE DEVELOPMENT OF THE "PEOPLE'S ARMED FORCES": 1948-1956

Many changes took place after the takeover. The first
casualties were high-ranking, pro-Western officers. Gen.
Ludvik Svoboda joined the Communist party and retained his
position as minister of defense. Svoboda is an interesting
and rather puzzling case. His first military experience
was as an infantry soldier in the Austro-Hungarian army
where he deserted to the Russian side and joined the
Czechoslovak Legion in World War I. Returning home in
1920, Svoboda played no important role in the armed forces

of the republic, but upon fleeing to the Soviet Union in
1939, was named to head the First Czechoslovak Army
Brigade. He was not officially a Communist in 1945 when
he was named minister of defense. Svoboda later claimed
that Gottwald had asked him to remain outside the party
for political expediency.[21] Though unsubstantiated, this
claim would explain Svoboda's survival in the postrevolutionary era in one of the key positions in the new government. Svoboda retained his position, but other Moscow-
based officers did not. Most notably, Bohumil Boček was
replaced by Gen. Simon Drgač. Boček, unlike Svoboda, was
not a member of the First Army Corps. He had been in
Moscow during a portion of the war, but as a representative
of the military-in-exile. These connections apparently
made him a liability in the revolutionary era.

In general, the period was marked by the meteoric rise
of political officers to military commands and by the
ascension of officers who had served with the First Army
Corps. In fact, the similarity of backgrounds among the
men who rose to the upper echelons in this period is
remarkable. With only three exceptions these officers
gained their middle-level experience as members of the
Moscow-based group. The officers filled vacancies left
by the purge of pro-Western officers. A few defected;
others, like Gen. Helidor Pika, the former chief of the
military mission in Moscow, were charged with espionage and
sentenced to death in 1948. A few others, like General
Janoušek of the air force, committed suicide. As a consequence of the purges, one year after the revolution 700
military officers had been dismissed. In addition to the
arrests and executions, the Parliamentary Defense and
Security Committee approved a resolution for demotion of
some officers to reserve private status.[22] The men were
deprived of their ranks but retained pension privileges
as long as they remained in the reserves. Many of these
professional officers were reinstated when the leadership
turned to the buildup of an efficient new force in the
middle 1950s. This was an interesting tactic by which
military men were deprived of a base of political activity
during the consolidation of the revolution, but enticed
to remain within easy reach for future use.

Further purges took place on the heels of an alleged
attempted military coup. In January 1949, Gen. Karel
Kutlvašr, a pro-Western general, supposedly was to lead a
coup to overthrow the regime. Planned by the political
underground, the coup was to take place in conjunction
with uprisings in western Czech lands. The history of
the alleged coup is shrouded in mystery. Although U.S.
intelligence at the time maintained the authenticity of
the plot and reported stepped up underground activity
in January 1949, it should be noted that the Czechoslovak
government rehabilitated Kutlvašr late in the 1960s.
Although it was never admitted that he was framed, his

rehabilitation casts doubt on the authenticity of the plot. Whatever the case, the affair was a convenient rationale for massive military purges, and its impact on the military was great. Initially, 14 officers were arrested, but the number grew to well over 200.[23] All aircraft were grounded for a week while the political reliability of the still heavily pro-Western air force was checked, and military personnel were confined to barracks on several occasions.

The purges and the efforts to reform the military officer corps had a dramatic effect. In three years, the Communist membership of the officer corps rose from 37.9 percent to 64.9 percent.[24] The backgrounds of members of the 1952 corps were as follows: 53.8 percent workers, 8.3 percent from families of government service, and 13.9 percent from "poor" or peasant backgrounds. The remainder were listed as intelligentsia.[25]

But as quickly as the pro-Western and anti-Communist officers were dismissed, the old Communists who replaced many of them found themselves out of favor. In 1949 and 1950, the officer corps underwent tremendous upheaval. The leadership was turning to the establishment of a military that was efficient and loyal. Many of the old Communists were ousted. Over 75 percent of the officers of general rank promoted in the period from 1948 to 1949 disappeared by 1952. Svoboda himself was removed and sent to a collective farm. Drgač, Boček (who had been demoted in 1948), and Prochazka were also removed. The purges were begun in 1948 and culminated in the terror of the Slansky trials. Many Czechoslovak military leaders were purged. In fact, the Slovak representation in the officer corps was substantially reduced, creating a chronic shortage of Slovak officers that persisted for some time. The purge facilitated the rapid promotion of the junior and middle officers who had been in training since 1945. It was during this time that most of the senior officers of the present-day Czechoslovak military rose to the middle grades. With only a few exceptions, these were officers whose military careers began as enlisted men in the First Army Corps.

The job of overseeing this new elite was entrusted to Alexej Čepička, Klement Gottwald's son-in-law and an old Communist. Promoted to army general just after his appointment as defense minister, Čepička was a party apparatchik who had never held military rank. As minister of defense Čepička enjoyed tremendous power, rising to the Politburo and in 1953 to the position of deputy prime minister.

Čepička completely reformed the political education system. Even before his rise to power in 1950, the political education apparatus had been maturing. Shortly after February 1948, Prochazka's education and enlightenment unit was replaced by the familiar, Soviet inspired, Main Political Administration (MPA). From 1950 onward, considerable effort was devoted to filling the many vacant posts among political offices. Political education classes were institutionalized within the military. Party control and education now slavishly followed the Soviet model.

Under Čepička the military was transformed into an efficient instrument. Like its East European counterparts, Czechoslovakia concentrated tremendous resources upon military development after 1951. Military spending reportedly reached its highest levels after the Korean War, skyrocketing to an estimated 11.7 percent of the budget in 1953.[26] New military academies, which were now devoted to functional specialities, were opened and staffed by Soviet officers. The practice of sending officers to the Soviet Union for training was accelerated, and the study of Russian language became compulsory in military academies.

The size of the military grew remarkably. United States intelligence and Communist sources placed the size of the 1945 ČLA at about 177,000.[27] In 1948 the ČLA numbered only about 130,000, organized into eleven incomplete divisions.[28] By 1951 and throughout Čepička's tenure, it is believed that the ČLA numbered over 250,000.[29] With the revitalization of its armament industries, Czechoslovakia became nearly self-sufficient in artillery and small arms by the end of the 1950s.

In 1955 the consolidation and strengthening of the ČLA was almost complete. The military establishment was trustworthy enough that it was branching into foreign policy, serving Soviet interests in the Third World. The Czechoslovaks were heavily involved in on-site training of military men from several "progressive" Third World nations. Czechoslovak armaments industries were assisting in the transfer of arms to several countries, most notably Israel in 1948 and Egypt in 1955. Ironically, Čepička, a political man with no military background, had managed to greatly enhance the prestige, size, and importance of the military establishment. In fact, he was presiding over the most prestigious non-Soviet military establishment in the Eastern bloc.

THE CZECHOSLOVAK PEOPLE'S ARMY IN THE KHRUSHCHEV ERA

The death of Stalin and the rise of Khrushchev brought profound changes in the Czechoslovak armed forces. Khrushchev began to pursue policies that would change the status of the East European states from totally dependent satellites to semisovereign allies. The new socialist interstate system was to depend more heavily on cooperation than on coercion. The plan didn't always work. Poland followed the prescription of domestic variance coupled with strict adherence to the Soviet foreign policy line. Hungary did not, threatening unilateral withdrawal from the Warsaw Pact, and the Soviets found it necessary to invade. But the plan for the new relationship survived the upheavals of 1956, and treaties and multilateral organizations gave legal justification to Soviet influence in Eastern Europe. In the military sphere, the reemergence of national diversity took the form of renationalization of insignia, uniforms, and emblems and the gradual rewriting of military history to include the traditions of the past. Thus, the exploits of the Czechoslovak Legion in World War I and the excellent record of Czechoslovak forces in World War II were selectively written back into history.

The prestige of the Czechoslovak military was further enhanced by the development in 1955 of the Warsaw Pact. This replaced the obvious reliance of the Czechoslovak state upon the Soviet Union with dependence on a military alliance in which the ČLA played an integral role. The development of the Warsaw Treaty Organization has been studied in detail and will thus be afforded little attention here. It is enough to note that the framework for integration was now set down. In truth, the process of integration and standardization has been slow.

Khrushchev's reevaluation of Soviet military doctrine, which placed emphasis on the development of strategic forces and upon nuclear-supported ground operations, further enhanced the importance and consequently the modernization of these armies. The militaries were given well-defined missions and an important role in Soviet theatre defense.[30] Increasingly sophisticated equipment and training followed. It was also during this period that Czechoslovakia's domestic armaments industries began to pursue development of more advanced weaponry. The success of advanced Czechoslovakia jet trainers brought considerable prestige to the domestic industry.

But under the surface of this growth in military prestige, signs of discontent were brewing. Čepička, the man responsible for Czechoslovakia's military growth, was accused of "cult of personality" in the military and dismissed. Moreover, several problems festered below the surface from 1956 until 1968. One problem was the slow review and rehabilitation of purge victims, an issue of particular interest to the military, which lost so many officers during the terror of the late 1940s and early 1950s. A second problem was the persistent isolation of Slovak officers from the higher echelons of the military elite. This problem led to considerable tension between the nationalities. The key problems, however, revolved around questions of doctrine and of party leadership in the armed forces. In the 1960s the first hesitant remarks began to appear on the differentiation of Czechoslovak military doctrine from Soviet doctrine, but little progress was made. The question of the role of the party in the armed forces was more openly debated, however, and small concessions were won. The effort to modernize the ČLA brought about a need for more highly educated and professional officers. In order to bring qualified officer candidates to service, the military had to compete with the civilian sector as never before. The party wished to concentrate on incentives like pension reform. Professional officers argued, however, that the real issue was a proper balance between political education and technical training. The ČLA was quickly becoming an organization of technicians, and many resented the long hours of political course work. The number of university-educated officers in 1963-1964 was roughly ten times that of university-educated officers in 1953-1954.[31] Furthermore, every fifth officer in 1963-1964 was a graduate of a military or civilian graduate school. But most important, 32 percent of all officers in the ČLA declared themselves to be engineers and technicians, an increase of 12 percent from 1954.[32] The military elite won small battles on this matter. Most notably, the Ministry of Defense agreed to consider a reduction in the number of days spent in political classes and did in fact agree to a separation of political and technical classes in the curriculum.[33] Still another victory for the military was the appointment of a man with military experience to the minister's post. In 1956, Gen. Bohumir Lomsky, a man with considerable military experience, replaced Čepička.

In spite of these changes, the military must still be viewed as a nonactor in the Khrushchev and early post-Khrushchev era. Nonetheless, the military did become involved in the political debate of the 1968 crisis. Figures from the entire spectrum of the military community, professional and political officers, the intelligentsia, and the leadership displayed an interest in the liberalization debate. The dialogue between the party and military leadership was quite remarkable and produced innovative ideas about the proper role of the military in society.

THE MILITARY AND THE 1968 CRISIS

From the beginning of the crisis, the military was subjected to severe tensions. The catalyst for military involvement in the political debate was an alleged attempt by high-ranking political officers to interject the military into the political deliberations of the Communist party's Central Committee. In December 1967, Antonin Novotny was called to account for years of inadequate political and economic leadership. Liberal elements felt that Novotny's power should be broken and that the functions of the party secretary and president should be separated. It is believed that Maj. Gen. Jan Šejna, the secretary of the Party Collective of Communists in the Armed Forces and ambitious Gen. Vladimir Janko, deputy minister of defense, intended to use the military to intervene on behalf of Novotny and the conservative cause. Unscheduled and indeed rare winter maneuvers took place on the days immediately preceding the Central Committee Plenum. In apparent conjunction with the exercises, a letter was delivered to the Central Committee from the Presidium of the Party in the

Armed Forces, which Šejna headed, supporting Novotny's position. The letter arrived too late. The vote had been taken, and Novotny lost the secretaryship. A few months later he was removed as president. The entire affair was exposed when the general staff of the army published an open letter charging that a coup had been attempted. When Šejna fled the country and Janko committed suicide, rumors and accusations were rampant. Reports surfaced about the military maneuvers, and the highest members of the military elite were implicated. Miroslav Mamula, Šejna's immediate superior as chief of the Central Committee's Eighth Department, was openly accused and eventually dismissed. The situation was so serious that Defense Minister Lomsky appeared on Czechoslovak television in order to deny association with the plot. By all accounts, the coup failed because Maj. Gen. Vaclav Prchlik, chief of the Main Political Administration, alerted anti-Novotny forces in the Central Committee.

Though the evidence in the Šejna affair is patchy, it is rather persuasive. Šejna himself denies that any such plan was intended, but the sequence of events would seem to suggest that something unusual was brewing. Indeed, during the spring of 1968 and after the crisis was settled, commentators from both the liberal and conservative camps admitted that the military was trying to influence the political developments.[34] It should be noted, however, that the alleged coup was a military coup in name only. Šejna was the consummate political general and was attempting to use the military in support of one political faction against another. A few professional officers, though possibly involved as accomplices, seemingly had little to do with planning the coup. One probable exception was co-conspirator General Janko.

Whatever the case, the alleged coup outraged society and military men alike. The question was asked, "How could the Šejna affair happen?" Most of the blame was placed upon the ability of a few party members to dictate and control internal military affairs. In particular, Šejna's Collective of Communists in the Armed Forces was considered to have operated well outside the eye of the Ministry of Defense. Šejna's group was accused of usurping many of the functions of the Main Political Administration. Šejna's group reported directly to the powerful Eighth Department for military and security affairs, but was housed in the Defense Ministry. Thus party policy was being disseminated and monitored by two quite independent entities. The following schematic identifies the complex links between party organs in the military as they were described by the chief of the Main Political Administration, Gen. Egyd Pepich.[35]

Pepich explained, "The relationship between the MPA and the collective of Communists at the Ministry has been and still is ill defined. It is said...that the Communists

CENTRAL COMMITTEE
EIGHTH DEPARTMENT

| Military Affairs | Police Affairs |
Ministry of Defense	Ministry of Interior
Main Political Administration General Staff Commands Inspector General	Party Organization in the Armed Forces (also referred to as the Presidium of the Party in the Armed Forces) Reporting directly to the Eighth Department but housed in the Ministry of Defense

at the Ministry are a great asset...but if we take a closer look...we must admit that everything is not exactly perfect in this respect."[36]

The activities of Šejna's group became a cause célèbre, crystallizing liberal sentiment and leading to a relentless evaluation of the role of the party in military affairs. Conversely, the pro-Novotny cause was seriously damaged, as most officers who did not support liberal ideas were discredited and branded as traitors. Within a few months, leading conservatives like Defense Minister Lomsky, chief of the general staff Otakar Rytir, and Miroslav Mamula all fell. Countless other conservatives who knew nothing of the Šejna episode were ridiculed and isolated from the military-political mainstream. In fact, the military was disgraced in general as the population branded men in military dress as "šejnovites."

As the conservatives faded, the tenor and issues of the military liberalization drive became radicalized. The military's own Action Program, paralleling the government manifesto of April 1968, called for democratization of the armed forces. It was suggested that party influence had to be diminished and that nonpartisan, truly democratic organizations should be instituted within the military in order to make certain that the military could never again be used against the people.

The concern over party influence was reflected in the intention of the liberal forces within the government and within the military to create watchdog institutions that would report to the National Assembly. The Committee on Defense and Security Affairs would have replaced the Eighth Department and reported only to the National Assembly. These changes would have left the Central Committee with only the MPA as a direct lever of influence in the Ministry of Defense. A related proposal would have diminished party influence in personnel decisions and appointed nonpartisan personnel collectives to evaluate soldiers for promotion.

But by far the most startling developments involved military press debates on the role of the Czechoslovak military in the Warsaw Pact. The Dubček leadership had been very careful to assure the Soviet Union and the other Warsaw Pact states that the military alliance was not being questioned in the process of democratization. But in the early spring, the radicalized military press organs Lidova Armada and A-Revue began openly to discuss the nature and organization of the Warsaw Pact. Initially the question centered upon the expense of Warsaw Pact membership but quickly developed into criticism of certain aspects of the alliance. Then, in July 1968, two memoranda were published by the staff of the Gottwald Military Academy. In essence the memoranda questioned the raison d'être of the pact, suggesting that the NATO threat might indeed be overstated.[37] The memoranda further called for a reconsideration of Czechoslovak national concerns based on geopolitical rather than class analysis.

Then, in July of 1968 the head of the Eighth Department and former MPA chief, Gen. Vaclav Prchlik, sent shock waves through the pact when he stated openly that perhaps membership in the Warsaw Pact was not as equal as it should be. The Soviet Union was furious and appalled to find that Martin Dzur, the new defense minister, had not totally disavowed the Prchlik statements. In deference to Soviet anger, Prchlik's department was abolished. This was only a partial victory for the conservatives, however, as the abolition of the Eighth Department was already planned. In fact, the military leadership reacted hesitantly to the Prchlik events. There was tremendous popular support for his position, and the leadership was in the unenviable position of trying to placate the Soviets without disavowing the democratization. The response of the leadership was slow, and it was a full two weeks before the Ministry of Defense disavowed the statement in principle. Students of the Soviet invasion have stated that the Soviet officers who held direct responsibility for the East European forces favored invasion. Among these Yakubovsky, certain officers of the Ground Forces Command, and General Yepishev of the MPA are identified. It is not surprising that Yepishev would be concerned about the liberal positions of Czechoslovak MPA chiefs Prchlik and Pepich. Yepishev must have thought that the loss of party control was imminent given the position of the MPA, the party's guardian institution.

In the weeks leading to the invasion of Czechoslovakia, the Soviet press openly questioned the ability of the ČLA to defend socialism. Though Dzur publicly defended the ČLA, there are those who claim that during the frequent

visits to Prague in the preinvasion period of General
Yakubovsky, Warsaw Pact commander in chief, Dzur denigrated
the cohesiveness and preparedness of his own military establishment.[38] Even without Dzur's comments, Yakubovsky
and numerous other Soviet officers were constantly on hand
during the extended maneuvers in the summer of 1968 and
could not have been oblivious to the situation in the
Czechoslovak military.[39] Furthermore, conservatives such
as Rytir and František Bedřich, now on the outskirts of
power, probably delivered alarming reports about the
dissolution of the ČLA. It is reasonable to suggest that
the state of the ČLA was one consideration in the Soviet
decision to invade. A few concessions were made prior to
the invasion. Most important, the conservatives began to
reassert control over the MPA, and arch-conservative
General Bedřich replaced the liberal Pepich as MPA chief.

INVASION AND NORMALIZATION

The August invasion of Czechoslovakia by Warsaw Pact
forces aborted all reforms in the Czechoslovak military.
The subsequent normalization was thorough in the military.
The hegemonic function of the party was reasserted, and
thorough control of the party over the military was reinstituted. General purges and a massive political reeducation campaign were launched. The chief radicals were
dismissed, and the center of radical debate, the Gottwald
Academy, was temporarily closed. In addition to the
officers who were forced out of the military, many left
voluntarily. Hardest hit were the junior officer grades,
where 57.8 percent of the officers under the age of thirty
left the armed forces.[40]

Considerable effort was made in trying to wipe the
story of the military's involvement in the crisis from the
pages of history. Every officer of general rank was asked
to write an addendum to his biography, presumably to explain his part in the events of the spring of 1968. A
few high-ranking officers were even prosecuted as
criminals--most notably Vaclav Prchlik, who was convicted
of participation in activities detrimental to the state
and jailed. Other officers, like Minister of Defense Dzur,
simply developed amnesia, renounced the liberal cause that
they had publicly supported, and were within a year praising the "fraternal intervention."

The most significant organizational change in the
postinvasion period was the creation of the Defense Council
in February 1969. The council, headed by the first party
secretary was given far-reaching control over military
affairs and through its charter reaffirmed the beginning
of the party.

Interestingly, the purges that occurred in the next
phase of the normalization victimized both residual liberal
elements and the most radical conservatives. The new

leadership apparently feared both radical right and left. There is even speculation that there was once again a threat of military intervention before Dubček's dismissal in April 1969. This alleged plan was apparently abandoned when Husak accelerated the normalization process. Husak was able to satisfy the Soviets, but had to purge Rytir, Bedřich, and others to make certain that they would not intervene on their own initiative. Normalization purges continued throughout 1972 and 1975.

A major consequence of the invasion was the reinstitution of a strong Soviet presence. A thorough network of Soviet advisers, reminiscent of Stalinist days, was reinstituted and five Soviet divisions installed on Czechoslovak territory for the first time in the postwar era. In the immediate postinvasion period, rumors of Soviet troop abuses (including breaking into student hostels) surfaced.[41] Though never confirmed, the rumors inflamed already volatile Czechoslovak public opinion. Further tensions were created by the scarcity of living accommodations and market goods for ČLA personnel. It was thought that Soviet troops were being housed at the expense of Czechoslovak military and civilian personnel.[42] This problem persisted for some time but was alleviated by the construction of permanent facilities for the occupying troops.

The Czechoslovak military continues to feel the repercussions of the invasion. Military officials readily admit that recruitment of young men to military careers has become increasingly difficult. Numerous incentives have been offered to attract young men to military service. Typical of the effort to recruit officers is a program, begun in 1969, that reduced basic military service (one year instead of two, the second year to be spent in officer training school). Bonuses (including five to six months' pay after leaving the military) are awarded to those who commit themselves to three to six years' service. Higher grants and privileges are awarded graduates of secondary- and university-level schools.[43] In addition, considerable resources have been expended on upgrading military academies and schools. These well-publicized efforts are aimed at attracting students to military rather than civilian education.[44]

It has also been increasingly difficult to interest military personnel in party membership, in spite of the career benefits that membership offers. In fact, military personnel are constantly reprimanded for their general lack of interest in the political life of the society. Concern that military men are failing to exercise their right to vote is a manifestation of this problem.[45]

All of these difficulties have led many to question the effectiveness and reliability of the ČLA. Indeed, the size of the ČLA has declined since 1968.[46] In this era of increasing involvement of Soviet allies in the Third

World, the Czechoslovak military has been much less active than the East German military. The ČLA, it seems, has an image problem, both with the Soviet sponsor and in the domestic environment. The mammoth media effort to publicize the technical proficiency of the ČLA and to herald its importance to the Czechoslovak society continues, though there is no evidence that it has been successful.

The fact is that in always antimilitaristic Czechoslovakia, the events of 1968 have destroyed the carefully sculptured prestige of the military. The failure of the army (reasons notwithstanding) to fight upon invasion in 1968 reinforced the old image of the military as subservient, expensive, and useless. In 1968, the military was changing and becoming an interested party in the political rejuvenation of the society. But the inability to defend the sovereignty of the country was a stigma from which the ČLA has apparently yet to recover.

The postinvasion period has been marked by a return to political inactivity on the part of the military. In the absence of the political upheavals of the 1968 period, party checks and military disinterest have once again relegated the ČLA to political isolation. Without the active participation of the Czechoslovak Communist party in reshaping the society and without the party-military dialogue that developed in 1968, the military once again appears disinterested. With the return of the Czechoslovak Communist party to full client status, the important actor in military and foreign policy matters is once again exclusively the Soviet sponsor. Participation in the indigenous political process could not possibly guarantee a voice in the matters that concern the military elite. This circumstance contributes to, perhaps in part causes, the political isolation of the military elite.

NOTES

    1. Communist sources claim that there were 531 Soviet military personnel in the Czechoslovak army in 1945-1946. At the same time there were 16,396 in the Polish army. Colonel M. Monin, "Internationalizm v Deistvi," Voenno-Istoricheski Zhurnal 6 (Moscow, 1967), p. 12. This claim is supported by United States intelligence, which claims that few Soviet advisers were in evidence in Czechoslovakia until 1949. Department of State telegram, June 7, 1949 (files of the U.S. Department of State, declassified United States intelligence). Both reports insist that the number of Soviet advisers decreased during the coalition period.

    2. Program prvé československé vlády národni fronty čechu a slováku přijatého na schuzi vlády v Košicich dne: 5 dubna (Nase Vojsko, 1961). (Hereafter referred to as Program prve československe vlady narodni fronty.)

3. Ibid., p. 1.
4. Ibid., p. 2.
5. Ludvik Svoboda, "Z Buzuluku do Prahy," Mlada Fronta, April 12, 1960.
6. A. V. Antosyak et al., Zarozhdenie Narodniya Armii Stran Uchastnii Varshavskogo Dogovora (Izdatelstvo Moscow: "Nauka," 1975).
7. Program prvé československe vlády národni fronty, p. 3.
8. Jaromir Navratil, "K Otazce Boje o Politicky Character Armady v Predunovem," Historie a Vojenstvi, vol. 3 (Prague, 1958), p. 425.
9. Ibid., p. 9. Also corroborated by a United States intelligence Report of the Strategic Services Unit, September 16, 1946 (files of the Department of State, declassified United States intelligence).
10. Antosyak, Zarozhdenie Narodniya Armii, p. 82.
11. Ibid.
12. Ibid., p. 83.
13. Report of the Central Intelligence Group, May 20, 1947 (files of the U.S. Department of State, declassified United States intelligence).
14. Antosyak, Zarozhdenie Narodniya Armii, p. 86.
15. Program prve ceskoslovense vlady narodni fronty, p. 4.
16. Ibid.
17. "Věcni Věstník Ministererstva Národní Obrany dne 10, záři, 1945," in Jaroslav Žižka, Volby a Ozbrojené Síly CSSR: Pracovníci Archivni Správy (Naše vojsko, Prague, 1976).
18. Report of the Central Intelligence Group, May 24, 1949 (files of the U.S. Department of State, declassified United States intelligence).
19. Report of the Strategic Services Unit, May 6, 1946 (files of the U.S. Department of State, declassified United States intelligence).
20. "Z Projevu Ludvika Svobody Na Zářijovem Plénu Uv KSC," Svědectvi (Paris) 10, no. 38 (1970), pp. 293-294. Svoboda claimed that he played a role in forcing Beneš to accept the "solution of February, 1948." Since the "admission" was made in the immediate postinvasion environment when it was expedient for Svoboda to emphasize his long-standing Communist commitments, however, this interpretation must be subject to some doubt.
21. Report of the Central Intelligence Group, May 24, 1949 (files of the U.S. Department of State, declassified United States intelligence).
22. Report of the United States Political Adviser for Germany, May 26, 1949 (files of the U.S. Department of State, declassified United States intelligence).
23. Antosyak, Zarozhdenie Narodniya Armii, p. 90.
24. Ibid.
25. Ibid.

26. United Nations Statistical Yearbooks: 1952-54 (New York: United Nations).
27. Antosyak, Zarozhdenie Narodniya Armii, p. 77.
28. Report of the Joint Intelligence Committee, April 1, 1948 (files of the U.S. Department of State, declassified United States intelligence).
29. A Ross Johnson, Robert Dean, and Alexander Alexiev, East European Military Establishments: The Warsaw Pact Northern Tier (Santa Monica, Calif.: RAND Corporation Report R-2417/1-AF/FF, December 1980).
30. A fuller discussion of the changing role of the ČLA in Soviet security plans may be found in Johnson et al., East European Military Establishments.
31. A-Revue, July 12, 1965.
32. Ibid.
33. Ibid.
34. See interviews with Maj. Gen. Egyd Pepich in Obrana Lidu, February 23, 1968 and in A-Revue (with Jiří Reindl), 1969, no. 10.
35. Ibid.
36. Ibid.
37. "How Czechoslovak State Interests in the Military Are to be Formulated," Lidova Armada, no. 3, July 2, 1968.
38. Zdeněk Mlynář, Nightfront in Prague: The End of Humane Socialism (New York: Karz Publishers, 1980). p. 148.
39. For extensive treatment of the question of Soviet military elite attitudes on the state of the Czechoslovak military see Jiri Valenta, Soviet Intervention in Czechoslovakia (Baltimore: Johns Hopkins Press, 1979), pp. 108-114.
40. Robert W. Dean, "The Political Consolidation of the Czechoslovak People's Army," Radio Free Europe Research, Czechoslovakia/April 29, 1979.
41. "Rumor or Fact?," Mlada Fronta, March 19, 1969.
42. "General Korbela Explains New Soviet Troop Accord," in Foreign Broadcast Information Service, Daily Report on Eastern Europe, February 14, 1969, p. D1.
43. Rude Pravo, June 12, 1970, p. 2.
44. Albin Pukančik and František Sčučka, New Training Equipment in the Antonin Zapotocky Military Academy, translation from the Czech by the Defense Documentation Center (Prague: Nase vojsko, May 21, 1974).
45. "Soldiers Urged to Vote in General Election," in Zapisnik, September 17, 1971 (Joint Publications Research Service, October 21, 1971).

9
The Romanian Army

Alex Alexiev

One of the most significant developments in Eastern Europe during the past decade and a half has been the remarkable Romanian challenge of Soviet interests and hegemony in the foreign-political field. Alongside the well-publicized Romanian foreign-political deviation there has also been an important, if largely unexplored, Romanian military deviation from established norms of behavior in the Soviet-dominated Warsaw Pact. As a result, the Romanian army has been transformed from an obedient, Soviet-controlled tool of party policy into a truly national military establishment, responsive only to the national political authority and espousing a national military doctrine that openly questions Soviet military hegemony in the bloc and negates the coalition warfare doctrine dominant in the Warsaw Pact. This chapter will attempt to document this transformation of the Romanian military by following the various stages of its evolution from the Communist takeover to the present.

Prior to the establishment of Communist rule, the Romanian army had an undistinguished record. Its most significant and certainly most consequential military involvement had been Romanian participation in World War II on the German side. Eager to recover the Romanian territories of Bessarabia and northern Bukovina, seized by the Soviets in the aftermath of the Nazi-Soviet pact in 1940, the Romanian army participated enthusiastically in the Nazi onslaught of the Soviets from the very beginning of the war. In the process, the Romanians occupied sizable Soviet territories above and beyond

---

This chapter is based in part on material contained in Alex Alexiev, <u>Romania and the Warsaw Pact: The Defense Policy of a Reluctant Ally</u>, The Rand Corporation, P-6270, January 1979.

the Romanian irredenta, took part in battles as far as Stalingrad, and suffered tremendous casualties.¹

In late August 1944, the Red Army pursuing the retreating Germans crossed the Romanian border and occupied the country. Several days earlier, on August 23, a palace coup had resulted in the removal of the pro-German government, and Romania gingerly switched sides, participating in the war against its erstwhile allies until the end. As in all other East European countries, the introduction of Soviet troops in Romania marked the beginning of the process of establishing a Communist social system in the state and all of its institutions, including the military.

THE SUBORDINATION OF THE ARMY TO PARTY CONTROL

The imposition of party control over the Romanian army, despite Soviet occupation of the country, proceeded at a rather slow pace at first and was not completed until the end of 1947. There are several reasons for this uncharacteristically deliberate process. First, the Soviet high command was obviously determined to avoid anything that might undermine the Romanian contribution to the war effort until final victory over Germany was achieved. Second, for the first six months after the Romanian coup d'etat of August 23, 1944, the government, although under strong pressure from the Communists and the Soviet authorities, was by no means totally dominated by them and did preserve a modicum of independence. Finally, there was an acute shortage of reliable party cadres that could be entrusted with the reorganization of the military establishment along traditional Communist lines. Unlike the situation in some other East European countries, in Romania there had been no significant partisan movement during the war. The Romanian Communist party, with a pre-1944 membership of little more than 1,000, could hardly provide the needed activists. Under these circumstances, the only readily available pool of cadres on which the party could rely was to be found in the ranks of the former Romanian prisoners of war on the eastern front who had been "reeducated," indoctrinated by the Soviets, and organized in an infantry division named after the nineteenth-century Romanian hero Tudor Vladimirescu.² Yet even those cadres were not immediately available as most of them were at the front.

In the period between August 23 and the installation of the first completely Communist-dominated government in March 1945, initial efforts toward the political and propagandistic penetration of the army were mainly undertaken by Soviet occupation authorities and the Soviet-dominated Allied Control Commission. Apart from purging the most pro-German and compromised Romanian generals immediately upon entering the country, the Soviets engaged in wide-ranging propagandistic activities in the Romanian army

designed to prepare the ground for the politicization of
the military. Although Romanian law prohibited political
activities in the army, an exception was made under Soviet
pressure for a newly formed society for Soviet-Romanian
friendship (ARLUS) that became extremely active as an
agitprop organ and published the only all-army newspaper
at the time. Considerable propagandistic effort was also
expended by the political administration of the Second
Ukrainian Front occupying the country, which, among other
things, published its own Romanian language newspaper and
other propaganda materials.

During the same period, the Soviets also provided
the fledgling Romanian party with considerable help in
setting up special paramilitary units called Patriotic
Combat Formations (<u>Formatiunile de Lupta Patriotice</u>),
which were directly subordinated to the party. Although
a few of these units may have been organized as early as
the spring of 1944, it was only after August 1944 that
their numbers grew significantly, reaching 60,000 by
March 1945.[3] These paramilitary units were to play a
crucial role in the consolidation of Communist rule in the
country as a whole and in the military later on.[4] Despite
these early efforts, however, the Romanian army remained
by and large independent of Communist control as late as
February 1945, when military units were used by the government
to suppress a pro-Communist demonstration.

The consolidation of Communist power in the military
was dramatically accelerated upon the installation of the
first Communist-dominated regime under Petru Groza on
March 6, 1945, following a Soviet ultimatum. The new
regime almost immediately initiated a wide-ranging purge
of high-ranking officers considered particularly unreliable.
By the end of the month, 71 generals and 120
colonels had been ousted.[5] The purge, which was conducted
under the direct supervision and perhaps on the instructions
of the Soviet representatives in the Allied Control
Commission, continued unabated in the months to follow.
According to one Soviet source, the number of officers
purged during 1945 amounted to 30 percent of the entire
officer corps.[6]

A further important step toward the political
<u>gleichschaltung</u> of the Romanian military was taken in
May 1945 with the introduction of Soviet-style political
controls in the army. This was accomplished with the
creation of a Main Administration for Culture, Education,
and Propaganda on May 8, 1945. The first contingent of
the so-called cultural-educational workers, whose functions
were patterned on those of the Soviet <u>zampolit</u>, were recruited
from the ranks of party activists serving in the
Tudor Vladimirescu Division. There is some evidence,
however, that the political penetration of the army by
party militants met with considerable resistance in the
officer corps for some time, which required direct Soviet

intervention on a number of occasions.[7]

A new source of reliable party activists became available to the regime after the formation of a second Romanian volunteer division in the Soviet Union in the spring of 1945. This new division, called <u>Horia-Closca-Crisan</u>, did not and probably was not intended to take part in combat operations but did play a significant political role upon its return to Romania. Another 500 thoroughly reeducated and indoctrinated former Romanian officers were repatriated from the Soviet Union and integrated in the army in 1946.[8]

Under Soviet tutelage, the party also took steps to assure its control of the military-educational institutions. The old system of military education was replaced by a new network of officer and noncommissioned officer schools that offered admission and preferential treatment on the basis of social origin and political loyalty. A school center for training of political officers established in October 1945 was given the task of producing reliable cadres in short intensive courses. By July 1947 it had placed at the disposal of the party 331 officers.[9] At about the same time, the Romanian Communist party began setting up party organizations and cells in military units, despite the fact that political activities and organizations continued to be illegal according to the country's laws.

Nineteen forty-five also marked the beginning of direct control of the Romanian armed forces by Soviet "advisers." In the summer of that year, for example, Soviet officers were directly appointed to key positions in the general staff, the navy and coastal defense commands, the military school centers, etc.[10]

The determined efforts of the Romanian Communist party and its Soviet sponsors, initiated in 1945, to establish political hegemony in the army were pursued energetically in 1946-1947. Politically suspect officers continued to be subjected to pressure and purges. In August 1946 alone, 9,000 officers and 5,000 noncommissioned officers were removed from the army for suspected disloyalty.[11] Attempts were made to alleviate the resulting shortages of qualified military professionals through the rapid promotion of trustworthy cadres. Thus, by mid-1946 close to 16,000 officers and sergeants were reported to have been promoted, with loyalty to the party often being the sole criterion.[12]

The process of consolidating party control in the military as well as in the country as a whole was largely completed by December 1947. Politically, the establishment of unquestioned Communist hegemony was signaled by the forced abdication of the king and the proclamation of the Romanian People's Republic on December 30, 1947. In the military realm, party supremacy was marked by the appointment of Politburo member Emil Bodnaras as minister of defense.

THE SOVIETIZATION OF THE ROMANIAN ARMY

With party control of the armed forces firmly secured, beginning in 1948 the Romanian army entered a period characterized by a massive restructuring of the military establishment patterned on the Soviet model. In every area of military life traditional Romanian practices were abandoned and Soviet ones introduced instead. Red Army military regulations, training manuals, and service practices were introduced throughout the army. The military-educational system was brought into conformity with the Soviet one, as were uniforms, equipment, and armaments. Direct Soviet control was assured by the appointment of advisers in all key command positions, as well as in all units down to the regimental level.

To a much greater extent than before, the political leadership sought to mold the army into an obedient and ideologically militant tool of party policy. Although party supremacy in the military had already been accomplished, the number of dedicated Communist activists remained relatively small. At the end of 1947, for instance, only 5.5 percent of the officers and 7.5 percent of the noncommissioned officers were party members.[13] There continued to serve large numbers of professional officers who had begun their careers under the pre-Communist regime and who were of doubtful ideological militancy. There were also many officers who were suspect because of their "undesirable" social origin, from the party point of view. As of December 1947, for example, only 29 percent of the officer corps had a "progressive" social origin, that is, were proletarians and poor peasants; 71 percent were from other less desirable categories. Included among the latter were 28 percent kulaks and capitalists--categories that were considered actively hostile to the new order.[14] It became an overriding goal of party efforts in the military field to totally politicize and indoctrinate the officer corps and assure that its members were not only loyal but committed to the Communist world view.

Several decisive steps toward accomplishing this objective were taken at various party forums early in 1948. The main effort was directed toward perfecting the instrumentalities of political control and the replacement of apolitical or suspect officers with activists. The new cadres were selected in several different ways. For many of the most important positions the leadership simply mobilized trusted political functionaries, assigned them the appropriate military rank, and entrusted them with key responsibilities, although most of them had not had any prior military experience or training. Three hundred eighty-five such functionaries were commissioned in 1948, 509 the year after, and 1,053 in 1950.[15] Among them was the present Romanian party boss and president, Nicolae Ceausescu, who was given the rank of major-general and appointed chief of the Main Political Administration in 1950.[16]

Large numbers of new officers were selected from among the noncommissioned ranks and the politically active soldiers. Usually they were commissioned as junior officers after attending several weeks of preparatory courses. Some 600 sergeants were commissioned in this way in 1949 alone.[17] These efforts brought quick results in the direction desired by the party. The percentage of new officers was only 3.51 percent in December 1947, but it had jumped to 18 percent in 1948, 46 percent in 1949, and 51 percent in 1950.[18]

Particular attention was paid to increasing the number of officers with proletarian and, to a lesser extent, peasant backgrounds. Social origin became a major if not the only criterion in such matters as military school admissions and promotion policies. Quotas were introduced at most military-educational institutions that severely limited the prospects of students from nonproletarian origins.

Throughout the late 1940s and early 1950s, the purging of officers from the ancien régime kept pace with the new commissions. The early 1950s also witnessed the first purges of Communist officers accused of various deviations and often tried on fabricated charges. Although the evidence available at present is scant and does not permit an elaborate examination, there are nonetheless some clues that such purges may have been rather large-scale. One Romanian source reveals, for example, that the number of party members and candidate-members in the army had declined from a high of 18,207 in 1950 to 14,700 in 1951 and 13,885 in 1953.[19]

The complete subordination of the officer corps and the restructuring of the military establishment was largely completed by 1955, at which time close to 90 percent of the officers corps consisted of new cadres, and some 85 percent had a progressive social origin.[20]

THE RENATIONALIZATION OF THE ROMANIAN MILITARY

In the second half of the 1950s, the Romanian military, along with most other East European military establishments, began to undergo a gradual process of modernization and renationalization triggered by the destalinization process in the Soviet Union. The military modernization, which was expressed mainly in the increasing professionalization of the officer corps and the reequipment of the army with modern weaponry, picked up momentum in the late 1950s and early 1960s, and by the mid-1960s the army was a far cry from the politically pliant but militarily incompetent establishment of the earlier period. An important watershed was reached in 1958 with the withdrawal of Soviet troops from Romania and the drastic curtailment of the activities of the Soviet advisers.

The development of the Romanian establishment and defense attitude from the mid-1960s on increasingly reflected the country's changing political realities brought about by the Romanian drive for independence from Soviet hegemony. Originally started as a revolt against Soviet policies of economic integration in Eastern Europe, considered detrimental to Romanian national interests, the pursuit of independence quickly resulted in a marked deviation from foreign-political, economic, and military-political behavior in the Soviet bloc. An early turning point was reached in August of 1968 when party leader Ceausescu boldly denounced the Soviet invasion of Czechoslovakia and declared Romanian resolve to resist militarily any Soviet incursion into Romania. At the basis of the country's new course was a determination to place perceived national interests above those of the Soviet Union or international communism whenever they conflicted. The new external political conditions created by the party's challenge of the Soviet Union dramatically changed the role and political importance of the army. Faced with a serious external threat from Moscow, the Romanian Communist party has now come to rely on the army for protection and support of its new policies. As a result of this unique--for a Warsaw Pact country--situation, the Romanian army has undergone some startling changes in terms of its position in society: party-military relations, defense doctrine and its role, and participation in the Warsaw Pact.

Perhaps the aspect of the Romanian challenge of Soviet hegemony most salient for the military has been the intensive propagation of nationalism as the surrogate ideology of the Romanian deviation. In the process of mobilizing public support on the basis of a nationalist revival, the party has sought to present itself as the legitimate guardian of traditional national interests and historic Romanian aspirations. An important corollary of this policy has been a wide-ranging reassessment and rehabilitation of the role of the military in Romanian history. The official party reinterpretation of the historical role of the army has been characterized by an effort to present it as an invariably progressive force in the struggle for achieving Romanian national ideals. In pursuing this objective, the Romanian Communist party has not only parted company with the traditional Marxist condemnation of bourgeois military establishments as reliable tools of oppression but also admitted its own erroneous stands in the past. Of particular importance here have been attempts to exonerate the role played by the Romanian army during World War II.[21] No less significant have been the numerous rehabilitations of officers who were purged after the Communist takeover.[22] These new party attitudes have resulted in the restoration of the Romanian military to its traditional place in society as a repository and defender of cherished national ideals.

In practical terms, the renationalization process has found its expression in the reintroduction of Romanian military norms and traditions and the wholesale abandonment of Soviet precepts and practices in the army. On yet another level, the party has significantly relaxed its once pervasive political control of the military through a thorough reorganization of the political apparatus.[23] This has given the professional military considerable autonomy. The relative emancipation of the military has led to its growing responsibility in such areas of traditional military jurisdiction as military doctrine, defense organization, and armaments that had been exclusively the party preserve. The net result has been the establishment of a much more equitable relationship between the military and political elements as well as the emergence of the Romanian army as a modern national military establishment enjoying a substantial degree of professional autonomy and free of subservience to an external political factor--Soviet hegemony. For the first time in Romanian postwar history, the army also assumed its traditional role as the societal institution solely responsible for the country's defense.

THE NEW ROMANIAN DEFENSE DOCTRINE

During the years of the Romanian drive for political and economic autonomy from Soviet tutelage, Romanian defense concepts and priorities have undergone some startling changes resulting in a defense posture radically different from that of the other pact partners--one that assumes a Soviet threat and prepares only for defensive war on Romanian territory. These changes have affected both the doctrinal-theoretical foundations of Romanian defense and the practical objectives and organization of the armed forces.

The most important development in the military theoretical field has been the evolution of a coherent Romanian national defense doctrine based on a set of principles designed to reflect specific Romanian conditions and defense priorities. The critical innovation of the new doctrine has been the elevation of the concept of *national* defense as the guiding principle of Romanian defense.[24] This, of course, represents a major break with traditional Warsaw Pact doctrine, which is premised on the collective, Soviet-led defense of the "socialist commonwealth." National defense in the Romanian concept is proclaimed the exclusive prerogative of the nation-state and is only valid within the national territory.[25] Its sole objectives are the preservation of national independence, state sovereignty, and the territorial integrity of the country.[26] Implicit in the above concept is a rejection of supranational mechanisms and military integration, which is the

professed goal of the Warsaw Pact. In this respect the
Romanians have consistently stressed their determination
to maintain strictly national command over the armed forces.
Party leader and President Ceausescu, for instance, has
stated bluntly that "it is impossible to conceive ceding
the right to command and lead the Armed Forces to an outside organ,"[27] and Defense Minister Ionita has rejected
surrendering sovereignty in military matters to "supranational bodies."[28]

The Romanian defense doctrine further specifies the
type and manner of conduct of a potential war in which the
country could be involved. Except for an occasional vague
reference to fulfilling Romania's international obligations--that is, Warsaw Pact commitments--military theoreticians and party leaders alike continually assert that the
only war in which Romania may be forced to participate will
be a defensive war on Romanian territory. The official
Romanian attitude on this point is stated succinctly in
the following excerpt from a 1976 speech by Ceausescu to
the armed forces leading cadres:

> Given the country's geographic position, the equipment and training of the army should be based on
> the concept of defensive war....As you see, I do
> not speak of strategic objectives since we do not
> intend to go outside our frontiers....We have no
> other strategy than to make sure that Romanian
> land does not fall prey to imperialist aggression,
> to a policy of strength.[29]

The method of conducting a national war of defense,
according to the new Romanian doctrine, is the transformation of any armed conflict on Romanian territory into a
people's war.[30] This concept, which is quite similar to
the Yugoslav doctrine of Total National Defense, is without precedent in Warsaw Pact military doctrine and has a
specifically defensive and deterrent character. By incorporating the nation-in-arms principle, a notion long
rejected by Soviet military theoreticians as utopian and
"unscientific," the Romanians have sought an answer to
what they believe to be their most serious defense
problem--facing an aggressor who enjoys tremendous
numerical as well as technological superiority. Military
writers have argued, for example, that a people's war
strategy would allow the country to mobilize up to 50 percent of the able-bodied population, amounting to some 6
million people, for the defense effort.[31] Finally, the
Romanian defense doctrine envisions the possibility of
temporary occupation of the country and emphasizes the
imperative of a protracted and organized guerrilla warfare against the enemy.

In accordance with the postulates of the new Romanian
defense doctrine, the organization and structure of

Romanian defense has undergone some major changes that
have further accentuated its unique character among Warsaw
Pact members. The most important change has been the
restructuring of the defense organization to make it reflect the concept of people's war. Following the Soviet
invasion of Czechoslovakia, Romania undertook several
measures to enhance its defense credibility. These were
later codified in the 1972 Law on National Defense. Most
relevant among them were the setting up of an extensive
system of paramilitary organizations and compulsory civilian
participation in defense preparations. The most widespread
form of defense participation is in the Patriotic Guards,
a militia organization in which a majority of able-bodied
civilians are organized. These "worker-peasant" armed
units were first (and not coincidentally) proclaimed by
Ceausescu on August 21, 1968, the day of the Soviet invasion of Czechoslovakia, and officially decreed two weeks
later.[32]

Participation in the Patriotic Guards is compulsory
for all Romanian citizens, except members of the armed
forces and other military organizations, regardless of sex,
up to the age of sixty-two for men and fifty-seven for
women. The guards are organized on the territorial principle, they are trained and equipped by the Ministry of
Defense, and they will be under the jurisdiction of local
military commanders in case of war.[33] They are further
expected to perform internal security functions and form
the backbone of organized guerrilla resistance in case of
enemy occupation of the country. In peacetime, the
Patriotic Guards have an independent vertical structure
headed by a general staff. There have been reports that
in some cases up to 40 percent of the population has been
included in the guards' units.[34]

Another form of civilian participation in defense is
the Local Air Defense Formations. These units, participation in which is again compulsory, are organized at all
territorial administrative levels down to the borough,
as well as in economic enterprises and institutions with
more than 100 employees.[35] Local Air Defense Formations
are under the control of the Ministry of Defense through
a Local Air Defense command. Romanian defense doctrine
emphasizes involving Romanian youth in the preparations
for defense. The organizational form through which this
is achieved is the Youth Homeland Defense Formation,
compulsory for all Romanians between the ages of sixteen
and twenty and organized in all schools, places of work,
and communities.[36] The formations are organized in units
of up to sixty members under the command of a reserve
officer or noncommissioned officer and receive combat training at special military training centers set up by the
Defense Ministry. The proportions of this effort could be
glimpsed from a 1972 report that revealed 650,000 Romanian
students were receiving military training in the school

system alone.[37] The setting up of a complex system of civilian participation in defense has been accompanied by a reorganization of the command structure of Romanian defense to reflect the new posture. In particular, this has included the introduction of a new organ of defense authority--the Defense Council of the Socialist Republic of Romania.[38] The Defense Council, whose membership consists of the top military and political leaders and is headed by the commander in chief, is a decision-making body charged by law with all vital defense functions in peace and in war. It has no equivalent in any of the other Warsaw Pact countries.[39] It has centralized defense authority and has effectively subordinated other military decision-making bodies to the commander in chief. Introduced shortly after the Soviet invasion of Czechoslovakia, the Defense Council could be seen as a possible Romanian reaction to the failure of the Czechoslovak military to act, as well as an effort to streamline command channels. Local defense councils have also been established throughout the country down to the local level and given considerable authority at the local level in time of war, in an apparent effort to insure the continuation of military resistance in the event of a breakdown of national command channels or the occupation of the country.

INDIGENOUS ARMS

As an integral part of the Romanian deviation in the military sphere, the country has engaged in an intensive effort to achieve a degree of self-reliance in armaments. As one of the socialist countries with a low technological-industrial base, Romania became totally dependent on Soviet weapons after World War II. Realizing that such a dependence was not only incompatible with their new defense posture but effectively precluded it (particularly because the country's exclusive supplier also happened to be the potential aggressor), in the late 1960s the Romanians declared their resolve to develop an indigenous arms industry and seek alternative suppliers.[40] Since then, numerous writings have forcefully restated the rationale and the correctness of this Romanian policy. Its primary objective is seen as limiting as much as possible the influence of factors--that is, Soviet influence--outside the control of Romanian decision makers on arms supplies and production. Romanian domestic production is also said to be an answer to high import prices and especially to political pressures by "exporters who impose restrictive measures."[41]

The actual development of the Romanian defense industry has been characterized by two parallel trends: the massive production of low-technology weapons and equipment for the needs of the Romanian army and paramilitary forces; and a quest to procure high-technology-weapons expertise under license or in joint ventures with non-Soviet sources. Given the low starting point and their lack of technological capacities, the Romanians have already achieved considerable success. In the area of low-technology weaponry, outside of an assortment of small arms and ammunition, the Romanians produce artillery pieces, antipersonnel weapons, multiple-rocket launchers, and a variety of military vehicles. Romania has also begun production, jointly with Yugoslavia, of spare parts for equipment of Soviet origin.[42]

Of much greater interest militarily as well as politically are Romania's remarkable efforts in the high-technology area. The most spectacular achievement here has been the joint Yugoslav-Romanian construction of a modern twin-jet fighter named IAR-93 in the Romanian version and ORAO (Eagle) in the Yugoslav version. The plane, which is the first non-Soviet fighter to be introduced in the Warsaw Pact, is equipped with Rolls Royce engines. It was first test-flown in 1975 and is expected to enter serial production soon.[43]

The success of the Romanian military industry is apparently the result of a concerted drive dating from the late 1960s to build a Romanian aviation capacity. At present, the Romanians possess a modern aircraft plant at Bacau and produce both British and German civilian aircraft under license. In another related development, the Romanians contracted for French Alouette helicopters and have been producing them under license since 1971. As of 1976 Romania was also building the more advanced PUMA helicopters.[44] A considerable number of Alouettes are now reportedly deployed in the army. Further ventures have included the building of Chinese torpedo boats under license, which must be considered a major provocation to the Soviets.[45] A recent Romanian interest in acquiring a powerful West German diesel engine has prompted Western speculation that the Romanians are either planning to modify their Soviet T-55 tanks or are building a new tank.[46] It should be noted, however, that despite concerted Romanian efforts to build an indigenous arms industry, the country is still dependent on imports for a considerable share of its armaments. One Western source has estimated that Romania produces about 75 percent of its requirements for military hardware.[47]

RELATIONS WITH THE WARSAW PACT

Given the rationale of the Romanian quest for independence--autonomy from Soviet domination--it is not difficult to imagine that relations with the Warsaw Pact and the character of Romanian participation in the pact have experienced the greatest metamorphosis during the deviation. Realizing that the Soviet Union would not tolerate an outright Romanian withdrawal from the pact, Romania has remained a nominal member but has done everything possible to minimize the Warsaw Pact's organizational ability to influence the country's affairs. Although seeking with considerable success to hold its obligations to the Warsaw Pact to a minimum, Romania has continued to participate in the pact's military bodies and has from time to time actively sought to frustrate Soviet intentions in these organs.

A watershed in Romania's attitudes toward the Warsaw Pact was reached in 1968 with the Soviet invasion of Czechoslovakia. Romania felt acutely threatened herself and not only angrily denounced the invasion as a "flagrant violation of national sovereignty and recognized principles of international law" but openly declared her resolve to militarily resist any similar violation of her sovereignty by the "fraternal armies."[48] A recurrent theme in Bucharest's attitude toward the pact both before and especially after the invasion has been its consistent rejection of any Warsaw Pact right (a right asserted by the Brezhnev doctrine) to interfere in the internal affairs of any of the member states. As Ceausescu has put it, "We have never for a moment conceived the Warsaw Pact as a reason for justifying interferences in the internal affairs of other states."[49] Several other issues that run directly or indirectly counter to basic Warsaw Pact tenets have become an integral part of the Romanian military-political Weltanschauung. Among these are the issues of military blocs, foreign bases, and maneuvers, as well as character of the Warsaw Pact itself.

Romania has for years consistently advocated the dissolution of military blocs. Although the Soviets also usually pay lip service to this doctrine, the Romanians have introduced an important nuance by claiming that all military blocs (and not only NATO) are an obstacle to peace and cooperation among the peoples.[50] Bucharest's fear of another Warsaw Pact invasion, like the 1968 invasion of Czechoslovakia but at Romania's expense, has been reflected in its uncompromising views of foreign troops and bases and maneuvers across national borders. Ever since the mid-1960s, the Romanians have repeatedly stated that they regard all foreign military bases and the stationing of foreign troops as a violation of state sovereignty and have vowed never to allow such activities on Romanian soil. Foreign bases and troops are further said to create conditions for political pressure and interference in the internal affairs of sovereign states.[51] Romania has just as vigorously opposed multinational maneuvers and maneuvers outside the national territory. In one case, through its representative at the Geneva disarmament conference, Romania made a proposal outlawing maneuvers by troops of one country on another country's territory.[52]

Romania's interpretation of the Warsaw Pact's

objectives and character is also significant. From the very beginning of their independent stance, the Romanians have tended to see the Warsaw Pact more as a traditional military alliance of sovereign states than as a military fraternity of socialist countries who share an identical ideology, social system, and the same objectives. They have firmly denied that the pact has any bloc internal political or integrative functions and have rejected the Soviet interpretation of the organization as a supranational form of socialist cooperation and integration. The only purpose of the alliance is seen as joint defense in case of aggression against one of the member states. The Romanians are also careful to show that they do not consider themselves obligated to assist their allies in any non-European or nondefensive conflict. In a typical commentary, the pact's provisions are said to become binding "only in the event of aggression against one of the European socialist countries which are members of the Pact." The provisions "refer to the event of an armed attack in Europe...and do not allow extension of the attributes of the Pact to areas not under the jurisdiction of the Pact."[53] In addition, Bucharest has its own unique position on the question of military cooperation in the Warsaw Pact. The basic principle of this position in effect indirectly denies the need for such cooperation by arguing that the strength of the pact is best served by the independent improvement of the national armies.

Given the circumstances of their continuing membership in the pact, the Romanians have practiced what they preach to a remarkable degree. Since 1962 they have refused to allow foreign troops on Romanian soil for maneuvers and have themselves not participated in any exercise outside Romania since 1969.[54] The presence of foreign troops on Romanian territory, for whatever reason, has been made extremely difficult by a special Defense Law stipulation that such a presence requires the specific approval of the nation's highest forum--the Grand National Assembly. The only exceptions have been a few limited map exercises for Warsaw Pact staff officers. Romania has further refused to grant transit rights to Soviet troops going to maneuvers in Bulgaria and has apparently firmly rejected Soviet demands for a permanent corridor and a broad-gauge railroad line through eastern Romania.[55] Romanian recalcitrance in cooperation with the Warsaw Pact has not been restricted to the issue of maneuvers. On numerous occasions, the Romanians have disagreed with their allies on various pact matters, and they have gone so far as to challenge Soviet domination of the pact by suggesting that the leading positions be rotated among the member countries. In addition, the Romanians have stopped sending their officers to Soviet military schools and staff academies and, according to a knowledgeable Czech defector, terminated intelligence cooperation with the Soviets as early as the mid-1960s.[56]

CONCLUSION

The foregoing analysis of the evolution of the Romanian army offers some insights pertinent to the study of Communist armies in general. First and foremost, the Romanian military deviation has shown rather conclusively that nationalism remained a powerful force in a Communist society subjected to decades of Soviet domination and inculcation in Leninist universalist dogma. The Romanian military establishment and its officer corps have remained loyal to the national political authority in its quarrel with Moscow despite long years of tutelage and indoctrination in Soviet-style proletarian internationalism. The ease with which the Romanian military rejected long-espoused Soviet military norms and doctrine and reverted to a national orientation in all facets of military endeavor is a testimony that Soviet military practices and values may have been only superficially accepted during the years of Soviet hegemony. Finally, the study of the Romanian army shows that even in a Communist society the military often exhibits the traditional predilection for a degree of professional autonomy and continues to view itself as the guardian of national interests.

NOTES

1. According to Marshal A. Grechko, ed., <u>Osvoboditelnaya Missiya Sovetskikh Vooruzhenikh Sil V Vtoroi Mirovoi Voine</u> (Moscow: Voenizdat, 1974), p. 133, Romania fielded some thirty divisions on the Soviet front and suffered 600,000 casualties of which 400,000 resulted in death.
2. For details see A. B. Antosyak, ed., <u>Zarozhdenie Narodniya Armii Stran Uchastnii Varshavskogo Dogovora--1941-1949</u> (Moscow: Nauka, 1975), pp. 176-183.
3. Ibid., p. 202.
4. See, for example, Maj. Gen. Paul Marinesku and Col. Constantin Olteanu, "Formatiunele Patriotice in Sprijinul Luptei Fortelor Democratice Conduse de Partidul Comunist Roman Pentru Insaurarea Puterii Populare," in Col. Al. Em. Savu, ed., <u>Romania Si Traditiile Luptei Armate A Intregului Popor</u> (Bucharest: Editura Militara, 1972), pp. 182-189.
5. A. B. Antosyak, <u>V. Boyakh Za Svobodu Rumunii</u> (Moscow: Voenizdat, 1974), p. 257.
6. M. M. Minasyan, <u>Osvobozhdenie Narodov Yugo-Vostochnoi Evropii</u> (Moscow) p. 202. See also Ithiel de Sola Pool, <u>Satellite Generals: A Study of Military Elites in the Soviet Sphere</u> (Stanford: Stanford University Press, 1955), pp. 85-88.
7. See Antosyak, <u>Zarozhdenie</u>, pp. 207-209.
8. De Sola Pool, <u>Satellite Generals</u>, p. 85. It is

worth noting that apart from the above-mentioned officers and the personnel of the two volunteer divisions, very few other Romanian POWs returned from the Soviet Union. According to de Sola Pool, a total of 460,000 Romanians were taken prisoner by the Soviets; of these 280,000 were captured after the August 23, 1944, coup turned Romania into a Soviet ally (p. 84).

9. Col. Dr. Aurel Petri, "Activitatea Partidului in Armata in Perioada 1944-47," in Momente din Faurirea si Intarirea Armatei Republicii socialiste Romania (Bucharest: Editara Militara, 1970), p. 116.

10. Antosyak, Zarozhdenie, p. 220.

11. Dionisie Ghermani, "Die Rumanische Volkarmee," in Peter Gosztony, ed., Zur Geschichte der europeaishchen Volksarmeen Hohwacht (Bonn: Verlag, 1976), p. 192.

12. Anale de Istorie, 1964, no. 5, p. 15.

13. Antosyak, Zarozhdenie, p. 222.

14. Col. Mihai Inoan and Col. Oliver Lustig, eds., Armata Romana in Primii Ani Ai Revolutei Si Constructiei Socialiste (Bucharest: Editura Militara, 1973), p. 137.

15. Ibid., p. 140.

16. De Sola Pool, Satellite Generals, p. 93.

17. Inoan and Lustig, Armata Romana, p. 142.

18. Petri, "Activitatea Partidului," p. 90.

19. Lt. Col. Niculae Niculae, "Aspecte Privind Istitutionalizarea Si Dezvoltarea Activitatie Partidului Comunist Roman," in Ilie Ceausescu, ed., File Din Istoria Militara A Poporului Roman (Bucharest: Editura Militara, 1974), vol. 2, p. 138.

20. Inoan and Lustig, Armata Romana, p. 156.

21. For a detailed examination of this issue see A. Alexiev, Party-Military Relations in Eastern Europe: The Case of Romania (Center for Strategic and International Affairs, University of California at Los Angeles, January 1979).

22. Ibid., p. 20.

23. Ibid., pp. 21-23.

24. The most elaborate discussion of all aspects of Romanian defense doctrine is to be found in Apararea Nationala A Romanici Socialiste: Cauza si Opera A Intregului Nostru Papor (Bucharest: Editura Militara, 1974).

25. Col. Trajan Groza, "National Defense Concepts and Principles," in Era Socialista, no. 4, February 1973.

26. Col. Iulian Cernat, "O Manifestare De Prestigiu a Gindirii Militare Romanesti," Viata Militara, November 1973, pp. 16-17.

27. Scinteia, February 6, 1971. Speech to armed forces basic cadres.

28. Romania Libera, June 14, 1976.

29. Scinteia, October 2, 1976.

30. See National Defense: The Romanian View, especially Ch. 4, "General Characteristics of National Defense"

(Bucharest: Military Publishing House, 1976), pp. 74-101.
   31. Ibid., p. 92.
   32. Radio Bucharest, August 21, 1968; and **Bulletinul Oficial**, Decree 3765, September 4, 1968 (Bucharest).
   33. See Col. L. Loghin and Col. Alexander Petricean, "Garzile Patriotice din Romania" (Bucharest: Editura Militara, 1974). See also Lt. Gen. Vasile Milea, "Garzile Patriotice in Sistemul National de Aparare," in **Politic Si Social in Doctrina Militara a Romaniei Socialiste** (Bucharest: Editara Politica, 1974), pp. 99-108.
   34. Radio Free Europe Research (RFER), 1, January 4, 1973, p. 20.
   35. The decree of the Establishment of Local Air Defense Formations was published in **Buletinul Oficial** on December 30, 1972.
   36. See **National Defense: The Romanian View**, pp. 196-200. The draft bill on compulsory military training in youth was passed by the Grand National Assembly in November 1968.
   37. Radio Bucharest, February 2, 1972, translated in FBIS.
   38. The law introducing the Defense Council was published in **Scienteia**, March 15, 1969.
   39. **National Defense: The Romanian View**, p. 255.
   40. The decision to sharply expand and intensify domestic arms production was taken at the April 1968 Plenum of the Romanian Communist party.
   41. Colonel Dinu Buznea and Lieutenant Colonel Georghe Bondei, "The Technical-Scientific Potential and its Role in Providing a National Defense Capacity," in **Lupta de Clasa**, January 1972, translated in JPRS 55539, March 24, 1972.
   42. **Sueddeutsche Zeitung**, April 25, 1975.
   43. The first test flight was reported by the Romanian **Agerpress** news agency and the Yugoslav **Tanjug** in April 1975. The plane's technical specifications can be found in **Air International** 9, no. 1 (July 1975).
   44. **Armees D'Aujourd'hui**, no. 22 (July-August 1977), p. 69.
   45. Ibid. The deployment of six Hu Chwan-class hydrofoil boats and fourteen Shanghai-class MGB boats are reported. See also **Jane's Fighting Ships 1976-1977** (London, 1976).
   46. **Armees D'Aujourd'hui**, no. 22 (July-August 1977), p. 69.
   47. Ibid.
   48. See the communiqué of the plenary session of the Romanian Communist party and leading Romanian bodies, Radio Bucharest, August 21, 1968, and Ceausescu's speech at August 21, 1968, Bucharest rally. Both items are translated in FBIS, August 21, 1968.
   49. See Ceausescu's speech at Galati on July 15, 1968, Radio Bucharest, July 16, 1968, translated in FBIS

Eastern Europe, July 16, 1968, p. H16. For a thinly veiled criticism of the Brezhnev doctrine, see Col. Traian Grozea, "Despre Modele Apararii" [On Defense Models], in Viata Militara, January 1974.

50. See Ceausescu's speech of June 11, 1966, Agerpress, June 11, 1966.

51. See a speech on European security by Gheorghe Apostol, member of the Romanian Communist party's Executive Committee, in Scinteia, July 26, 1967.

52. Christian Science Monitor, March 2, 1970.

53. Radio Bucharest, April 12, 1969, commentary on Budapest meeting of Warsaw Pact Political Consultative Committee by Ion Cirje, translated in FBIS, Eastern Europe, April 14, 1969.

54. Reuters, February 22, 1973, and TASS, May 20, 1969.

55. Soviet pressures on Romania for a corridor have been reported by Western sources on numerous occasions, most recently in June 1974. Romanian officials have neither denied nor confirmed such speculation but have, in one case, stated that even the expression of such a Soviet desire would be "unthinkable." See, for example, the International Herald Tribune, June 13, 1974; Frankfurter Allgemeine Zeitung, June 20, 1974; Deutsche Zeitung, June 20, 1974; and Die Presse, July 11, 1974.

56. See U.S., 98th Congress, Senate, Committee of the Judiciary, Communist Bloc Intelligence Activities in the United States, testimony of Josef Frolik, November 18, 1975.

10
The Mongolian Army

Robert A. Rupen

The Mongolian People's Republic possesses a very small population, about 1.5 million in 1980, and a very large area, approximately 600,000 square miles. It lies between Russia and China and has been politically tilting away from China and toward Russia for most of the twentieth century. Since 1921 it has been governed by a Soviet-style Communist regime and has often been termed the first satellite of the USSR. The MPR, called Outer Mongolia before 1924, retains only remnants of its traditional culture, and its indigenous nationalism has suffered severe blows from Soviet-inspired purges and decades of systematic Communist indoctrination. The country has improved significantly in the areas of health and education and recently has begun notable modernization; a formerly backward traditional society has moved into the mainstream (Soviet-style) of the twentieth century.

China considers Outer Mongolia its own territory and believes that Russia took it illegally. Throughout most of this century the Chinese have unsuccessfully sought ways to retain or restore control over the area. China's military capability was totally inadequate to the task, and her claims usually amounted to no more than empty rhetoric. Russia successfully employed military superiority to deny large-scale settlement in Outer Mongolia, which neutralized almost the only effective weapon the Chinese possessed.

Japan possessed military means, an aggressive will, and immense ambition. For four decades Japan threatened Russia and Mongolia. The USSR feared that large-scale permanent Chinese settlement and/or military aggression by the Japanese army would threaten the narrow Baikal Corridor, which the Trans-Siberian Railroad traverses. The railroad connects European Russia and western Siberia with the thinly populated but territorially vast Transbaikal and Soviet Far East.

Russian, Chinese, and Japanese military-strategic moves, manipulations, and reactions left but a very small field of independence to the Mongols. Russia maintained predominant influence in Mongolia, in great part for defense of Siberia against what it perceived as Japanese and Chinese threats.

EARLY REVOLUTIONARY PERIOD: 1911-1919

Establishment of a Mongolian national army was one of the first moves of the Outer Mongolian government formed after the revolution of 1911. Russia inspired its formation and provided money, arms, instructors, and training to maintain it. Problems of conscription, a high rate of desertion, and riots, rebellions, and mutiny plagued it. The army was unable ever to attain the desired goal of 2,000 men. Perry-Ayscough reported his impression: "These men as seen on parade in March 1913 do not give the idea of trained soldiers in the accepted sense of the term. They are armed with old-style Russian rifles and long calvary sabers. Their appearance is slovenly in the extreme. They wear no uniform, and drill in their native boots."[1]

The national army's political importance probably outweighed its obviously slight military significance. It represented evidence of Russian commitment, support for the shaky central government, encouragement for the Sain Noyan Khan and other pro-Russian Mongols, and a warning to China. It sent other more ambiguous or threatening messages. For example, although the army reinforced the central authority of the Jebtsun Damba Khutukhtu, it also strengthened a potential secular political rival (the Sain Noyan Khan). The Buddhist hierarchy generally was suspicious or openly opposed, even though its organization of 100,000 lamas was not challenged very seriously. The secular princes usually sent only the poorest human material to man the new army. Because the army was such a marginal operation in the society, its effects were limited, but it did represent potential for nation-building, modernization, and even revolutionary change.[2]

Some Russian military units had operated in Outer Mongolia before 1911, but the czarist government committed troops sparingly and reluctantly and attained most of its goals in Mongolia without military confrontation. The Chinese Revolution of October 10, 1911, that overthrew the Manchus (the "Double Tenth") in effect immobilized Chinese forces and opened Urga to predominant Russian influence without a fight. The main battle of the revolution took place in western Mongolia, at Kobdo, where Mongols did the fighting, and the Russians exploited the victory by a subsequent commitment of only a small number of Cossacks. During the 1911-1917 period several kinds of military units were more significant in determining the fate of the area than the tiny Outer Mongolian national army: Russian Cossacks, the Japanese Kwantung Army in southern Manchuria, the forces of charismatic adventurers such as Ja Lama, traditional nomad cavalry units serving independent Mongolian princes (especially Inner Mongols such as Babujav), and the armies of Chinese warlords (such as Chang Tso-lin).

REVOLUTIONS: RUSSIA IN 1917 AND MONGOLIA IN 1921

The Red Army swept across Siberia in 1920, returning to Irkutsk in February, Verkhneudinsk (now Ulan Ude) in March, and Chita in September. Elements of that army occupied Urga, the capital of Outer Mongolia, on July 6, 1921. That occupation resumed the czarist commitment to protect the vulnerable Baikal Corridor by controlling Outer Mongolia, protected Russia's traditional national interest, and was not made for the benefit of the Mongols. The anti-Chinese implications of Russian control of Outer Mongolia accounted for Mongols' pro-Russian orientation. The Mongols needed a powerful Russian protector against the Chinese threat of thorough assimilation that could end the separate culture and perhaps even the existence of the Mongols. They could not possibly defend themselves against Chinese absorption.

During the Russian civil war the Chinese tried to abolish Outer Mongolian autonomy and reestablish full control. Their chances were most favorable while Kolchak was winning in Siberia and driving the Bolsheviks back into European Russia during most of 1919. But Semenov's Pan-Mongol movement, backed by at least 2,000 troops of the Special Manchurian Detachment (OMO), posed a military threat and a political challenge. Semenov, a Buryat Mongol Russian Cossack, had formed a unit of Transbaikal Cossacks while the Provisional Government still ruled. He began to receive Japanese support in February 1918, and that support escalated after Japanese intervention forces landed at Vladivostok in April.

Active Buryat Mongol participation in the Semenov movement, influenced by Pan Mongolism, very likely was one factor influencing Khalkhas, a Mongol sect, to avoid the movement: The lamas of Outer Mongolia never liked or trusted the Buryats, whom they considered half Russian. The holdover Russian representative in Urga, Orlov, and the veteran Chinese government representative, Chen I, united in helping to convince the Jebtsun Damba that he should take no part. The Russian-trained Mongolian national army at that time numbered about 4,000, but Chen I indicated that only 500 of them were actually equipped and ready to fight. Chen I brought the Mongols around to asking China to send troops to fend off the threatened Semenov invasion.[3] Meanwhile the Chinese reinforced their military strength in Urga, and the Japanese stopped aiding Semenov. The danger from Semenov dissipated substantially.

Moreover, the cruel Chinese oppression of the next

eight months overlapped the time when the Bolsheviks returned to Irkutsk (February 1920). The dissension-torn OMO, without Semenov, was captured by the Chinese garrison at Maimaicheng in January 1920, and the figurehead lama leading the Pan-Mongolian movement, Neisse Gegen, was shot, along with twelve brigade commanders. Return of the Bolsheviks and escalation of Mongolian anti-Chinese nationalism were setting the stage for dramatic political and military developments. After cruel Chinese treatment, "Mongols of all classes began to look to the White Russians to deliver them from the Chinese. Ordinary Mongols enlisted in great numbers in the Baron's army."[4] In October 1920 Baron von Ungern-Sternberg laid siege to Urga unsuccessfully but returned with more troops and greater success in January, actually occupying the city in February 1921 and ruling until July 6 in coordination with Semenov and his Japanese allies.

Some Mongols sought assistance in Russia. The "Khalkha Seven" crossed the border into Russia during July and August 1920: Sukhe Bator, Choibalsan, Bodo, Chakdorjav, Danzan, Doksom, and Losol. Danzan even met Lenin, who expressed concern about Mongolian anti-Chinese nationalism that seemed far stronger than class consciousness. Some Russian supplies and other support began coming through to the Mongols at Kyakhta. Military training began there in November 1920, a date that represents the beginning of the new Mongolian army with only a few hundred Mongol soldiers. Many were veterans of the czarist-trained national army that had been dissolved by the Chinese in November 1919. The operation for the Mongols at Kyakhta continued somewhat lackadaisically, without clear direction. Although the headquarters of the Far Eastern Republic moved to Chita in October 1920, the Russian representatives Krasnoshchekov and Boris Shumyatsky disagreed about many things, and their rivalry affected Mongolian policy. The Russians made clear to the Mongols that direct Russian intervention could occur only if anti-Bolshevik Russians established themselves in Outer Mongolia and the Mongols stopped joining von Ungern-Sternberg's forces. Opposition to Ungern-Sternberg would win Soviet support.[5]

Ungern-Sternberg's initial reception as an anti-Chinese protector was warm. But his savage cruelty, including the killing of forty Jews and eighty Russians and the raping of Mongols, led to widespread disillusionment and to the desertions and ultimate betrayal that weakened and destroyed his movement. The enthusiasm of the Mongols waned as Ungern-Sternberg's priority target shifted from the Chinese to Bolshevik Russians. Although Mongols were not enamored of Bolshevik ideology (especially the anti-religion aspect) it became clear that the Bolsheviks controlled Russia, which offered the best chance of limiting or denying China's return to Outer Mongolia. The Jebtsun Damba, the high lamas, and the princes turned against

Ungern-Sternberg along with the masses; it was not a
class struggle of lamas, princes, and Ungern-Sternberg
against the people.

Bolshevik exploitation of revolution in a small
country initially proceeded slowly. Once the Chinese were
out, Ungern-Sternberg was in, and Shumyatsky's position
was clarified, a flurry of activity occurred from March to
July 1921. The Revolutionary Military Council of the Fifth
Soviet Red Army at Irkutsk began organized assistance to
Sukhe Bator and his troops. Russian advisers, Russian
training, Russian models of organization, and Russian
equipment formed an indispensable attribute of the new
Mongolian army. The civil-military pattern included a
Revolutionary Military Council and an Army Political
Administration linking the army to the new revolutionary
government. The Mongolian People's Revolutionary Army
(MPRA) was officially founded in March 1921 in Kyakhta on
Russian soil.

In 1921 Red Army and Bolshevik partisan units pursued
and destroyed most anti-Bolshevik units fleeing from
Russia in battles that raged throughout 1921, from
Sinkiang to the Kobdo district and Ulyasutai into Tuva.
This military spillover into Outer Mongolia subjected the
small indigenous Mongolian independence and revolutionary
movement to Russian methods and goals. The Red Army in
effect unified outlying lands for the central government
in Urga and finally ended the destruction and havoc caused
by all the fighting.

The MPRA of about 900 cavalry soldiers accompanied
more than 10,000 Soviet Red Army troops into Urga on July
6, 1921, and established a new revolutionary government
there on July 11. Russians served as top staff officers
of the Mongolian army, and a Soviet citizen--Altai Oirat--
headed the army's Political Administration. A Kalmyk Mongol, also a Soviet citizen, was appointed first military
commandant of the city of Urga, representing the new
revolutionary Mongolian government.[6]

A tiny indigenous Mongolian revolution was being
carried along on the mighty torrent of the Bolshevik
revolution and buffeted yet more by waves and tides coming
from the political maelstrom in north China. A clear
pattern of close Russian-Mongolian cooperation against
China was already established.

THE ESTABLISHMENT OF A REVOLUTIONARY GOVERNMENT: 1921-1926

An army of 17,000 men, nominally ready reserve of
50,000 men, and annual training of 10,000 men strained
the manpower resources of the country. In 1926 Mongolia
had a population of half a million and supported tens of
thousands of lamas. A few lamas served in the army, and
Strasser reported that "the young men...no longer become
lamas, but soldiers."[7] Ma Ho-tien visited the Military

Academy in Urga in 1926 and saw anti-Buddhist posters prominently displayed there: One showed "soldiers shooting down nobles and lamas."[8]

The Military Academy had 400 students, of whom 31 were in party affairs. Cavalry was always the essence of the Mongolian army; there was no infantry. Military service was compulsory for all males over eighteen. Soldiers trained for six months in Urga and then returned to their home districts as reserves. In 1922 there was no registration apparatus, and the draft was generally ignored. Desertions were commonplace, and trying to find AWOL nomads was an unrewarding task.[9]

The army constituted part of a domestic military-political complex that enforced primarily internal control. It was closely connected with border troops, secret police, "justice" (courts and prosecutors), and the Revsomols (RSMs, the party youth movement). This complex formed one of three parallel interacting syndromes, which might be termed Soviet dogmatist, Chinese revisionist, and Japanese traditionalist.

Jadamba, head of the RSMs and of the army's Political Administration in 1923, and Choibalsan, a member of the organization's Central Committee, were the leading Soviet dogmatists. Russians served as army chiefs of staff in the early 1920s (Kosich and Kangelari), established Mongolian army intelligence (Sarakovikov), and organized Mongolian border troops (Shchetinin). Ma Ho-tien reported six Russians running the Mongolian secret police in 1926. Choibalsan was in the USSR shortly after Bodo and fifteen other Mongolian leaders were arrested for treasonable activities in January 1922. He went to Moscow after their arrest, returned in time for the RSM Congress in June, and then the "traitors" were executed in August. Choibalsan and Maksorjav (an early Mongolian leader) were in Moscow with Russian military advisers when Danzan (another early leader) and his Revsomol-supporter Bavasan were trying to wrest control of the army from the Russian advisers and when Danzan and Bavasan were executed in August 1924. Soon after that Maksorjav went again to Moscow, and Mongolia received a Soviet loan.

Choibalsan was appointed chairman of a newly founded Political Court in January 1926; Jadamba became head of the Revolutionary Military Council; Gursec, also a member of the RSM Central Committee in 1922, became chairman of the Supreme Court in 1926; and Dendyp headed the Juridical Commission. Roland Strasser described the political situation in Urga in 1926 as army and secret police united against the Buddhist establishment.

The dogmatists strongly opposed Japan, condemned any overtures to China, opposed attempts (specifically by Danzan) to establish regular Urga-Kalgan automobile connections, tried to eliminate all private trade and to expel the Chinese merchants who controlled most of it, and

waged a campaign against the lamas and the Buddhist
church generally. That is, they were anti-Japanese, anti-
Chinese, antibourgeois, and antifeudal. They were the
group most intimately connected to the Russians.

The regular party organization included many pro-
Chinese revisionists who wanted a Russian-Chinese alliance
against Japan and ties with Inner Mongolia. Ideologically
they were moderate neo-Buddhists. The connections with
Feng Yu-hsiang, a Chinese warlord, and the accompanying
Pan-Mongolian developments, were expected to amplify Soviet
relations with the Guomindang, weaken ideological ortho-
doxy, and lead to a greater degree of bourgeois nationalism
and more "democracy." Ma Ho-tien, a representative of
Feng, noted the political situation in 1926-1927:

> Most of the leaders in the Mongol People's Party
> are Rightists who advocate union with China.
> Damba Dorj, the present Chairman of the Central
> Executive Committee, is an example. Although
> educated in Russia, he is antagonistic to that
> country and is strongly in favor of joining with
> the Chinese Kuomintang in order to reduce the
> power of the Russians. He is especially disliked
> by the Revolutionary Youth League.[10]

Finally, the pro-Japanese traditionalists, including
the church and the feudalists, favored anti-Communist
Japan. Japan, in turn, used Manchurian warlord Chang
Tso-lin and Pan Mongolism as its weapons of penetration.
Japanese aid to Chang in 1925 allowed him to defeat Feng
and thereby break the Urga-Kalgan connection and close
the double window of Russian-Chinese alliance and Outer-
Inner Mongolia relations. Chiang Kai-shek's turn against
the Chinese Communists and Borodin's flight from China
sealed Mongolia's borders after 1927 for decades.

THE JAPANESE THREAT: 1927-1947

The Russians never doubted that Japan intended to
take over Mongolia and attack the USSR. Japan's occupation of Manchuria in September 1931 confirmed this
opinion. But opening hostilities in Manchuria did not
involve the Japanese. When Manchurian warlord Chang
Tso-lin defeated Feng Yu-hsiang in 1925-1926, several
Inner Mongolian nationalists fled to the MPR. The
assassination of Chang Tso-lin by the Japanese in June
1928 left a power vacuum until December, when his son
joined Chiang Kai-shek and the Guomindang. In the inter-
regnum, Mongols led by emigré Inner Mongolian nationalists--
according to some reports, under Russian officers--launched
a raid from the MPR into Barga, obviously hoping to spark
a Mongol uprising and profit from the uncertainty of
political-military control in Manchuria. But Chang

Hsueh-laing's troops easily drove the invaders back into the MPR and nothing further came of that attempt.

The raid on the Soviet consulate general in Harbin in May 1929 and the forceful takeover of the Chinese Eastern Railroad (CER) in July caused stern and effective Soviet reaction, which deflated a now-united Guomindang China. A Soviet troop buildup from 34,000 to 113,000 soldiers and the formation in August 1929 of the Special Far Eastern Army under Blyukher was followed in October and November by a punitive Soviet military raid into Manchuria. The Russians occupied the border town of Manchuli, took 8,000 prisoners on November 20, and occupied Hailar on November 28. Chang Hsueh-laing lost his taste for battle and accepted Soviet terms in the Khabarovsk Protocol of December 22, 1929.[11]

Under these conditions a test of MPR military preparedness took place. The 1929 test-mobilization brought out 2,000 instead of the expected 30,000 reservists. A special Red Army inspector, A. I. Gekker, dispatched in 1930 to investigate and report, narrowly escaped an assassination attempt. The forced collectivization and other radical measures in Mongolia led to a nascent civil war. Livestock losses were immense, the Buddhists were seething, the whole society was in an uproar--at the very time when Japan occupied neighboring Manchuria in mid-September 1931.

Professor Nicholas Poppe has testified about the situation in Mongolia: "In 1932 the entire population revolted against the Soviets. The Red Mongolian Army and many members of the Mongolian People's Army took the side of the revolters, and this rebellion was crushed by the Russian Red Army, tanks and aircraft were rushed from Russia to Mongolia."[12] The small Mongolian army (8,000 men) was revealed as an empty shell, the draft and reserve system as a farce. The task officially set for the army for 1932-1940 was "to form an entirely modern system of defense sufficiently powerful to beat off the attacks of Japanese imperialism."[13] That would not be easy.

It was no coincidence that Japanese establishment of Manchukuo and Autonomous Hsingan in March 1932 was followed in July by complete reversal of policy in the MPR. An "extraordinary plenum" of the party substituted the moderate New Turn policy for "left deviation," canceling the abortive First Five Year Plan and the disastrous livestock collectivization. Choibalsan left for Moscow, where he remained the next four years. Soviet troop buildup continued: eight divisions in the Far Eastern Army in 1932, eleven in 1934, and fourteen in 1935. A Soviet-MPR gentlemen's agreement was concluded in November 1934. In 1935 Russia sold the Chinese Eastern Railroad.

Pravda of April 9, 1936, indicated the Soviet

assessment of Mongolia's part in Japanese ambitions: "Outer Mongolia is a base desired by the Japanese military, which aims to seize the MPR and to threaten the Soviet Union. The seizure of Outer Mongolia would create a direct threat to the Soviet Pri-Baikal region, the Siberian trunkline, and to the entire Far Eastern Krai."[14]

In March 1936 the Russians announced a Soviet-Mongolian Treaty of Friendship, including a Mutual Defense Protocol. The Soviet Far Eastern Army increased in strength from twenty divisions in 1937 to thirty in 1939. The Mongolian army followed Red Army precedent by reintroducing ranks and appointing to the new rank of marshal both Choibalsan and Demid in February 1936 and by reestablishing control-by-commissar in November 1937. Russians moved into Mongolia. F. N. Voronin directed the Political Administration and the commissars. I. A. Pliev served as instructor of the general staff from 1936 to 1939. Rokossovsky participated in training the First Mongolian Cavalry Division, and V. A. Sudets had begun to form a Mongolian air force in 1933. N. V. Feklenko's 57th Rifle Corps established headquarters in Ulan Bator in September 1937. Mongols attended Soviet military schools. Soviet Foreign Minister Molotov warned the Japanese on May 31, 1939: "I give warning that the borders of the MPR, by virtue of the mutual assistance treaty concluded between us, will be defended by the USSR as vigorously as we shall defend our own borders."[15] Zhukov came to the MPR in June.

Military purges and public trials in both Mongolia and Russia undoubtedly encouraged the Japanese to expect easy victory despite the vigorous Soviet and Mongolian statements and warnings. Tukhachevsky was shot in June 1937 and Blyukher disappeared in August 1938. Of twenty-eight leading officers of Blyukher's Special Far Eastern Army, half were dead by the time of the Nomonhan battle. Marshal Demid died mysteriously on August 22, 1937, and was linked to an alleged and undoubtedly imaginary treasonous plot with the purged Gendun in a show trial in October 1937.[16]

The MPR's comparatively moderate New Turn policy of 1932-1936 included the possibility of avoiding military service by becoming a lama at age eighteen. The number of lamas increased from 57,000 in 1932 to 94,000 in 1936, and a report of 1934-1935 indicated that 48 percent of eighteen-year-old males chose the church that reporting year. Only after a change in this legislation did the number of lamas decline by 22,000 in 1937 and 49,000 more in 1938. By the end of 1939, only 15,000 remained. Opposition to the Soviet Union and the Communist regime was equated with helping Japan, and the crisis with Japan provided justification for destroying the church.

A fairly serious Soviet-Japanese military incident occurred on the border between eastern Manchuria and the Soviet Far East at Changkufeng (Lake Khasan) in July-

August 1938. The USSR was the victor, despite a purge-imposed change of command in the middle of the fighting (Shtern replacing Blyukher). The confrontation at Nomonhan (Khalkin-gol), on the MPR-Manchuria border, lasted from May to September 1939 and again ended in Soviet victory. Mongolian army units participated in the fighting and suffered a reported 1,131 casualties. There were probably no more than two Mongolian cavalry divisions in the fight, so their contribution was minimal. But a Mongolian army did participate in a major battle and did not disgrace itself. It passed one important test. Edmund Clubb attributed great importance to Nomonhan:

> The battle...proved to be one of those critical turning points in history....It led directly to the defeat of the Japanese faction that gave priority to a war with the Soviet Union, and the consequent rise to predominance in the Japanese Government of those who favored a grand strategy built around a plan for collision with the sea powers.[17]

Even if the quagmire of China had already absorbed considerable Japanese strength by the time the battle took place, and the Hitler-Stalin Pact of August 23 may have eased Soviet fears of a two-prong war, the outcome at Nomonhan marked Soviet victory in the confrontation of Russia and Japan after a rivalry of almost half a century.

Pearl Harbor, United States aid to China, American naval successes in the Pacific, and the U.S. war effort against Japan overall diverted Japanese focus and preoccupation away from Mongolia, Manchuria, and Russia. The Soviet success at Stalingrad (decisive defeat of the Germans, January 1943) assured ultimate Russian victory and weakened the pressure on Moscow to transfer men and arms from the Far East. Soviet troop strength tied down a large Japanese army that never participated in war against Russia, China, or the United States. Throughout the war the Japanese forces represented a potential danger to Mongolia and Siberia, but their freedom to attack was denied by Soviet forces that remained in the Far East despite war in Europe.

Mongols thus avoided direct fighting in World War II. Citizens of the MPR were not drafted into the Soviet army, nor were any volunteers accepted. The Russians did require Mongolia to supply horses and meat in quantity, both for Soviet Far Eastern troops and for the army in Europe. Strict rationing resulted. Mongols "volunteered" substantial war loans, equipping a tank regiment and an air squadron. Sacrifices were imposed by the lack of Soviet imports. A wartime atmosphere prevailed even though the war was very remote.[18]

Although it was more like a giant war game than a

genuine military engagement, the massive joint Soviet-MPR two-week campaign in Manchuria and Inner Mongolia in August 1945 represented the Mongolian army's largest action, and along with Nomonhan (September 1939) its most important battle. The Mongols suffered 1,131 casualties in 1939 and 675 in 1945. The Mongolian contingent in the 1945 operation was of course dwarfed by the 1.5-million-man Soviet army, but it did include four cavalry divisions, artillery, some tanks, and even a few airplanes. At that time the Mongolian army probably totaled 80,000 men, with most of them participating in this Manchurian-Inner Mongolian campaign. Soviet reports referred to "liberation of the territory of Inner Mongolia by soldiers of the Soviet Union and the MPR....The arats demonstrated massively for...the union of Inner Mongolia with the MPR."[19] But plans for such Pan Mongolism quickly collapsed as the Chinese Communists' Liberation Army took over the area and incorporated it under their own effective control.

The area of Peitashan in the mountains separating northeast Sinkiang (almost directly north of Urumchi) from the southwest MPR was disputed by China and the MPR. Events in Sinkiang in 1944, after Sheng Shih-stai had deserted the Russians and redefected to the Guomindang, included revolts of ethnic minorities against imposition of oppressive Guomindang measures. The Kazakh leader, Osman Bator, was pursued by Chinese troops to his Peitashan refuge, whereupon Mongolian cavalry and Soviet pilots, or Mongols flying Russian planes, attacked the Chinese. This Peitashan Incident alternately smoldered and burst into flame several times between 1944 and 1947. Kazakhs, Uighurs, and other minority ethnics in full rebellion against Guomindang repression appealed for and apparently received Soviet assistance for their "liberation" cause. Mao's People's Liberation Army (PLA) entered Sinkiang in early 1950.

The Mongols claimed to have represented a "barrier against the Japanese," but they exaggerated considerably--a tripwire describes the situation more accurately. The MPR functioned as part of the Soviet army's forward position, not simply as a buffer. It provided important maneuvering room. At Nomonhan, units of the Mongolian army sometimes operated as independent patrols under Mongolian command, but in Manchuria and Inner Mongolia in 1945 they were thoroughly integrated into the Soviet command structure. In any case the Mongolian People's Army never fought an independent major engagement.

Although actual fighting was limited and casualties were few, the symbolic and propaganda manipulation of the effort in World War II was considerable. Military victory provided legitimacy, and the defeated enemy provided a scapegoat to charge with every evil deed and failure. Military victory justified the revolution, and some considered that it justified purges and terror. Victory was used to justify destruction of the Buddhist church, the expulsion of ethnic Chinese, and the special "elder brother" status of the Russians in Mongolia. It added legitimacy to the close Russian guidance and direction that has prevailed for so many years.

A NEW ERA FOR MONGOLIA: 1947-1954

The People's Republic of China (PRC), under Mao Zedong's leadership, accepted the result of the 1945 Plebiscite, recognized the MPR, and sent the first Chinese ambassador to Ulan Bator on July 10, 1950. Mao, however, had indicated to Edgar Snow in 1936 that "when the People's Revolution has been victorious in China the Outer Mongolian Republic will automatically become a part of the Chinese federation, at their own will."[20] The PRC's Mongolia policy can probably best be understood as a vigorous but unsuccessful attempt to return to dominant control in Outer Mongolia, and the USSR's Mongolia policy as a successful attempt to frustrate China's policy.

Constraints limiting the USSR-MPR joint force from fully exercising its military superiority in Inner Mongolia in 1945-1947 included the MPR's desire to join the United Nations, Soviet concern about adverse effects elsewhere if they were judged to have taken excessive advantage of the Yalta agreement, and the Communist leader Ulanfu's unexpectedly rapid and effective consolidation of Inner Mongolia. The establishment of the Inner Mongolian Autonomous Region (IMAR) on May 1, 1947, would have required the Soviet Union to engage in open military confrontation to take over the area. There was no doubt of an eventual Russian military victory in such a confrontation, but the political cost would have been very high. The Russians and Outer Mongols quietly withdrew. Eyewitness reports indicated that the MPR troops "were well fed, well trained, and well equipped, and...made a favorable impression."[21] Ulanfu added Hsingan and Barga (Mongol areas in Manchuria) in 1948, and moved into Kalgan early in 1950.

The veteran Mongolian military and political leader Choibalsan died in January 1952. Tsedenbal emerged as successor to Choibalsan only after an unexplained four-month delay. As the head of MPR delegations just a few months later, Tsedenbal was received by Stalin in Moscow on September 5 and by Mao in Beijing on September 29. The Stalin-Tsedenbal-Mao negotiations of September 1952 included an agreement to complete the Trans-Mongolian Railroad, improving the Moscow-Beijing rail connection. Tsedenbal was replaced by Damba as party first secretary in April 1954.

Beginning in May 1955, an influx of Chinese workers and an exodus of Russians started to shift the correlation of forces. As Harrison Salisbury has argued, "The momentum of the Chinese initiative is so great, the attractive force of Chinese dynamism is so overpowering, that it is hard to see how, over the long run, Russia can maintain her position. She is still the first power in Outer Mongolia, but five years from now this may well be no longer true."[22] The Chinese laborers going to the MPR attained a maximum total of about 20,000; the number of Russians declined from 1956 to 1963 to a low of about 8,900. Russian troops withdrew from the MPR in 1956, after twenty years of unbroken presence. The decline in Russian civilian presence in the MPR and the troop withdrawal certainly suggested major reorientation of Mongolia. Khrushchev in October 1954 asked Mao for a million Chinese workers to go to Siberia, of whom 200,000 did go to Siberia. Khrushchev concluded:

> What had the Chinese been up to? I'll tell you: they wanted to occupy Siberia without war. They wanted to penetrate and take over the Siberian economy. They wanted to make sure that Chinese settlers in Siberia outnumbered Russians and people of other nationalities who lived there. In short, they wanted to make Siberia Chinese rather than Russian....[23]

Sending Chinese workers to Mongolia was obviously a related and very similar project, and at one point the Chinese discussed sending 300,000 Chinese laborers to the MPR!

CONSOLIDATION ERA: 1955-1980

An official appointment put an army general into a job usually held by civilians, that of minister of foreign affairs. In 1955-1956 S. Ravdan served in that position. Ravdan had been deputy head of the Political Section with the Mongol troops that accompanied Soviet General Pliev into Inner Mongolia in 1945. After his brief stint as minister of foreign affairs, at a very sensitive time, he became head of the army's Political Administration and then, in 1962, deputy minister of defense. He died in about 1975.[24]

Preliminary moves in 1961 and major reorganization of the Mongolian defense establishment in 1962 opened the process of escalating militarization that culminated in the Sino-Soviet confrontation at Damansky Island in 1969. A visit to Ulan Bator in 1961 by Malinovsky and Pliev, emphasizing propagandistic recall of joint Soviet-Mongolian operations in World War II, was followed by formation of the Mongolian Society for Support of the Army. The year 1962 was marked by a struggle involving the approved handling of the reputations of two dead men: Choibalsan and Genghis Khan. Choibalsan, the USSR, and

the military won; Genghis Khan, China, and the civilians
and intellectuals lost. The hawks defeated the doves.
Major military reorganization occurred during May-August
1962. Ilichev in Ulan Bator in January 1963 laid down a
tough ideological line, and Soviet General Danilov came
to the MPR as senior military adviser in 1963.

A visit by Brezhnev, the conclusion of a Soviet-MPR
Mutual Defense Treaty, and reentry of regular units of the
Soviet army into Mongolia marked 1966. The Soviet military buildup throughout the Far East spanned the whole
Sino-Soviet border. Three divisions from the Transbaikal
military district were stationed on the Mongolian border
with China when the Damansky altercation erupted.

In 1969, a few months after the Damansky Island incident, John Erickson judged that "it would be too much to
draw a straight analogy between conditions pertaining between 1932 and 1946 and those prevailing today, but there
are similarities which command some attention."[25] High-level Soviet military advisers came into the MPR to improve Mongolian defense in 1933 and 1963. USSR-MPR
treaties of mutual defense were concluded in 1936 and
1966 and in both cases were quickly followed by the return
of regular Soviet army units to the MPR. The pattern of
the 1930s, building up Mongolian forces and then bringing
in regular Soviet units, was similar. Confrontation at
Nomonhan in 1939 and at Damansky Island in 1969 in both
cases threatened to expand into larger war--and did not.

But the USSR synthetically enhanced actual parallelism with a tenuous transference of the genuine Japanese
threat of the 1930s into an exaggerated version of the
actually limited Chinese threat of the 1960s. The
Mongolians went on in the 1970s to employ a symbiosis of
Soviet and Mongolian military symbols involving anniversaries, awards, catafalques, cemeteries, ceremonies,
eternal flames, holidays, honors, memoirs, monuments,
and museums. Soon after Brezhnev was appointed a marshal
of the USSR, Tsedenbal became a marshal of the MPR.
Brezhnev and top Soviet military officers have been
awarded Orders of Sukhe Bator and other high Mongolian
decorations; Tsedenbal has received high Soviet military
awards. Marshal Choibalsan and Marshal Stalin have been
rehabilitated, as have Marshals Tukhachevsky, Blyukher,
and the Mongolian Marshal Demid. Sukhe Bator Square
copies Red Square, and military parades are held in both.
The highest monument in Ulan Bator is raised to commemorate
joint Mongolian-Soviet military cooperation. Visiting
officials pay tribute to Soviet army dead at the monument
atop Mt. Ziasan, where an eternal flame burns. The
Zhukov Military Museum recently opened in Ulan Bator, and
a major street in the capital city bears Zhukov's name.

The Chinese threat in the 1950s and early 1960s to
develop Darkhan and colonize the Selenga valley reminded
the Russians that an empty and undeveloped Mongolia would

always invite challenge to Russian dominance. Mongolia and Siberia would both be "unstable" as long as they continued empty and undeveloped. Soviet actions in the 1970s included the opening of the major mining complex of Erdenet to Darkhan, the formation of state farms, expanded electric power and communications from the Soviet side of the border, and increasingly intensive use of the northern part of the Trans-Mongolian Railroad from the Ulan Ude connection on the Trans-Siberian Railroad to the border town of Naushki to Ulan Bator. Economic planning in Mongolia puts locational economics at the service of military-strategic requirements.

The general buildup of troops in the Far East included three divisions from the Transbaikal military district assigned to the Mongolia-China border. The southern part of the Trans-Mongolian Railroad, almost unused for civilian freight and passenger service because of the Sino-Soviet dispute, became a useful adjunct to military operations.

Tsedenbal's unusually tough speech to generals and officers of the army and border troops on September 30, 1980, accused China of "intention to annex Mongolia." He indicated that

> the Soviet Union is taking concrete measures to equip our People's Army and units of the border and internal troops with the most modern types of armament and military equipment....The modern tanks, infantry combat vehicles, armored carriers, self-propelled artillery and antitank guided missiles increase many times over the firepower, strike force and mobility of troops on the battlefield....Utilization of modern infrared devices raises the combat opportunities of troops and increases the maneuvering speed of tanks and armored carriers.[26]

The Mongolian government expelled several Chinese and claimed they were guilty of espionage or otherwise threatening the interests of the MPR. A tougher and more aggressive Soviet-Mongolian line developed in 1980 without any evident Chinese cause.

Organizationally, the intimate connection of the army with the secret police and the courts continues. The present minister of defense, General Avkhia, served several years as state prosecutor and was described by one Soviet source in 1974 as a leading writer on law. The present head of the Political Administration of the army, Lieutenant General Yondonduichir, also served several years as state prosecutor. The chairman of the Supreme Court from 1970-1978, Major General Gunsen, had been deputy minister of public security and then state prosecutor. In 1974, while serving as head of the

Supreme Court, he received a doctor's degree from the Moscow Institute of State and Law, Academy of Sciences of the USSR; his dissertation topic was "Legal Protection of State Property in the MPR."[27]

CONCLUSIONS

For almost seventy years the Mongolian national army has existed as an important part of Russian influence in the country. The army has never been a defender of Mongols against Russians except for a few instances of mutiny that were never serious enough to threaten Russian control. Neither has the Mongolian army been an important element of defense against Japan or China, as it was necessarily much too small to operate independently against such large adversaries. The Mongolian army has not been involved very often or very intensively in actual fighting and may have been more important as a symbol of Russian influence and of Russian-Mongolian cooperation than as a military unit. Serious fighting always required commitment of Russian troops.

Although it may fairly be charged that Russia detached Mongolia from China and persistently refused to permit China to reassert its legal claim, it must also be recorded that the Chinese government repeatedly failed both militarily and politically to fulfill sovereign functions. Chinese exploited and mistreated Mongols and proved incapable of defending Mongolian territory against Japan or even against Ja Lama and von Ungern-Sternberg.

The Russian judgment that the Baikal Corridor, and therefore much of Siberia, was vulnerable to an attack from Outer Mongolia, led them to classify the area as vital to their national interest. That in their eyes justified interference when China failed to defend the country effectively. But the Russians also moved to keep the Chinese at a distance and did not really want them in Outer Mongolia at all, even if they had effectively defended the territory.

Both czarist Russia and Soviet Russia supported the Mongolian army, but the army included new aspects after 1921: a Political Administration, a Revolutionary Military Council, and a party organization. It also implied ancillaries not part of the military establishment until 1921: secret police, military courts, and special border troops. The czarist-supported Mongolian army was never very effective, nor was the Soviet-supported one, either, for many years. Only in the 1930s did it show discipline, organization, and a modicum of reliability. Its appearance and performance were markedly more professional and impressive in 1945 than in 1939.

The army was Russian-organized and supported and served as an anti-Chinese agent. The army was part of the Soviet-encouraged Mongolian establishment that excluded

Chinese and closed the country to foreigners generally. It helped to isolate Mongolia. The army in the Soviet period also participated in the revolution. It engaged in domestic operations to limit and ultimately destroy the Buddhist church. Soldiers displaced lamas. But the Mongolian army always relied on the Soviet army to crush foreign and domestic enemies, and Soviet troops were officially in the country from 1921 to 1925, from 1936 to 1956, and from 1966 to the present. Scattered reports suggest that sometimes USSR units operated in the MPR at other times as well. There were few years when the Soviet army was not on the scene.

For many years the Mongolian army represented revolutionary transformation of Mongolian society and dramatic far-reaching revolutionary change, but it also functioned to a large extent to keep Mongolia unchanged. By expelling Chinese, yet not supplying any economic investment, the USSR and the Mongolian army it organized and supported maintained a static and backward condition in the country for decades. Military force kept the society in abeyance: The Soviet Union put the MPR on hold. Only in the 1960s, and more so in the 1970s, did economic development become part of the program, and that was obviously in response to the PRC's attempts to return to Mongolia. For several decades the Mongolian army has helped to limit, divert, exclude, and eliminate change.

Substantial Soviet military presence diminished the importance of the Mongolian army and emphasized its subordinate and dependent position. But general knowledge that the powerful Soviet army stood behind the not-so-powerful Mongolian army lent the lesser force prestige and clout. The Mongolian soldiers could swagger confidently and act with arrogance because they knew that they would never have to face resistance alone. That they depended on and took orders from their "elder brothers" was clear.

The USSR strictly controls the sources, direction, and content of change in the MPR, and it controls the army that constitutes one significant element in that domination. The Mongolian army has always been ultimately an auxiliary of the Russian army.

NOTES

1. Henry Perry-Ayscough and R. B. Otter-Barry, <u>With the Russians in Mongolia</u> (London: John Lane, 1914), pp. 113-114.
2. The Russian military mission introduced the Mongols for the first time to modern military methods. It was only from the poorer class that soldiers were recruited into the Mongol army from 1912 onward. The military training they received had the wholly unexpected result of providing a nucleus of trained men, who knew one

another from the old days, for the embryo revolutionary army mobilized in early 1921. Sukhe Bator, the revolutionary general, was for seven years a professional soldier who was demobilized as a sergeant major of machine guns in 1920. He was able to recruit many old comrades who had suffered along with him from overbearing Buryat and Mongol officers, bad food, and irregular pay. Charles R. Bawden, The Modern History of Mongolia (New York: Praeger, 1968), pp. 201-202.

3. Robert Rupen, Outer Mongolian Nationalism (Ann Arbor, Mich.: University Microfilms, 1954), pp. 290-291.

4. Bawden, Modern History of Mongolia, p. 216.

5. Isono, "Soviet Russia and the Mongolian Revolution of 1921," Past and Present (May 1979), p. 134.

6. Thomas Hammond, "The Communist Takeover of Outer Mongolia: Model for Eastern Europe?," The Anatomy of Communist Takeovers (New Haven, Conn.: Yale University Press, 1964), vol. 1, 155, n. 67; and Sow-theng Leong, Sino-Soviet Diplomatic Relations, 1917-1976 (Honolulu: University of Hawaii Press, 1976), pp. 168-169.

7. Roland Strasser, The Mongolian Horde (London: Jonathan Cape, 1930), pp. 112-113.

8. Ma Ho-tien, Chinese Agent in Mongolia, trans. de Francis (1949), pp. 105-106.

9. Marguerite Harrison, in Rupen, Mongols of the Twentieth Century, p. 208.

10. James E. Sheridan, Chinese Warlord: The Career of Feng Yu-hsiang (Stanford: Stanford University Press, 1966), pp. 141; 145-146; 151-153; 164; 167; 169-172; 183-184; 190-191; 198-202; 208; 230-231; 339, n.57; 343, n.25; and 343-344, nn. 35-41. See also Sow-theng Leong, Sino-Soviet Diplomatic Relations, p. 232; and Ma Ho-tien, Chinese Agent in Mongolia, p. 115.

11. Text in Harriet Moore, Soviet Far Eastern Policy, 1931-1945 (Princeton: Princeton University Press, 1945), pp. 182-184.

12. Rupen, Mongols of the Twentieth Century, p. 249, n.35.

13. Ibid., p. 230.

14. Pravda, April 9, 1936.

15. Rupen, Mongols of the Twentieth Century, p. 226; and How Mongolia Is Really Ruled (Stanford: Hoover Institution Press, 1979), pp. 38-39; 172, n.9.

16. Bawden, Modern History of Mongolia, pp. 335-342, 354-357; Rupen, Mongols of the Twentieth Century, pp. 235; 250, n.47.

17. O. Edmund Clubb, China and Russia (New York: Columbia University Press, 1971), p. 318.

18. Livestock exports to the USSR in Rupen, Mongols of the Twentieth Century, p. 268, n.25. Bawden points out concerning eighteenth-century Manchu demands on the Mongols: "Animals in colossal numbers were requisitioned for mounts, transport and provisioning" (Modern History of

Mongolia, p. 100); and Ramstedt refers to the situation in Russia at the end of the nineteenth-century: "All Kalmyk horses were officially under the authority of the Ministry of War, and a Kalmyk was not allowed to sell his horse unless it had been examined by the local military command" (p. 114). Bibliography in HMHR lists three books dealing with this relationship: "Aviaeskadril'ya," p. 199; Narody Brat'ya, p. 208; Semenev, "Eskadril'ya," p. 212.

19. John Erickson, Soviet Military Power (London: Royal United Services Institute, 1971), pp. 27, 73; Harrison Salisbury, War Between Russia and China (New York: Norton, 1969), pp. 158, 161.

20. See especially History of the MPR, trans. and annotated by William A. Brown and Urgunge Onon from a work edited by Bagaryn Shirendyb et al. (Cambridge, Mass.: East Asian Research Center, Harvard University, 1976), n.85 (by Brown), p. 802.

21. Doak Barnett, China on the Eve (New York: Praeger, 1963), p. 212.

22. Harrison Salisbury, "Soviet and China Compete for Power in Outer Mongolia," New York Times, August 4, 1959; Salisbury, To Moscow--and Beyond (New York: Harper & Row, 1960), p. 229.

23. Strobe Talbott, trans. and ed., Khruschev Remembers: The Last Testament (Boston: Little, Brown & Co., 1974), pp. 249-250.

24. S. Ravdan, "MNRP--organizator i rukovoditel' narodnykh voisk MNR," Kommunisticheskie vooruzhenie sil, no. 5 (1961), pp. 80-83.

25. Erickson, "Reflections" (1969), p. 87.

26. Alan Sanders, "Shield Against China's Hordes," Far Eastern Economic Review, October 31, 1980, pp. 47-48.

27. "The Mongolian Military Elite," in Rupen, How Mongolia Is Really Ruled, pp. 114-116. Ewing notes, "There is no question...that the Soviet secret police is active in Ulan Bator" (p. 319).

11
The Chinese Militia

June Teufel Dreyer

    Located at the interface of civil-military relations, the militia has occupied a delicate and frequently controversial position in the People's Republic of China (PRC). It is ironic that this situation should exist in a society characterized by a high degree of overlap between civil and military leadership. Available evidence suggests that these controversies have arisen because of ambiguities in the role of the militia, and that these ambiguities have in turn been brought about by the interaction of three factors--ideological principles contained in the Marxist-Leninist canon, the developmental pattern of the Chinese revolution, and elite politics within the PRC. This chapter will describe these three factors, analyze their interactions, and assess their impact on civil-military relations in the PRC.

IDEOLOGY

    Early Communist theorists considered professional armies to be tools through which the ruling classes sought to keep themselves in power. They believed that socialist societies could best be defended by locally recruited militias. Trained in the martial arts at the same time as they participated in the economic activities of peacetime society, these citizen soldiers would fight outside enemies with a spirit that could not be matched by that of any professional army. Because they were defending their own families and homes, amateurs were believed capable of overcoming even modern armies equipped with more sophisticated equipment.[1] Thus, the existence of a militia was considered a significant part of a socialist state and an important guarantee of its safety, not only from outside attack, but from takeover from within by a professional military.

DEVELOPMENT OF THE CHINESE COMMUNIST REVOLUTION

The idea of reliance on the armed masses had considerable appeal for leaders of the nascent Chinese Communist party (CCP). In the late nineteenth- and early twentieth-century environment that formed these leaders' frame of reference, standing armies had not served China well. Incapable of defending the country from foreign invasion, they were a domestic scourge as well. For several decades after the fall of the Qing dynasty in 1911, large parts of China were ruled by warlords. Acting in frequently shifting coalitions, warlords fought one another for territorial gain. Their armies regularly looted and pillaged the areas through which they passed.

The CCP considered the training and organization of militarily skilled and politically aware citizens important not only for external defense but for internal revolution. The National Institute of the Peasant Movement, set up in Canton in the early 1920s and much celebrated in party mythology, included military training on its curriculum. And Mao Zedong's widely read 1927 <u>Report of an Investigation Into the Peasant Movement in Hunan</u> advocated the destruction of the landlords' power by armed peasant groups. Groups of armed peasants, workers, and students were established by CCP organizers in various parts of China, and during 1927 they launched a series of insurrections. The failure of any of these insurrections to consolidate gains for the revolution convinced many Chinese leaders that victory could not be won without a regularized, professional military. In due consequence, the Chinese Workers' and Peasants' Red Army was founded.

Army and militia were to fight a united people's war against the class enemies. Although some differences of opinion must have arisen concerning the division of labor between army and militia, the common dangers of their situation and their belief in a common revolutionary goal served to mute many of the disagreements. The CCP's very survival was in doubt during this period, and neither army nor militia achieved spectacular gains.

In 1936 the CCP's collusion in a daring and successful attempt to kidnap Chinese President Chiang Kai-shek led to Chiang's Guomindang (GMD) government granting a degree of legitimacy to the CCP. Ostensibly, the purpose was to encourage the CCP to fight China's Japanese occupiers, and this in turn facilitated the growth of both the party's regular army and its militia organizations. The declaration of war on Japan by the United States after Pearl Harbor left the CCP and GMD more free to fight one another, and the Communist militia played a significant part in what became known as the War of Liberation. Militia groups mounted guerrilla operations in support of the regular army, provided the army with rear services, and served it as a source of recruits.

During this period the militia was divided into two segments, an elite main-force group and the ordinary militia, which was known as the People's Self-Defense Corps. Communist sources credit the militia with an important part in achieving victory in the War of Liberation and an important role in the strategy of people's war.

CHINESE ELITE POLITICS AND THE ROLE OF THE MILITIA

Disagreement over the role of the usefulness of the militia has apparently existed since its inception, with the first head of the CCP, Chen Duxiu, accused of disbanding armed groups of peasants and workers (probably on orders from the Soviet Union, which wished to form an alliance with the GMD) and handing their weapons over to "reactionaries."[2] At a later date, Mao Zedong was credited with "correctly solving a series of problems" concerning the building and operations of the militia system.[3]

However, the organization of the militia, like many of the arrangements under which the CCP waged its war for control of China, was often of necessity ad hoc and informal. It was not until the war had been won and the PRC founded that the party confronted the problem of formalizing and institutionalizing the role of militia. Questions concerning this role have led to frequent disagreements among ranking members of the PRC elite. Typically these disagreements reflect underlying ideological differences with significance far beyond the militia itself. At the same time, they have led to profound changes in the composition and function of the militia forces. Although virtually no facet of militia work has been exempt from these controversies, disagreements have tended to cluster around three principal issues: first, command and control; second, the proper mix of civilian and military functions; and third, the optimum size for the militia.

COMMAND AND CONTROL

Command and control issues have focused on the mix of powers that party and military are to exercise, separately or concurrently, over the militia. Subsidiary issues have concerned the degree of central versus local control and the matter of control over weapons. Theoretically, the issue of party versus army control of the militia should not arise. The party's authority is supreme, as enshrined in Mao Zedong's phrase, "The party must always control the gun; the gun must never control the party." In reality, the party's supremacy is less clear cut. While the party sets general guidelines for militia work and reviews the militia's nonmilitary functions, the People's Liberation Army (PLA) must train the militia, supervise and control its equipment and inventories, and inspect the militia's performance. Thus, a dual system of control exists.

This duality is faithfully reflected in the militia chain of command. The Mobilization Department of the PLA oversees militia work. The commander of a military district--generally coterminous with a province in area--directs militia operations, and the provincial party secretary serves as political commissar of the district and assists in militia work. The same is true at military subdistrict level.

At county level and below, militia work is supervised by People's Armed Forces Departments (PAFDs), whose commanders are usually PLA officers appointed by the military district. The PAFDs also have party representation, as well as that of local civilian authorities. However, the PAFD is an element in the military chain of command. Party directives are transmitted to the PAFD through the party's Political Officers Department at any given level in the administrative hierarchy. The PAFDs serve as local command, administrative, and supply organs for the militia; they are also responsible for militia conscription and veterans' affairs.

In this dual system, either party or army may seek to enlarge its sphere of influence at the expense of the other. So also may the local area. PAFDs have frequently become quite independent of any higher authority: While dutifully repeating party and PLA directives, they tend to interpret these directives in light of perceived local needs. Often, senior military officials have had to be dispatched to PAFDs to bring their behavior into line with the standards laid down by higher levels.

Although this command and control system generally describes militia organization since the founding of the PRC, several interesting variations have occurred in response to differences among the elite group over the proper role of the militia. For example, in 1958, with China embarking on a massive radical socioeconomic experiment known as the Great Leap Forward, control over the militia was transferred from the PLA to the CCP. The PAFDs, their functions gone, disappeared from mention and seem to have been abolished. Mass media criticized Minister of Defense Peng Dehuai for his handling of militia work. It appeared that this shift from army to party control was part of radicals' efforts to undercut the power of moderate, professionally oriented military officers and enlist the militia in its socioeconomic program.

There is no evidence that the military was opposed to devolution of its responsibilities toward the militia. On the contrary, professionally oriented elements within the PLA tended to regard militia work as burdensome and a waste of time. Although relieved to be rid of this burden, these professionally oriented elements are also known to have opposed many of the Great Leap Forward's programs and doubtless also disapproved of the use of the militia and PLA in support of these programs.

The Great Leap Forward proved an abject failure, resulting in several years of economic crisis and social chaos. Central control over the militia, by either party or army, virtually disappeared. Food shortages were severe and widespread, so that the first priority of most of China's citizens was survival. At this point, local and personal interests became dominant, with some militia organizations disbanding so that their members could tend to farming. Other militia groups stayed together and, using militia weapons, attacked government warehouses or the fields of neighboring areas in search of food. A reassertion of central control over the militia was clearly needed. Eventually, after several years and considerable effort, this was accomplished--only to reopen the question of party versus army control.

In December 1959 a three-year program for improving the organization of the military was announced, with the consolidation of militia work as one of its aims. A few months later, in April 1960, a national conference on militia work was convened. Here Lin Biao, who had replaced Peng Dehuai as defense minister, launched a movement to rectify the militia. In January 1961, the party's Military Commission issued a directive calling for, among other items, strict central control over the utilization of the militia, thorough accounting for militia supplies and weapons, and consolidation of militia organization. That such a directive should be needed seems to indicate that previous efforts to assert central control had had limited success. In 1962, control of the militia was removed from the party and returned to the army.[4]

However, during the following year, public security forces began to assist in militia training, and the amount of time the militia devoted to political work increased. Both these changes indicate efforts to bring the militia more under party control. These efforts continued until the outbreak of the Cultural Revolution in 1966, after which it became difficult to tell who controlled the militia.

The official media reported militia groups supporting Mao Zedong and pro-Cultural Revolution elements who were loyal to him. However, other evidence indicates that militia units frequently acted in support of local causes that might or might not reflect the ideas of radical party ideologues in Beijing. Many years later, Beijing Radio praised the militia of a certain county in Shanxi province because it had not entered the area's towns during the Cultural Revolution to cause trouble[5]--the implication being that the opposite phenomenon had been prevalent at that time.

However loyal militia members may have wished to be,

lines of authority were highly confused during the Cultural Revolution, and it was difficult to judge to whom one's loyalty was due. Militia groups took part in factional fighting, sometimes on their own initiative, sometimes on party orders, and sometimes in response to military directions. Militia weapons were extensively used in support of factional fighting and became accessible to non-militia members as well. In light of allegations that would be made many years later about this period, it is interesting to note that several recorded examples of militia misbehavior occurred in or near Shanghai.[6]

One effort to rein in this chaos involved putting the militia under army control again. During a rather brief period in 1967 known as the "February adverse current" or the "evil wind of March," the army attempted to use the militia to shore up the country's faltering economy. However, the "adverse current" was reversed during the early spring, with militia groups reportedly highjacking trains and looting PLA arsenals for weapons. Several attempts were made to confiscate militia weapons, but with no discernible results. In some parts of the country, it was simply not feasible even to try: Where the Cultural Revolution decimated public security functions, militia units sometimes took over their duties. Here, the militia's possession of weapons often enhanced their effectiveness.

During the show trial of radicals held in late 1980, the prosecution charged that the radical group known as the Gang of Four had begun at this time in 1967 to organize the militia as its own armed force. The Gang of Four allegedly tried to use the militia to implement radical policies, as it felt that the army opposed these policies.[7] Whatever the intent of radical leaders during this period, however, the militia did not assume a clear-cut role in the Cultural Revolution.

Eventually the army was used to restore order and emerged from the Cultural Revolution in a strong position, not only with regard to the militia, but in terms of its place in society as a whole. As a result the army had become deeply involved in maintaining social order, eclipsing any role the militia may have played in public security functions during the latter part of the Cultural Revolution. The militia, in fact, was scarcely mentioned in 1968 and received attention in official media only after border clashes with the Soviet Union in 1969 heightened Chinese fears of attack by the USSR. Not surprisingly, these newly important militia units were very much under army control.

This remained the case until the autumn of 1973 when yet another shift to party control occurred. Joint editorials in the People's Daily and Liberation Army Daily--the official party and army publications, respectively--called for local party committees to forcefully reassert direct control over the militia.[8] As before, there is no record of army resistance to this reassertion of party control. PAFDs were abolished, with their functions assumed by party organs. Militia headquarters were created in major cities, with plans to create a militia command at national level as well.

The precise degree of control exercised by the party over these militia headquarters is unknown. Although the radical elements in the Chinese leadership who advocated this reassertion of party control insist that the militia headquarters were under party control, their moderate opposition sees the militia headquarters as tools of radicals rather than of the party and views the headquarters as subversive rather than constructive in aim. Both sides agree, however, that the radicals aimed at ending the army's control over the militia. The very carefully contrived evidence presented at the 1980 show trial that China's moderates held to convict leading radicals quoted one defendant as having said in March 1974, "The army must not be allowed to lead the militia, whose command should be in the hands of the municipal party committee."[9] Two years later he allegedly added, "I'm certainly going to keep firm control over (the militia). You must run it well for me...the army isn't so reliable."[10]

In the view of the radicals, the strong position the military had held in the PRC power structure since the Cultural Revolution was being used to buttress moderate, ideologically unacceptable economic and social policies. Thus, radicals saw their mission as returning power in China to the party, to which it clearly and rightfully belonged, and hoped to use a militia that had been strengthened and removed from military domination as a tool to this effect.

The mid-1970s saw considerable tension between the army, supported by moderate Vice-Premier Deng Xiaoping, and the militia, championed by the radical Gang of Four. For example, in August 1975, the New York Times reported that Deng had ordered the PLA in the coastal city of Hangzhou to put down a militia disturbance there. After considerable difficulty, the army succeeded in disarming and disbanding the militia.[11]

By contrast, Deng's purge in the wake of violent demonstrations in Beijing's Tiananmen Square in April 1976 led to a much greater role for the militia. The militia was in fact touted as the savior of the Tiananmen riots, and Deng's steadfast opposition to the creation of militia headquarters was listed among his many traitorous acts. Following Deng's removal from office, Taiwan sources reported that radical-led militia units were replacing PLA personnel on garrison duty in Beijing.[12] At the same time, Soviet sources charged that radical leaders were using the militia in opposition to the regular army.[13] Although one must be wary of both Taiwan and Soviet interpretations of the PRC, these particular reports are corroborated by statements made by official Chinese sources during the 1980 trial of radical leaders.

The issue of who was to control the militia was joined again after Mao's death in September 1976, with the radicals the clear losers. Their leaders were taken into custody during the weeks following Mao's death, and the militia was temporarily disbanded. Several months later a very different organization began to emerge, with militia headquarters abolished and PAFDs revived. At the same time, Deng Xiaoping returned to a position of power.

In 1978 a national-level militia conference convened in Beijing. New militia regulations were issued that re-established the dual system of control by party and army. Local party committees and military regions were admonished to pay attention to militia work and to exercise unified leadership over it.[14]

This remains the situation at present writing. However, both the military conference and several subsequent pronouncements left little doubt that neither party nor army is especially enthusiastic to shoulder the burdens of military work. As phrased by Politburo member Nie Rongzhen: "All local committees must attach importance to militia work, place it among the most important items on their agendas, and effectively strengthen leadership... some (PLA) comrades...feel that to do militia work means they are inferior to others and that it means a lack of faith in them by their organizations."[15] Repeated admonitions that party and military organs must pay strict attention to militia work seem to indicate that, despite central government pronouncements and formal organizational charts, the system of dual control does not accurately describe reality in a significant number of cases. With both army and party seemingly indifferent, an important portion of militia command and control may devolve on the local areas, as has happened many times in the past. As we shall see, there is, in fact, evidence that this may be occurring.

CIVILIAN VERSUS MILITARY FUNCTIONS

In theory the militia member is both civilian and soldier--a productive member of society in peacetime and a valiant warrior in time of hostilities. This is epitomized in party slogans describing militia members as striding forward "with a rifle on one shoulder and a shovel on the other." In reality, the functions of the militia are much more complex.

To extend the party's metaphor, it is difficult to aim one's rifle accurately with a shovel on one shoulder and hard to do farm work while carrying a gun. To be ready for war implies a fairly rigorous and systematic peacetime training program. Yet to participate in such training means time must be taken away from production work. How the militia member shall be compensated for the time spent on training and whether this training increases the state's security to a degree at least equal in value to the goods and services the trainees would have produced had they remained at their jobs have been recurrent questions during the past thirty-odd years.

Militia members have traditionally been expected to perform a variety of both military and nonmilitary tasks. In time of hostilities, they are expected to provide mass support for the army and to mount mobile, guerrilla-type operations. Both tasks are integral parts of Mao Zedong's concept of "people's war," and indeed it is in official descriptions of people's war that the militia's place in party mythology has been enshrined. The militia is considered a bridge between the people and the army. As such, its members are to provide reserves for regular troops and to serve these troops in an auxiliary capacity. In the latter role, they may transport supplies to troops, serve as guides in their local areas, give medical treatment to the wounded, and guard prisoners. In areas further removed from battle lines, militia members are to secure lines of communication against sabotage and enemy attack, to organize the civilian population against air attack, and to assist in such recuperation and evacuation efforts as may be needed after such attacks.

During peacetime, militia members are expected to play leading roles in increasing production and to perform public security duties. Militia members are frequently called upon to serve as a shock force in a drive to increase production and to render aid in time of emergency such as earthquakes or floods. Their public security duties involve coordination with PLA and regular public security departments; the performance of guard duty at border areas, warehouses, and factories; and reporting of suspicious persons, prevention of sabotage, suppression of rebellion, and the like. Militia have a political-ideological role as well, being expected to promulgate and conform to whatever may be the current party line. At the same time, militia members are expected to carry out normal work activities.

Clearly it is impossible to play this wide variety of roles with any degree of skill, and the militia has been criticized frequently for its deficiencies. Lin Biao, who was Mao Zedong's designated heir from the Cultural Revolution period until his death in 1971, allegedly felt that the militia was a "heap of loose flesh," and the Gang of Four is said to have described its composition as "officers sitting on a wall and soldiers trained in a chest of drawers."[16] Many efforts have been made to remedy these deficiencies; all have involved making choices as to which roles of the militia to emphasize and, by implication, which to downgrade in importance. Any particular choice of roles is apt to be criticized by the enemies of those leaders responsible for making the choices.

With the CCP's victory over Chiang Kai-shek in 1949, it is hardly surprising that the militia's domestic tasks were emphasized over their military duties. Militia members helped to implement the sweeping reforms the CCP introduced into most areas of the Chinese socioeconomic system. Some also served as "volunteers" in the Korean War and helped to suppress internal resistance from those who continued to oppose a Communist government.

Regulations passed in 1957 changed the militia's role from basically domestic to predominantly military. In effect, the militia became the reserve force for the PLA, being assigned both those young people who were eligible for the PLA but not selected for service and those who had already served their tour of duty with the PLA. The change from civilian to military emphasis reflects the increased concern with military professionalism generally associated with Defense Minister Peng Dehuai.

The militia's role as reserve force for the PLA was short-lived. In 1958, when radical leaders introduced their Great Leap Forward program, the role of the militia shifted again. Radicals considered mass mobilizations the crucial element in tackling most of China's problems, whether domestic or foreign, and the militia was expected to play an important part in both. Domestically, the "everyone a soldier" campaign emphasized the militia's role in increasing production. In foreign policy, radical leaders assessed that the world balance was shifting toward socialist countries and adopted a much more militant stance toward "decadent" capitalist states. Considering military professionalism tainted by association with bourgeois capitalism, radicals touted the superiorities of people's war as fought by armed civilians. These again enhanced the role of the militia, albeit not in a way that emphasized training or war preparedness.

The collapse of the Great Leap Forward and the reassignment of the militia to army control did not, as might have been expected, lead to an emphasis on military training for the militia. Military training was given to the militia, with official media reporting marksmanship competitions and demonstrations of martial skills. But the main focus of militia work was on activities designed to increase production. In part this focus reflected the exigencies of China's situation at the time. The Great Leap Forward had devastated the PRC's economy and it was absolutely necessary to revive the production system that serviced the daily needs of the country's population. However, this reduced military role for China's militia also reflected the army leadership's feeling that time spent training the militia was time lost from other activities that were more beneficial to the national defense. Advocates of military professionalism again predominated in leadership positions, and they tended to consider the militia of marginal value.

The Socialist Education Movement of the mid-1960s led to a downgrading of production-related activities in favor of emphasizing the ideological role of the militia. Radical elements were gaining power; they tended to consider the internal political role of the militia of foremost importance. Ideological education occupied a much larger part of militia members' time than previously, and more attention was given to the public security duties of the militia. The underlying premise was that, having been ideologically purified, the militia would be equipped to perform internal surveillance functions.

Radicals were opposed to militia contests and demonstrations of skill, believing them to be manifestations of the "bourgeois military line." The competitions ceased--although paradoxically, official propaganda gave increased attention to the role of the militia in time of war. This apparent contradiction has a ready explanation: Although militia competitions were ideologically unacceptable to radicals because they represented bourgeois military professionalism, radicals were firm believers in the principles of people's war, in which the militia plays an important part.

Radical pronouncements on the military value of the militia were not meant exclusively as assertions of ideological principle aimed at a domestic audience. The concept of the unassailability of a China defended by scores of millions of stalwart militia members was also useful internationally during the 1960s. Should the American imperialists desire to extend their aggression from Vietnam to the PRC, they were forewarned that the valiant Chinese militia awaited them.

The greater the defense role given to an armed citizenry, the less the prestige of the regular army--and in particular the less the prestige of a professionally oriented, highly specialized army equipped with modern weapons. That we know of no instance of the PLA protesting this diminution of its role may simply mean that its protests were delivered privately. However, the PLA was itself highly politicized during this period. The military rank system was abolished in 1965, and emphasis was put on the PLA's role in civilian society, its duties toward the masses, and on the folly of relying on advanced technology rather than ideological purity to win wars. Many professionally oriented officers were purged or demoted. Thus the PLA's seeming indifference to its diminished role vis-à-vis the militia may also reflect changes in its structure that brought to power less professionally oriented people who were more in sympathy with the concept of citizen soldiery.

The Cultural Revolution, which followed close on the

heels of the Socialist Education Movement, intensified
the changes brought by the latter. Save for a brief
period in 1967 when the army was put in command of the
militia and attempted to use it to repair damages to the
country's faltering economy, the militia was utilized in
ideological education and public security duties. The
value of people's war and the importance of the militia's
role therein was stressed. It was apparently also at this
time that radicals came to reorganize Chinese society in
line with revolutionary principles and when they first
devised their plan to make the militia into a counterforce
to the PLA. Given the strong position the PLA attained
as a result of the Cultural Revolution, plus Mao's dictum
that the party must always control the military, this use
of a radicalized militia to combat a moderate PLA may be
seen as entirely justifiable.

Radicals plans to use the militia in this way were
temporarily halted by relatively serious border skirmishes
with the Soviet Union during much of 1969. The resulting
fear of war led to close PLA supervision over the militia
and an intensification of training activities. However,
as the threat of war receded, PLA control diminished. In
1973 radicals began to popularize a new form of militia
that incorporated the functions performed by public
security and fire departments. This new "three in one"
militia, said to be based on a prototype model in
Shanghai, was to guard against both internal and external
enemies. Two years later, a change in the Chinese constitution elevated the militia to parity with the PLA and
reaffirmed the authority of the party over both--"The
Chinese PLA and the people's militia are the workers'
and peasants' own armed forces led by the Communist Party
of China."[17]

Although its creators touted the new militia's role
in protecting China against both internal and external
enemies, it was the former function, and not its usurpa-
tion of PLA prerogatives, that became more controversial.
Militia members were used as guardians of the standards of
ideological purity introduced by the Cultural Revolution.
They reportedly sought out "counterrevolutionaries,"
"deviationists" (from the party line), and "revisionists"
(of Marxist-Leninist doctrine). In keeping with the
radicals' conviction that legal procedures were a bourgeois
device that hindered justice, suspects were typically
apprehended without warrants, detained without indictments,
and convicted on the basis of forced confessions.[18] The
militia was also used in support of power struggles at the
highest level: It suppressed the Tiananmen demonstrations
of April 1976 that led to Deng Xiaoping's dismissal from
office.

Radicals also planned to use the militia to ensure
that their views would prevail after the death of the
aging and ill Mao Zedong. Factories in Shanghai were

reportedly ordered to manufacture large quantities of rifles for militia use, and heavy-duty weapons such as rockets, howitzers, and tanks, which are not normally issued to militia, began to be stockpiled. Although the militia uprising was to take place in a number of urban areas, only in Shanghai did it assume major proportions. The PLA, presumably acting on the orders of antiradical leaders, put down the uprising and concomitantly broke the power of radical leaders.[19]

A new state constitution promulgated in March 1978 removed the militia from its position of parity with the PLA, and other regulations divested the militia of its formal connection with public security and fire-fighting departments. The present leadership's view of the militia's proper functions focuses on its role in increasing production and organizing relief work in time of emergency. In addition, part of the militia is to have a role in wartime. Although the main energies of the militia are to be consumed by the Four Modernizations Programs, designed to bring China into the ranks of industrialized countries by the year 2000, the militia's role in people's war has been reaffirmed. Terming the concept of people's war and the militia's place therein "a revolutionary heirloom which we must pass on from generation to generation," a vice-chairman of the party's Military Commission argued that the role of the militia would be greater rather than less in a war fought under modern conditions.[20] However, subsequent actions made clear that only a small, carefully selected percentage of militia members would be thoroughly trained and given the necessary familiarity with modern weapons to play a significant role in such a war. In effect this group, known as the armed militia, serves as a reserve for the army; the remainder of the militia would focus on production activities. In order to reduce the burdens of militia work on the work units to which they belong, flexibility is to be the guiding principle of militia training. Local areas are to avoid using the militia at unnecessary functions such as parades; they may fix training periods to coincide with slack periods in their production activities, and they may choose which kinds of training activities best suit local needs.[21]

Although the role of the militia as guardian of ideological purity is no longer mentioned, the militia retains a peripheral role in public security functions. Given the criticism the militia sustained for their public security role under the Gang of Four, one might suspect that many militia members would be loath to participate in public security duties. Indeed, the official media have stressed a need to reeducate these comrades so that they understand that it is not militia participation in public security itself that is wrong, but rather participation in the erroneous manner advocated by the Gang of

Four. Indications are that they have not yet succeeded in convincing militia members of this.

OPTIMUM SIZE

Controversy over the size of the militia has been closely connected with elite assessments of its value to the society as a whole and of its particular worth as a military force, aid to production, and/or mass organization. Generally speaking, the size of the militia has varied in response to perceptions of the imminence of conflict with an external enemy and with assessments of its ability to contribute to internal production and surveillance work. Views on the optimum size of the militia have ranged from a large mass organization of citizen soldiers on the one hand to a small well-trained elite usually serving mainly as reserves for the PLA on the other.

A note of caution on interpreting statistics on militia size is in order. The PRC government has frequently been reluctant to release any meaningful statistics at all and is particularly hesitant to do so on matters relevant to national security. Where statistics on the militia have been given, they do not reveal what percentage of the organization is combat-effective and what percentage exists mainly on paper. Many reports on militia size reflect Western computations derived from sporadically released Chinese figures for the number of militia members in a county or province whose total population is known. However, to calculate the total size of the militia from data based on a few counties or provinces is risky. Other Western estimates are based on immigrant and refugee interview data compiled in Hong Kong. This sample contains a disproportionate number of persons from the areas nearest Hong Kong, causing problems of extrapolation.

However, difficult as it may be to specify the exact size of the militia, we are able to chart the general growth, decline, and resurgencies in militia membership and to relate these shifts to elite perceptions of the militia. Before 1949 a large militia was considered important to the prosecution of the war against Chiang Kai-shek, and by the time the PRC was founded, the militia comprised approximately 10 percent of those Chinese under CCP rule. Militia organization, always informal, apparently disappeared after the CCP's victory. A People's Daily article of November 25, 1950, mentioned a three-year plan to bring militia strength to 23.75 million, or about 4 percent of the total Chinese population, by the end of 1953.

Even this modest figure was apparently never reached, and both the numbers and prestige of militia members remained low. The PLA at this time had its own reserve system, so that entry to the prestigious regular army could not be facilitated by service in the militia. In 1957, when new regulations made the militia the reserve force for the PLA, both its prestige and its numbers rose quickly. By the end of that year, militia membership was estimated at 30 million.

During the following year, China launched its Great Leap Forward, and the militia's prestige and numbers reached unprecedented heights--although not because of its function as a reserve for the PLA. In fact, the militia was elevated to virtual parity with the regular army, with any suggestions that it should play a lesser role condemned as examples of a bourgeois military line.

An important goal of the Great Leap Forward was to reduce specialization. In a scheme that aimed at erasing the differences between farm work and factory work and at making peasants into intellectuals and vice-versa, it is not surprising to find the assertion that ordinary citizens could be responsible for the country's defense. Indeed, as has been mentioned above, one of the slogans of the Great Leap Forward was "everyone a soldier." It should not be supposed that militia membership aimed only at enhancing the country's defense. Rather, the drive attempted to induce the broad masses of civilians to enthusiastically apply a military-like style of work to all of China's problems, domestic and otherwise.

As might have been expected, the "everyone a soldier" movement led to a denigration of professionalism within the PLA, and the recently ousted defense minister was criticized for saying that the militia had lost its function in postrevolutionary society. Large numbers of people were enrolled in the militia. Chinese sources report that an incredible 220 million people, or a third of the total population at that time, had joined. However, most of this membership was nominal, with probably no more than 10 to 15 percent of these receiving military training and not many more being mobilized as militia to tackle the economic and social tasks set by the Great Leap Forward.

With the failure of the Great Leap Forward, many of the actual policies that comprised it were revamped or dismantled, although a good deal of the movement's rhetoric was retained. Thus, the value of the militia continued to be affirmed even as its effectiveness declined. The size of the militia remained large, although most of its membership existed only on paper.

Militia regulations passed in 1961 reflect a differentiation between nominal and effective membership. All able-bodied male citizens between the ages of sixteen and forty-five and females between sixteen and thirty-five who were of good class background might participate and had an obligation to do so. However, a distinction was made between this ordinary militia and a backbone, or basic, militia with more stringent eligibility requirements to whom better training would be given. A still more elite organization, the armed militia, was to be recruited from the basic militia.[22]

This convenient fiction allows China to claim that virtually all able-bodied citizens are militia members, while requiring time and commitment from, and spending relatively little on, only a small percentage of them. The same membership criteria were reiterated by the 1978 militia regulations, except that the 1961 version's clause stipulating good class background was replaced with one providing that militia membership be on the basis of the individual's own free will. Provided that not too large a segment of the Chinese population chooses to exercise its free will thus, these regulations make the size of the militia a function of the age distribution of the Chinese population. Probably not many will opt out: As membership in the ordinary militia often involves no training at all, there are few disadvantages to joining.

The militia is presently estimated to comprise about 25 percent of the Chinese population, or 250 million people. However, membership in the basic militia is smaller--perhaps 10 percent, or 100 million people--and that of the armed militia is from 12 to 15 million. The wide swings in past membership from 4 percent to 33 percent of the Chinese population during the 1950s have not been repeated in recent years. However, controversy continues to exist on how many of these militia members will be given active roles in society in their capacity as militia members. The Gang of Four and, apparently, radical groups in general favor an activist role and high political salience for large numbers of militia members; more moderate governments tend to favor a low militia profile internally, with military training being given to a relatively small elite within the militia. Only in time of external threat does this radical-moderate split on the size of the effective militia diminish: A common response to border disturbances with the Soviet Union in 1969 and the Sino-Vietnamese confrontation in 1979 was an increase in the training exercises of larger numbers of militia members.

CONCLUSION

The Chinese militia seems to exist largely because it is expected to, rather than because it fills a needed function. Its roles in domestic society--as spearhead of production, vanguard of ideology, and in public surveillance and guard duty--can probably be better performed by organizations specifically directed toward these tasks. Similarly, its military functions might better be filled by the PLA or by a regularly constituted reserve of the PLA.

The militia's raison d'être rests on its alleged

value in the CCP's march to victory in 1949--a value for which there is little hard evidence.[23] Repeated disparaging remarks about the militia by former leaders indicates that many Chinese feel that the militia has been of little value since 1949.[24] The multiplicity of roles it has played since the CCP came to power and the vacillation on which roles to emphasize reinforce an image of the militia as an organization without a clear-cut function. Since ideology nowhere specifies the proper mix of roles, there is legitimate ground for disagreement about them, and controversy will probably continue. Questions of command and control and size have likewise proved intractable. What is perhaps the most fundamental problem, that of creating a powerful and efficient martial organization without making it too much like a standing army and without demanding more of the time and energy of both individual members and their production units than they are willing to give, has not been solved.

The militia has been the stepchild of both army and party, with neither anxious to assume responsibility for the militia unless it feels the other is usurping its prerogative. This has contributed to problems of morale in the militia, with official sources reporting members' complaints that "it doesn't pay to be a militiaman, as you are neither fish nor fowl."[25] Such attitudes inevitably affect the efficient functioning of the organization.

The one known attempt to use the militia as a counterweight to the army and in support of a particular faction in a power struggle resulted in failure. It is conceivable that other such attempts will be made, although this seems improbable in the near future. Present regulations divide control of the militia between party and army. Although this division was designed to make it difficult for either to usurp power, divided authority also weakens the respective feelings of responsibility of both army and party for militia work.

The repetition of official admonitions to military districts and party committees to take militia work more seriously indicates that they are not doing so. Thus, power frequently devolves to the local areas, with undesirable effects on social order. For example, in 1979 a dispute between the children of neighboring villages on Hainan Island escalated into a serious altercation between their elders. The village party secretaries each authorized the use of militia personnel and weapons against the rival village, and a battle involving nearly 700 persons ensued. Six people were killed and extensive property damage done.[26]

Recent directives allowing local areas more flexibility in recruitment practices and training schedules of the militia will doubtless reinforce this already extant localism. Interestingly, these problems of localism have a vivid parallel in imperial China, where interlineage feuding and militia organization had a reinforcing effect on one another.[27] In extreme cases the security of the state was jeopardized, with federations of village militia organizations rebelling against the central government. These were particularly hard for central government troops to quell because local ties were strong and it was impossible to distinguish militia belligerants from ordinary peasants. One official, writing in 1826, expressed a problem with contemporary relevance, lamenting that "when they congregate and oppose the government, they are rebels; when they disperse and depart, they are civilians once more."[28]

Such situations are unlikely to arise on any large scale in present-day China. Yet during the turmoil of the past few years, the government has several times publicly acknowledged that its enemies in widely different areas maintain links with one another[29] and that militia weapons have contributed to antigovernment violence.[30] Thus, the militia, despite its limitations both as an external fighting force and in its domestic duties, has the capacity to cause substantial harm to social order.

Although apathy rather than aggressive intent best describes the present posture of the militia, the government is well aware of the problems that the militia has posed in the past and is capable of posing in the future. Politburo member Nie Rongzhen's characterization of the militia as a revolutionary heirloom is apt--but it is an heirloom whose continued existence may impose costs to the society that are not worth the positive contributions it may make.

NOTES

1. Karl Marx and Friedrich Engles, "Elberfeld Speeches," 8 February 1845, Works (Moscow, State Publishing House of Political Literature, 1955), vol. 2, p. 539.
2. Lin Yun-cheng, "The Militia in Chinese People's Revolutionary Wars," Beijing Review (BR) 7, no. 34 (21 August 1964): 21.
3. Ibid., p. 22.
4. Yang Lu-hsia, "The Chinese Communist Militia," Part I, Issues and Studies (Taibei), June 1973, p. 56.
5. Xinhua (Beijing), 13 August 1980, in Foreign Broadcast Information Service, China, 1980, no. 164, p. L/4 (hereafter FBIS-CHI-80-164): L/4).
6. See, for example, Shanghai Radio, 13 January 1967; Xinhua (Shanghai), 25 January 1967.
7. Xinhua (Beijing), 19 November 1980, in FBIS-CHI-80-226: L/27.
8. FBIS, Trends in Communist Media 24, no. 40 (3 October 1973): 3.

9. *Xinhua* (Beijing), 19 November 1980, in FBIS-CHI-80-226: L/27.
10. Ibid.
11. C. L. Sulzberger, "The Bear in the China Shop," *New York Times*, 10 August 1975, IV-15.
12. Hong Kong, AFP, 2 July 1976, in FBIS-CHI-76-129: K/3-4.
13. Radio Moscow, 19 June 1976, in FBIS-SOV-76-123: K/3-4.
14. These regulations are translated in *Issues and Studies* (Taibei), February 1980, pp. 75-95. See specifically article 4 on p. 77.
15. *Xinhua* (Beijing), 8 August 1978, in FBIS-CHI-78-154: E/9.
16. *Xinhua* (Beijing), 8 August 1978, in FBIS-CHI-78-156: E/1.
17. *BR* 18, no. 4 (24 January 1975): 15.
18. *Pravda*, 31 July 1976, in FBIS-SOV-76-151: C/2.
19. *Xinhua* (Beijing), 13 December 1980, in FBIS-CHI-80-242: L/3.
20. Nie Rongzhen, "The Militia's Role in a Future War," *BR* 21, no. 35 (1 September 1978): 16.
21. See, for example, an account of the arrangements made by various areas near Tianjin, as reported in Joint Publications Research Service (JPRS), 75320, *China Report*, no. 67, 17 March 1980, pp. 45-59.
22. *Issues and Studies*, February 1980, pp. 88-89.
23. There may be a parallel between the Chinese experience and that of the United States. American mythology has tended to eulogize in a manner disproportionate to the facts the role of sturdy farmers and frontiersmen in winning the war against the standing armies of the British. See Marcus Cunliffe, *Soldiers and Civilians: The Martial Spirit in America, 1775-1865* (Boston: Little, Brown & Co., 1968), pp. 52-54.
24. Nie Rong-zhen, speaking in August 1978, listed Peng Duhai, Lin Biao, and the Gang of Four. *Xinhua* (Beijing), 7 August 1978, in FBIS-CHI-78-154: E/1. Other sources have added still more names to the list.
25. *Yunnan Ribao* [Yunnan Daily], 3 July 1978, in JPRS, 32-432, 28 February 1979, p. 7.
26. Haikou Radio, 21 March 1980, in FBIS-CHI-80-59: P/7.
27. Philip A. Kuhn, *Rebellion and Its Enemies in Late Imperial China* (Cambridge, Mass.: Harvard University Press, 1970), pp. 78-79.
28. Quoted in ibid., pp. 40-41.
29. Radio Beijing, 25 April 1980, in FBIS-CHI-80-83: L/0.
30. Shenyang Radio, 24 May 1980, in FBIS-CHI-80-103: S/3.

12
Conclusion

Jonathan R. Adelman

A major gap in the emerging literature on Communist civil-military relations has been the lack of systematic attention to armies other than the Russian or Chinese. Furthermore, most work in the area has been relatively ahistorical, with analysis heavily focused on the present and near past. The series of chapters in this book on the historical development of civil-military relations in nine Communist countries have provided important material in this area. The focus on the early development of the armed forces in the taking of power and consolidation phase has added especially valuable information. The evidence presented in this volume calls into question some commonly held ideas about Communist armies and civil-military relations.

It has often been asserted that Communist armies have never manifested the propensity toward violence so common among armies in developing countries. It is true that there has never been a successful army coup in a Communist country. But, these chapters have chronicled the 1932 Mongolian army uprising, the 1967 Sejna affair in Czechoslovakia, and the 1971 Lin Biao affair--all cases where military commanders evidently attempted to use their power for political purposes.

Theorists of civil-military relations traditionally have assumed a rigid separation between civilian and military institutions. Encroachment by the military into civilian affairs has been seen as "praetorianism" or the politicization of the army. But the chapters by Domínguez, Ting, Dean, and Turley have shown protracted periods of army-party fusion in Cuba, China, Yugoslavia, and Vietnam. In Cuba, for example, Domínguez has argued that the resultant ideal of the civic soldier has become "the norm for all, even in purely civilian organizations."

Another traditional concept of civil-military relations in need of revision in view of the material presented in this book is that of a unified, Soviet-inspired model of civil-military relations. The nine armies have demonstrated an enormous range of levels of political influence. On one extreme have been powerful political actors such as the Cuban and Chinese armies. On the other extreme have been weak and passive actors such as the Mongolian army and the Czechoslovak army after 1968, both excluded from a policymaking environment dominated by an external actor, the Soviet Union.

In this light, how can we reconceptualize Communist civil-military relations, especially if we continue to argue as we did in Chapter 1 that there are distinctive elements that separate Communist countries from non-Communist ones? Or, put more simply, what do these chapters imply about the validity of the historical developmental model outlined in Chapter 1?

On the whole, these chapters suggest that such a model can help to explain the development of Communist civil-military relations, especially in the first generation after the seizure of the power. At the same time serious revisions are needed to explain East European events, and lesser revisions are needed to flesh out the model. We should begin by broadening the path to power argument to explicitly include the consolidation phase after the seizure of power. This enables us to highlight more clearly the nature and extent of the military contribution to the ultimate success of the revolution.

The Russian civil war, coming after the October Revolution, saw the creation of a poorly legitimate and relatively ineffective Red Army; political concessions, extensive police terror, and repeated mobilizations of Communists and workers were all needed for the achievement of victory. The explicit inclusion of the consolidation phase is useful in fitting Cuba into the second pattern of countries in which civil war created a fused civil-military elite. Clearly the Chinese revolution, in which the Communists took twenty-two years to fight their way to power; the Vietnamese revolution, which took ten years (before 1954); and the bloody Yugoslav revolution all exemplify this second pattern involving lengthy and protracted fighting before the attainment and consolidation of victory. But Cuba, where Castro had less than 1,000 guerrillas mainly in Oriente province prior to Batista's flight from the country on New Year's Day in 1959, seems a deviant case. However, the matter is more explicable if we consider the consolidation phase period of 1960-1965 during which the fighting was often intensive and 2,000-2,500 deaths were recorded. This period, which included the abortive Bay of Pigs landing, saw a level of fighting equal that of the 1950s, according to Dominguez. Thus the creation of a strong army numbering several hundred thousand men, which was effective in eliminating counterrevolutionary activities, was a major element in the success of the Cuban revolution. This process lasted more than a decade and predated the creation of an effective Communist party, which was not to hold its first Party Congress until 1976. Indeed, the fact that Castro was initially a radical democrat and not a Communist in 1959 further strengthened the military's role in politics.

Our concept of the impact of the takeover and consolidation period when the military and military values are dominant is also reinforced by an examination of the unique Vietnamese experience. Having come to power in North Vietnam in 1954, the Vietnamese Communists under Ho Chi Minh resumed the battle for all of Vietnam in 1959. During this second, arduous, and ultimately successful sixteen-year struggle for power in South Vietnam, the North Vietnamese Communists, according to Turley, acted again not like rulers of an established state but as insurgents acting from base areas in the North, as political actors who subordinated everything to ultimate victory. Thus, the triumphant entry of the PAVN into Saigon in April 1975, achieved against tremendous odds and without significant local South Vietnamese Communist aid, greatly reinforced the legitimacy and aura of effectiveness of the North Vietnamese army.

Certain variations occurred among the various revolutionary armies who fought their way to power. The Chinese Communists, in Lin Biao's colorful description, encircled the cities from the countryside; the Vietnamese Communists controlled the cities in the latter part of 1945 and in 1946 before being forced back into the countryside by the return of the French army. The Chinese, Vietnamese, and Yugoslavs all developed a strong party apparatus together with a strong army; the Cubans under Castro did so only slowly after the taking of power. The Vietnamese Communists had no significant nationalist rivals in their battle against the French colonialists, but the Yugoslavs had to fight significant nationalist forces as well as the Germans. Similarly, the Chinese Communists had to fight the Japanese and then the Guomindang. Cuban military clashes were small-scale affairs, but Chinese battles often involved hundreds of thousands of men on each side.

Overall, however, certain basic uniformities pervaded the road to power and consolidation of the Cuban, Vietnamese, Chinese, and Yugoslav revolutionaries. All four countries were underdeveloped countries in which external intervention of one or more major powers had disrupted the traditional governing system. The Communists, combining nationalist and agrarian reform appeals, appeared as a popular force that could effectively reintegrate the country and regain the country's independence. In the struggle, usually protracted, against powerful forces, the military and civilian elites and their tasks became blurred and fused. The lengthy gestation period promoted a homogeneous and effective officer corps with a significant Communist stratum in the ranks.

The ultimate victory against foreign and domestic enemies gave the final proof of the legitimacy and effectiveness of the army--usually the first completed institution of the revolution in a country lacking such institutions. The relatively minimal Soviet role in the achievement of victory--and explicit Stalinist advice to Tito and Mao <u>not</u> to try to achieve final victory--ensured that an external Soviet role would not be great enough to deny the military its rightful fruits of victory.

Finally, we need to look at and revise our assessment of the seizure of power in Eastern Europe. None of the authors in this volume deny the important role of the Red Army that occupied these countries during the elimination of Nazi Germany in World War II. But we must completely revise our estimation of the difficulties in creating reliable domestic armies in the 1944-1948 period. Korbonski's chapter on Poland, the chapter by Valenta and Rice on Czechoslovakia, and Alexiev's chapter on Romania add valuable new material in this regard.

In Poland the Soviet-led Polish army, which numbered 400,000 men, did play a significant role together with the Soviet Red Army in the seizure of power by the Communists. Furthermore, there was a mini-civil war from 1944-1948 in which 100,000 partisans fought the new Communist regime and 20,000 casualties occurred on both sides. However, there were significant differences between the Polish situation and situations in which Communist armies fought their way to power alone. The external Soviet military role was great, both through the direct role of the Soviet Red Army and the Soviet role in the directing and training of the new Polish army. Furthermore, unlike the homogeneity and Communist domination of the army in China or Vietnam, the Polish army after 1945 included many heterogeneous and even non-Communist elements: former Polish POWs in German camps, members of the pro-Communist local <u>Armia Ludowa</u> partisans and Soviet-led Berling Army formed on Soviet soil, members of the non-Communist local <u>Armia Krajowa</u> partisans and the Anders Army, which fought in Italy. As a consequence, the Polish Communists relied on local security organs for the seizure of power while the Soviet-led Polish army fought the Germans in 1944 and early 1945. During the civil war both the secret-police troops and army troops fought the resistance. Thus, the takeover and consolidation periods left the Polish army by 1948 in the ambiguous position of a force of some legitimacy but not fully trusted, an army with some effectiveness but without the certainty of effectiveness.

The Czechoslovak case is also interesting. Unlike the German or Romanian cases, here was an intact prewar military untainted by fascism or defection in a country with the only strong Communist party in Eastern Europe. Unusual too was the high level of Czech industrial development and the existence of a mature arms industry. Furthermore the Soviet forces were welcomed as liberators, and the Czech First Army Corps helped liberate the Prague together with the Red Army.

No Soviet army troops remained in Czechoslovakia. Under these conditions, Valenta and Rice persuasively argue, the gestation period for the future Czechoslovak Communist army was the 1945-1948 period of the Beneš government. During this period a steady recruitment process brought the number of Communist officers in a heterogeneous officer corps to 3,000 by 1947. Although 98 percent of the political commissars in the army were Communists who reported directly to Prochazka, the Communist chief political commissar, the party assiduously fostered an enlightenment program in the army and established party cells in each unit. The pro-Western air force was downgraded, Soviet instructors taught in military schools, and officers were exchanged with the Soviet Union. By 1948 Communists and their sympathizers occupied such key posts as defense minister (Svoboda) and chief of staff (Boček); 37.9 percent of the officers were Communists. But significant bases of opposition still existed in February 1948 such that "the army was Communist in form and organization," but "pro-Western officers still controlled many elite positions." Thus, the February Revolution was accomplished against the background of the neutrality of the army rather than with its active support.

Finally, in Romania the creation of a new army was a lengthy and protracted process, involving widespread purging of the old Romanian army. Lacking a broad base from which to build, the party would need a number of years before it successfully could create a new army.

In short, we have seen an ambiguous role for the military in the takeover and consolidation phases. In both Poland and Czechoslovakia there were heterogeneous and positive elements from which to construct a new army. By 1948 the Polish army could certainly claim greater legitimacy and demonstrated effectiveness than its Czech counterpart. As for the Romanian army, it still suffered from serious problems of legitimacy and effectiveness. If we were to include other East European countries we might see other variations. This awaits further research.

CIVIL-MILITARY RELATIONS AFTER CONSOLIDATION

The chapters on the first two types of Communist civil-military relations--the Soviet model and that of powerful and effective armies--have basically confirmed our presentation in Chapter 1. In the Soviet case the relatively ineffective and vaguely legitimate Red Army played no significant political role in the two decades after the end of the civil war period. With no significant countervailing foreign influence (as the Soviet Union was to exert in Eastern Europe after World War II), the army did not place a single professional soldier on the Politburo in this entire period. Its representation on the Central Committee fell as low as 3 percent in the late 1930s, when the army was devastated by the Great Purges. It performed no significant societal functions apart from the creation of a Kolkhoz Corps in the Far East in the 1930s. The army's effectiveness was often questionable: In the late 1920s it was considered barely able to repel a Polish attack, and in the winter of 1939-1940 it had grave difficulties in the Finnish campaign (although it did beat the Japanese at Lake Hassan in 1938 and at Khalkin Gol in 1939). Overall, only after the great victories of World War II would the Red Army finally gain legitimacy and demonstrate its effectiveness. Even then the army had to wait for the death of Stalin before it would become a significant interest group in a highly developed Soviet society.

The chapters on Cuba, Vietnam, China, and Yugoslavia nicely flesh out our earlier description of the powerful political role of these armies that emerged as legitimate, effective, and highly important actors in the takeover and consolidation of power. As Dominguez wrote about Cuba, "Revolutionary Cuba has been governed, in large part, by leaders whose civilian and military roles were fused during the insurgency." Ting similarly writes about China of "a civil-military elite system...that adjusts periodically to systemic imbalances." Turley argues that in Vietnam the army has been the most prestigious institution. And Dean sees a very important role for the Yugoslav army as the arbiter of politics after Tito's recent death in 1980.

These four armies also share a number of key characteristics. All, unlike the Soviet army, have performed (at least sporadically) extensive societal functions. The Cuban army enthusiastically has participated in a variety of societal tasks. In 1970, 64 percent of all regular soldiers helped cut 20 percent of the large sugarcane harvest. The Vietnamese army was deeply involved in economic recovery and administrative work after 1954 and again after 1975. The Chinese army actually ran the country from 1950 to 1952 and was deeply involved in the Cultural Revolution and various grain harvests. Finally, the Yugoslav army assumed a role in production.

Furthermore, all these armies, which originally had flexible structures operating at rather primitive levels of military technology, showed significant signs of increasing professionalization during the first several decades after the takeover. The Cuban army regularized ranks in 1973 and 1976. The Chinese army introduced rank in 1955 and modeled itself on the Soviet army only to reverse these decisions in the 1960s. There has been a noticeable increase in professionalism in the Vietnamese officer corps under the stringent pressures of modern warfare. After the 1971 Croatian crisis there was a marked emphasis on professionalism in the Yugoslav army.

Finally, these armies demonstrated a marked effectiveness in battle, except for the Yugoslav army, which avoided warfare. The Cuban army easily defeated counterrevolutionary attacks in the early 1960s (highlighted by the Bay of Pigs invasion in 1961) and won a decisive victory in Angola in 1975 and 1976. The Vietnamese army defeated and ousted the French colonialists in 1954 and, despite massive American intervention, marched into Saigon in April 1975. Again in 1978 the Vietnamese army routed Pol Pot's army and occupied Kampuchea, and in 1979 it repulsed a Chinese invasion thrust. Finally, although the Chinese Poeple's Liberation Army had some difficulties in 1979 border skirmishes with Vietnam, during the Korean War it routed powerful American and Korean forces in North Korea and then stalemated them near the original Korean border. As with the Cuban and Vietnamese armies, the Chinese army accomplished this despite the massive military technological supremacy of its enemies.

The final mode of civil-military relations has been that of the East European armies. Here the chapters by Korbonski, Alexie, and Valenta and Rice have forced us to strongly revise our initial evaluation. Clearly the civil-military relations of East European countries fit into neither of the preceding modes. Influenced by the ambiguous legacy of the takeover and consolidation phases and the overwhelming Soviet domination of their politics in the last years of Stalin's life, these armies played no significant political roles in the 1948-1953 period. Instead, they were the objects of Stalinist-inspired purges of army officers. By 1952, 75 percent of the Czechoslovak Communist army generals of 1948 were purged. In Poland massive purges of army officers accompanied the appointment of Soviet Marshal Rokossovsky as Polish defense minister and commander in chief, an appointment that symbolized the new Soviet domination of Polish politics.

Stalin's death in 1953, followed by Malenkov's New Course in 1954 and Khrushchev's secret speech in 1956, signaled a new era in Soviet-East European relations. The newfound limits on Soviet intervention in East European affairs, symbolized by the recall of Rokossovsky and his 10,000 Soviet advisers to Moscow, now permitted a new stage in civil-military relations. Although these relations would never be close and intimate, as in the Cuban or Vietnamese model, neither would they be as remote or coercive as the interwar Soviet model.

In all three East European countries discussed in this book the army emerged as an actor with diverse interests and the potential, given nationalist sentiments and control over the instruments of violence, to be a veto group in domestic politics. This is most vividly seen in Poland; in his chapter on the Polish army, Korbonksi has outlined an emerging pattern of accommodation. In 1956 army support for Gomulka and putative resistance to Soviet intervention helped deter a Soviet invasion. In 1970 the refusal of the army under Defense Minister Jaruzelski to fire on Polish workers led within a day to revocation of a price increase. In 1980 military hostility to Gierek helped force his replacement by Kania, and military refusal to use force against the solidarity movement led to agreement with the unions. The epitome of this new military role was seen early in 1981 in the appointment of Jaruzelski as prime minister, and later in martial law.

Similarly, the Czech army became politically involved in the events that culminated in the 1968 Prague spring. In December 1967 a coup attempt in support of Novotny, led by Major General Šejna and Deputy Defense Minister Janko was uncovered and stopped, leading to Šejna's flight and Janko's suicide. Early in 1968 Defense Minister Lomsky and Rytir, the chief of staff, were purged as conservatives. After the Soviet invasion, which went unopposed by the Czech army, there was a renewed purge, this time of Dubček supporters. Soviet domination of Czech politics since 1968, accompanied by the permanent stationing of Soviet troops in Czechoslovakia, has again relegated the Czech army to a passive role in politics. Finally, the Romania army has emerged in Romanian politics since the removal of Soviet troops in 1959 and the creation of an independent Romanian foreign policy. As Alexiev has observed, the army has created a symbiotic relationship between itself and the party.

Thus, we have seen that where the Soviet military presence has been removed or is not locally dominant--as in Poland, Romania, and Czechoslovakia before 1968--the army may emerge as a political force of some importance. But where the Soviet presence is dominant--as in East Germany (twenty divisions) and Czechoslovakia after 1968 (five divisions), or during the Stalinist era--the army has tended to remain an emasculated passive object of external politics.

There remains considerable future work in this field. There are seven Communist countries not covered in this work and about whom little has been written in this connection. They are Laos, Cambodia, Albania, East Germany, North Korea, Bulgaria, and Hungary. Furthermore, more work remains to be done about a number of the countries examined in this volume; only Russia and China have been adequately covered in the literature as a whole.

Much more work needs to be done with regard to not only party-military relations but also to the relation of the military to militia forces and the secret police. June Dreyer's chapter on the Chinese militia discusses the attempts by China's radical Gang of Four to counterpose the militia to the moderate PLA. More work is definitely needed here on potential rivals for control of the instrument of violence--particularly the secret police, which especially under Stalin was a bitter rival and even executor of military purges in the Soviet Union in the late 1930s. Similarly, Korbonski suggests that the ascent of the secret police implied the decline of the army in Poland during the 1949-1953 period. In a forthcoming Westview Press book (<u>Terror and Communist Politics: The Role of the Secret Police in Communist States</u>), which I will also edit, we hope to begin filling this vacuum.

Contributors

JONATHAN R. ADELMAN, editor, is an assistant professor in the Graduate School of International Studies, University of Denver. He has written The Revolutionary Armies (1980) and will edit a companion volume, Terror and Communist Politics (1982), for Westview. His articles have appeared in a number of journals, including Survey, Armed Forces and Society, and Studies in Comparative Communism.

ALEX ALEXIEV is an analyst with the Rand Corporation who has written on Eastern Europe.

ROBERT W. DEAN is assistant national intelligence officer for the Central Intelligence Agency. He has written West German Trade with the East (1974) and has coedited Eastern European Perspective on European Security and Cooperation (1974).

JORGE I. DOMÍNGUEZ is chairman of the Committee on Latin American and Iberian Studies and professor of government at Harvard University. Among his publications are Cuba: Order and Revolution (1978); Insurrection or Loyalty: The Breakdown of the Spanish American Empire (1980); and Enhancing Global Human Rights (1979).

JUNE TEUFEL DREYER is director of the East Asian Program and professor of politics in the Center for Advanced International Studies at the University of Miami. She has written China's Forty Millions (1976) and contributed articles to Problems of Communisn, Annals, and Armed Forces and Society.

ANDRZEJ KORBONSKI is chairman of the Department of Political Science of the University of California, Los Angeles. He has written a number of pieces on various aspects of East European politics.

CONDOLEEZZA RICE is an assistant professor in the Department of Political Science at Stanford University.

ROBERT A. RUPEN is a professor in the Department of Political Science of the University of North Carolina, Chapel Hill. He has written Mongols of the Twentieth Century (1964), The Mongolian People's Republic (1966), and How Mongolia Is Really Ruled (1979), and has coedited Vietnam and the Sino-Soviet Dispute (1967).

WILLIAM PANG-YU TING is an assistant professor in the Department of Political Science of the University of Michigan. His articles have appeared in the American Political Science Review and Asian Survey.

WILLIAM TURLEY is an associate professor in the Department of Political Science at Southern Illinois University. He has edited Vietnamese Communism in Comparative Perspective (1980).

JIRI VALENTA is coordinator of Soviet and East European studies and associate professor at the Naval Postgraduate School, Monterey, California. He has written Soviet Intervention in Czechoslovakia, 1968 Anatomy of a Decision (1979) and numerous articles. He coedited Eurocommunism Between East and West (1980) and The Communist States in Africa.

Index

Acevedo, Roger, 55
Albright, David, 3, 4
Alexiev, Alex, 213, 214
Allied Control Commission, 159
All People's Defense, 87
Alouettes, 160
American army, 6, 10-11, 46, 63, 66, 73, 111, 129, 197, 205
American revolution, 10
Anders army, 105-106, 110, 114
Andropov, Yuri, 26
Angola, 46, 48-49, 56, 58, 213
Anti-Party Group, 24
Anti-semitism, 108, 117
Antonov-Ovseenko, Vladimir, 19
Arendt, Hannah, 1
Armia Krajowa, 105, 109-111, 115, 210
Armia Ludowa, 105, 109-110, 114, 210
Army for National Salvation, 64, 65
Army of Working Youth, 47, 50-51, 56, 58
Army party organization
  Chinese, 68
  Cuban, 52-54
  Czechoslovakian, 133
  Polish, 116
  Romanian, 152, 153
  Soviet, 52-53, 56, 68
  Vietnamese, 68-69, 78
  Yugoslav, 92-93
Arnold, Benedict, 11
August Revolution, 66-68
Avkhia, General, 181

Babjav, 169

Bacau, 160
Baikal corridor, 169
Bakaric, Vladimir, 89
Baltic coast riots, 117
Baltics, 17
Barga, 178
Batista, Fulgencio, 6, 47, 53, 208
Bator, Osman, 177
Bator, Sukhe, 170, 180, 184n
Bavasan, 172
Bay of Pigs, 46, 208, 213
Bedrich, Frantisek, 144
Beijing, 178, 191, 193-194
Belgrade, 84, 89, 97
Belorussia, 9, 17
Benes, Eduard, 131, 135
Beria, Lavrentiya, 24, 115
Berlin, battle of, 22
Berlin crisis, 26
Berling army, 106-110, 114, 123n, 124n, 210
Bermejo, Raul, 50
Bessarabia, 9, 149
Blau, Peter, 59n
Blyukher, Vasilii, 18-19, 174-176, 180
Bocek, Bohumil, 134, 136-137, 211
Bodnaras, Emil, 152
Bodo, 170
Bonapartism, 3, 8, 25
Borodin, Mikhail, 173
Brezhnev, Leonid, 8, 26-28, 117, 180
Brown, Harold, 41
Brzezinski, Zbigniew, 2
Bubnov, Andrei, 9, 17
Budenny, Semen, 16, 18-20, 22
Bukovina, 149

Bulgaria, 129, 162

Camaguey province, 55
Cao Bang, 64-65
Castro, Fidel, 10, 47, 50,
  208-209
Castro, Raul, 47
Ceausescu, Nicolae, 153-155,
  157-158, 161
Central Committee
  Chinese, 35, 38-40, 56
  Cuban, 50, 55, 58
  Czechoslovak, 140-142
  Polish, 116, 119, 124n
  Soviet, 18-19, 23-24, 27, 56
  Vietnamese, 63, 69, 72, 78, 81
  Yugoslav, 97
Central Military Affairs
  Commission (China), 37
Cepicka, Alexej, 137-140
Chakdorjav, 170
Chang Hsueh-laing, 174
Chang Tso-lin, 169, 173
Che Guevara Brigade, 49
Chen Duxiu, 189
Chen I, 169
Chiang Kai-shek, 173, 188, 196,
  200
Chinese army, 1-2, 4-8, 30-42,
  79, 121, 207-209, 212-213
  civil-military elite system,
  39-40
  military modernization and
  budget, 40-42
  path to power, 31-34
  post-1949 politics, 34-39
Chinese Eastern Railroad, 174
Chinese militia, 188-202
  Chinese elite politics, 189
  Chinese revolution, 188-189
  civilian versus military
  functions, 194-200
  command and control functions,
  189-194
  optimum size, 200-202
Chinese revolution, 1, 6, 9, 11,
  15, 66, 168
Chinovniki, 12
Chita, 169-170
Choibalsan, 170, 172, 174-175,
  178-180
Civic soldier, 46, 55, 57-58,
  63, 78
Civil wars, 5-8, 15-18, 31-34,
  46-47, 64-70, 73, 108-113, 169-170
Civil-military relations
  Chinese, 1, 4, 6, 8, 31-45, 121,
  207-209, 212-213
  Communist, 1-14, 208-215
  Cuban, 1, 4-6, 10, 46-62, 207-209,
  212-213
  Czechoslovak, 7, 129-148, 210-211,
  213-214
  Eastern European, 1, 4, 7-8, 121,
  129, 210, 212-213
  Korean, North, 5, 10
  Mongolian, 167-186
  Polish, 7, 103-128, 210-211,
  213-214
  Romanian, 7, 10, 149-166, 211, 214
  Soviet, 1, 2, 8-10, 15-30, 103,
  129, 208, 211-213
  Vietnamese, 1, 4-6, 8, 63-82, 207,
  209, 212-213
  Yugoslav, 6, 8, 21, 83-102, 121,
  207, 212
Clubb, Edmund O., 176
Collado, Carlos, 60n
Colton, Timothy, 3, 4
Comintern, 107
Commissars, 2, 3, 16, 20, 33, 36,
  51, 53, 67-68, 107, 190, 211
Communist Youth Organization (Cuba),
  52, 54
Croatian crisis, 83-84, 88-93, 98
Croats, 87, 93, 96, 213
Cromwell, Oliver, 1
Cuban army, 1, 2, 4-5, 10, 45-62,
  207-209, 212-213
  future, 58-59
  military mission, 46-49
  political mission, 51-58
  production mission, 49-51
Cuban missile crisis, 26-27
Cuban party, 51-52
Cultural Revolution, 2, 20, 36-38,
  40, 56, 191-193, 195, 198
Czechoslovak army, 7, 129-148,
  210-211, 213-214
  1945-1948, 131-135
  1948-1956, 135-138
  1956-1964, 138-140
  1968 crisis, 140-144
  1968 and after, 144-146

Damansky island, battle of, 179-180
Danilov, General, 180
Danzan, 170, 172

Darkhan, 180, 181
Dean, Robert, 207, 212
Demid, Marshal, 175, 180
Dendyp, 174
Deng Xiaoping, 36-37, 40, 193-194, 198
Denikin, Anton, 9, 17
Desertion, 6, 9, 10-11, 17
Djilas, Milovan, 95
Doksom, 170
Dominguez, Jorge, 2, 207, 212
Dong, Pham van, 67
Dorj, Damba, 173
Drgac, Simon, 136-137
Dubcek, Alexander, 143, 145, 214
Dubovoy, 19
Dung, Van Tien, 67, 69, 77

East European armies, 1, 4, 7, 8, 11
Egypt, 138
Eisenhower, Dwight, 23
Erdenet, 181
Erickson, John, 180
Escalante, Anibal, 58
Estonia, 9

Far Eastern Republic, 170
February Revolution (Russia), 130, 135, 211
Feklenko, N. V., 175
Finder, Pawel, 124n
Finland, 17
Finnish campaign, 21, 212
First Cavalry Army, 9, 20
Fishman, General, 20
Four Modernization Program, 199
French army, 6, 11, 63-64
French revolution, 1, 10
Friedrich, Carl, 2
Frunze, Mikhail, 16, 18

Gang of Four, 38, 192-193, 195, 199-200, 202
Gdansk agreement, 119
Gegen, Neisse, 170
Gekker, Anatoli, 174
Gendun, 175
Geneva conference, 6, 161
Genghis Khan, 179-180
German army, 6-7, 22-23, 104
German-Soviet war, 105, 149-150
Germany, 107
Germany, East, 7

Giap, Vo Nguyen, 64-65, 67, 69-71, 77, 82
Gierek, Eduard, 117-119, 214
Gomulka, Wladyslaw, 113, 115-118, 124n, 214
Gottwald, Klement, 133, 136-137
Gottwald Military Academy, 143-144
Gozze-Gucetic, Vuko, 96
Great Britain, 105
Great British army, 11, 111
Great British revolution, 1, 10
Great Purges (Soviet Union), 3, 19, 21-25, 28
Grechko, Andrei, 25-27
Griffiths, William, 3
Grigoriev (ataman), 17
Groza, Petru, 151
Gunsen, General, 181
Guomindang (China), 6, 32-34, 173-174, 177, 188, 209

Hailar, 174
Hainan Islands, 203
Hangzhou, 193
Harbin, 174
Hart, Armando, 55
Hassan (Lake), battle of, 175, 212
Herljevic, Franjo, 96
Herspring, Dale, 3, 4, 104
Historical development model, 104
Hitler-Stalin Pact, 176
Ho Chi Minh, 63, 209
Hong Kong, 200
Horia-Closca-Crisan division, 152
Hsingan, 178
Hungary, 129, 138
Hungarian army, 8, 114
Huntington, Samuel, 2, 5, 59n
Husak, Gustav, 145

Ilichev, 180
Ingr, Sergei, 133
Institute for Strategic Studies, 47
Institutional congruence model, 3-4
Interest group model, 3-4
Ionita, General, 157
Iran, 105
Irkutsk, 169-171
Israel, 117, 138

Jadamba, 172
Janko, Vladimir, 140-141, 214
Janousek, K., 134, 136
Janowitz, Morris, 1

Japan, 167-168
Japanese army, 6, 34, 63-64, 168, 173, 188, 209-210
Jaruzelski, Vojtech, 117-119, 127n, 214
Jews, 17, 108, 117, 170
Jiang Qing, 38
Jianxi, 32
Johnson, Chalmers, 5
Jovanovic, Djoko, 100n

Kalgan, 178
Kamenev, Sergei, 9, 16
Kampuchea, Vietnamese invasion of, 76-77, 79, 213
Kangelari, 172
Kania, Stanislaw, 119, 214
Kardelj, Eduard, 91
Katyn massacre, 105-106, 130
Kazakhs, 177
Kelleher, Catherine, 2
Khabarovsk Protocol, 174
Khaka Seven, 170
Khalkas, 169
Khalkin-gol, battle of, 21, 176, 212
Khan, Sain Noyan, 168
Khrushchev, Nikita, 8, 24-26, 28, 138-140
Khutukhtu, Jebtsun Damba, 168-169
Kiev salient, battle of, 23
Klapek, Karel, 135
Klimovskikh, General, 22
Kobdo, battle of, 168, 171
Kolchak, Admiral, 9, 17, 169
Kolkhoz Corps, 20, 212
Kolkowicz, Roman, 3-4, 103
Konev, Ivan, 24-25
Korbonski, Andrzej, 210, 212, 214-215
Korean, North, army, 2, 5, 10
Korean War, 6, 35-36, 39, 41, 213
Kosice Program, 130, 132-134
Kosich, 172
Kosygin, Aleksei, 26
Krasnoshchekov, 170
Kronstadt revolt, 9, 18
Kukoc, Ivan, 97
Kulik, General, 20
Kursk-Orel, battle of, 22
Kutlvasr, Karel, 136
Kuznetsov, General, 24
Kyakhta, 170-171

Kwangsi, 65

Lama, Ja, 169, 182
Lang Son, 64
Latvia, 9
League of Cuban Bandits, 46, 50
Lebedev, 16
Lee, Choong-sik, 2
Lenin, Vladimir, 17, 28, 170
Leningrad, 22
Lin Biao, 2, 36, 38, 40, 42, 56, 191, 195, 209
Liska, Alois, 134
Lithuania, 9
Liu Shao-yi, 11, 35-37
Ljubicic, Nikola, 97, 100n, 101n
Ljubljana, 97
Local Air Defense Formations (Romania), 158
Lomsky, Bohumir, 140-142, 214
London, 104
London exiles, 106, 109
Long March, 6, 33-34
Losol, 170
Lundquist, Colonel, 17
Lushan Plenum, 35

Ma Ho-tien, 172-173
Maimaicheng, 170
Makhno, Nestor, 17
Maksorjav, 172
Malenkov, Premier, 24, 213
Malinovsky, Rodion, 25, 179
Mamula, Mirolsav, 141-142
Manchuli, 174
Manchuria, 168, 174, 176-177
Mao Zedong, 2, 11, 32, 35-38, 40, 177-178, 188-189, 191, 194-195, 198
Mikhajlov, Mihajlo, 95
Mikoyan, Anastas, 26
Military Affairs Council (China), 35
Military coup, 1, 89, 136, 141
Militia, 11, 38, 111, 158, 187-205
Miscovic, Ivan, 94-95
Moczar, Miecslaw, 118
Molotov, Vyacheslav, 175
Moncado barracks raid, 6
Mongolia, 38, 64
Mongolian army
  1911-1917, 168-169
  1917-1921, 169-171
  1921-1926, 171-173

Mongolian army (cont'd)
  1926-1947, 173-178
  1947-1956, 178-179
  1956-1980, 179-183
Moscow, 22, 25, 136, 178
Moskalenko, Marshal, 25-26
Muraviev, Colonel, 17
Muscovites, 108

National Heroes of Labor (Cuba),
  50
National Institute of Peasant
  Movement (China), 188
Naushki, 181
New Course (Soviet Union), 24
New Economic Program, 19
Nie Rongzhen, 194, 204
Nomonhon, 177
North Atlantic Treaty Organization, 143, 161
Novotny, Antonin, 140-142, 214

October Revolution, 8, 66
Odom, William, 3-4
Oirat, Altai, 170
Olikov, Sergei, 17
Orel, 17
Oriente province, 208
Orlov, 169

Pan Mongolism, 177
Partisans, 16
Patriotic Guards (Romania), 158
Pavlov, General, 22
Pearl Harbor, attack on, 176, 188
Peitashan, 177
Peng Dehuai, 35-36, 39-40, 190-191, 196
People's Armed Forces Department (China), 190, 193-194
People's war, 198-199
Pepich, Egyd, 141-144
Petrine civil-military
  relations, 3
Pika, Heliodor, 136
Pliev, I. A., 175, 179
Podgorny, Nikolai, 26
Poland, 7-9, 17, 138
Polish army
  pre-1944, 104-108
  civil war era, 108-113
  1948-1955, 113-116
  1956 and after, 116-119

Polish Committee of National
  Liberation (Lublin), 107-108
Polish partisans, 132
Polish party, 105, 108, 111, 113-114
Politburo
  Cuban, 52, 55-56
  Czechoslovak, 140
  Polish, 118, 124
  Soviet, 18, 23-27
  Vietnam, 81
  Yugoslavia, 97
Poppe, Nicholas, 174
Poznan demonstrations, 115
Prague, 132
Prchlik, Vaclav, 141, 143
Prochazka, Jaroslav, 134, 137, 211
Professionalism
  Chinese, 190, 197, 212
  Cuban, 48-49, 212
  Czechoslovak, 139-140, 213
  Polish, 120, 213
  Romanian, 154
  Vietnamese, 64, 71-72, 75, 77-79, 212
  Yugoslav, 213
Provisional Government, 15
Purges
  Cuban, 56
  Czechoslovak, 136-137, 139, 141-142, 144
  Mongolian, 175
  Polish, 113, 117
  Romanian, 150-152, 154-155
  Soviet, 19, 21, 56, 175, 215

Qing dynasty, 188

Radek, Karl, 17
Rankovic, Aleksandr, 84, 90, 94, 96, 99n
Ravdan, S., 179
Red Guards, 37
Reicin, Bedrich, 135
Revolutionary committees (China), 38
Revolutions, 5
Rice, Condoleezza, 210-211, 213
Rokossovsky, Konstantin, 8, 19, 113-116, 175, 213
Rola-Zymierski, Michal, 109, 113
Romania, 7, 129
Romanian army
  early period, 150-152
  invasion, 144-146
  new defense doctrine, 156-159

Romanian army (cont'd)
  1968 crisis, 140-144
  renationalization, 154-156
  sovietization, 153-154
Rytir, Otakar, 142, 144-145, 214

Saigon, loss of, 7, 209, 213
Salisbury, Harrison, 178
SALT Treaty, 27
Sanchez School for Revolutionary Armed Forces, 51
Sarokovikov, 172
Sarac, Dzemil, 97
Secret police, 2, 8, 11, 214-215
  Chinese, 195, 199
  Czechoslovakian, 135
  Mongolian, 172
  Polish, 111, 113-114, 210
  Soviet, 23, 26, 109
  Yugoslav, 94, 96, 99
Sejna, Jan, 140-142
Selznick, Philip, 5
Semenov (ataman), 169-170
Serbian leaders, 90-91, 93, 99
Shanghai, 192, 198-199
Shanxi, 191
Shaposhnikov, Boris, 20, 23
Shchetintin, 172
Sheng Shih-tai, 177
Shtern, General, 176
Shumatsky, Boris, 170
Siberia, 16, 176, 179, 181-182
Sinkiang, 171, 177
Skilling, Gordon, 3
Slansky trial, 137
Slovakia, 129, 131-132, 137, 139
Slovenia, 93
Snow, Edgar, 178
Socialist Education Movement, 198
Sokolovsky, Marshal, 25
Soviet army, 1, 3, 5, 7-9, 11, 68, 103, 111, 119
  civil war, 15-18
  1921-1940, 18-21
  1941-1953, 21-23
  1953-1964, 24-26
  1964-1982, 26-28
Soviet-Mongolian Friendship Treaty, 175
Soviet Union
  advisers, 106, 109, 123n, 125n, 126n, 133, 145, 152-153, 155
  aid, 41, 47
  civil war, 8-9, 15-18

  foreign policy, 4-5, 32-34, 41, 87, 115, 144-146, 155, 160-162, 169-183
  intervention in Yugoslavia, 99
  invasion of Czechoslovakia, 87, 155, 158-159, 161
  liberation of Prague, 132
  occupation of Poland, 104
  October Revolution, 8
  State Defense Committee, 23
  Stavka, 23
Split, 97
Spychalsky, Marian, 115-117
Stalin, Joseph, 3-4, 6, 8, 10, 16, 18-20, 22-25, 28, 84n, 103, 108, 111, 113-115, 119, 121, 132, 138, 145, 178, 180, 212-213, 215
Stalingrad, battle of, 7, 22, 24, 150, 176
Stresser, Roland, 173
Sudets, V. A., 175
Sverdlov, Yakov, 17
Svoboda, Ludvik, 133-137, 211

Taiwan, 193
Tan, Le Trong, 77
Technology, level of, 6, 17, 21, 40-42, 71, 73-75
Tet offensive, 74
Thanh, Nguyen Chi, 69-72
Tiananmen Square, 193, 198
Timoshenko, Marshal, 19-20, 22
Ting, William, 207, 212
Tiso, Joseph, 129
Tito, Joseph Broz, 83-84, 86, 88-91, 95-98
Totalitarian model, 2-3, 103
Transbaikal Military District, 181
Trans-Mongolian Railroad, 178
Trotsky, Leon, 3, 9, 16-19
Tsaritsyn, battle of, 20
Tsedenbal, 178, 180-181
Tucker, Robert, 5
Tukhachevsky, Mikhail, 3, 9, 20, 25, 175, 180
Turley, William, 2, 207, 209, 212
Tuva, 171

Uborevich, General, 20
Uighurs, 177
Ukraine, 9, 16-17, 19
Ukrainian Insurgency Army, 111
Ulan Bator, 175, 178-181
Ulanfu, 178
Ulan Ude, 181

Ulyasutai, 171
Ungern-Sternberg, Baron von, 170-171, 182
United Nations, 178
Urga, 169-173

Valenta, Jiri, 210, 211, 213
Valley Forge, 11
Vatsetis, 9, 16
Vasilevsky, Marshal, 24
VE Day, 111
Verkhneudinsk, 169
Viet Minh, 64-65, 67
Vietnamese army, 1-2, 4-8, 11, 15, 63-82
  contemporary political role, 77-80
  impact of Second Indochina War, 73-75
  invasion of Kampuchea, 76-77, 79
  occupation of Laos, 79
  origins, 64-70
  post-resistance priorities and missions, 70-73
  post-war missions and wars, 75-77
  resistance to Chinese invasion, 76-77, 79
  Southern reunification, 70-71
Vietnamese revolution, 6, 9, 11
Vladimirescu, Tudor, 150-151
Vladivostok, 169
Voenspets, 9, 16-17, 19
Voice of America, 95
Vojvodina province, 91
Volgyes, Ivan, 3-4
Voronin, F. N., 175
Voroshilov, Kliment, 16, 18-20, 22

Warsaw, battle of, 9, 109
Warsaw Pact, 8, 27, 104, 119, 130, 138-139, 143-144, 149, 155-157, 159, 160-162
Whampoa Military Academy (China), 64, 67
Whitson, William, 33
Wiatr, Jerzy, 104
Wolf, Eric, 5
Wrangel, Baron, 17
Wuhan Incident, 37-38

Yakir, Iona, 19-20
Yakubovsky, Marshal, 143-144
Yalta agreement, 178
Yegorov, Marshal, 18
Ye Jianying, 2
Yepishev, Marshal, 143
Yondonduichir, General, 181
Yorktown, battle of, 11
Youth Homeland Defense Formation, 158
Yudenich, 17
Yugoslav army, 2-3, 7-8, 83-102, 121, 160
  Croatian crisis, 89-90
  disarray and consolidation, 84-85
  and domestic civil security organs, 95-96
  internal role, 96-99
  Miscovic case, 94-95
  national balance of officer corps, 93-94
  party organization, 92-93
  political metamorphosis, 85-87
  professional grievances, 94
  territorial defense, 87-88
  veterans, 90-92
Yugoslav party, 84
Yugoslav revolution, 6, 112

Zagreb, 84, 97
Zakharov, Marshal, 25
Zhou En-lai, 11
Zhukov, Georgi, 3, 23-26, 28, 175, 180
Zhu Teh, 32
Zinoviev, Grigori, 17